Louisiana Law of
Security Devices

LOUISIANA CIVIL CODE PRÉCIS SERIES

LOUISIANA LAW OF OBLIGATIONS IN GENERAL
Alain Levasseur
4th Ed. 2015

LOUISIANA LAW OF CONVENTIONAL OBLIGATIONS
Alain Levasseur
2015

LOUISIANA LAW OF SALE AND LEASE
Alain Levasseur & David Gruning
3d Ed. 2015

LOUISIANA LAW OF TORTS
Frank Maraist
2010

LOUISIANA LAW OF SECURITY DEVICES
Michael H. Rubin
2d Ed. 2017

LOUISIANA LAW OF PROPERTY
John Randall Trahan
2012

Louisiana Law of Security Devices

A Précis

SECOND EDITION

Michael H. Rubin
McGlinchey Stafford PLLC

2017

CAROLINA ACADEMIC PRESS
Durham, North Carolina

ISBN: 978-1-52210-193-2
eISBN: 978-1-52210-194-9
LCCN: 2016960222

CAROLINA ACADEMIC PRESS, LLC
700 Kent Street
Durham, North Carolina 27701
Telephone (919) 489-7486
Fax (919) 493-5668
www.cap-press.com

Printed in the United States of America

To my wife and best friend, Ayan,
with whose support all things are possible.

Contents

Index of Definitions and Abbreviations

AUTHOR'S NOTE: These definitions are intended to be abbreviated and incomplete; they are given as a way to easily find a more complete definition and description in the body of this work.

"Abstract of Title" is a compilation of documents obtained by a review of the public records as part of a title examination. See 23.2.

"Authentic Act" means a document signed in the presence of a notary public and two witnesses. C.C. art. 1833.

"C.C." means the Louisiana Civil Code. Instead of citations in this book being "LSA-C.C. art. X" all citations are given as "C.C. art. X."

"C.C.P." means the Louisiana Code of Civil Procedure. Instead of citations in this book being "LSA-C.C.P. art. X" all citations are given as "C.C.P. art. X."

"C.Cr.P." means the Louisiana Code of Criminal Procedure. Instead of citations in this book being "LSA-C.Cr.P. art. X" all citations are given as "C.Cr.P. art. X."

"Collateral Mortgage" means a mortgage which secures a collateral mortgage note, which in turn is secures an obligation. See 13.4(a).

"Collateral Mortgage Note" means a note perfected by a UCC9 security interest that both (a) secures a principal obligation and (b) is secured by a mortgage. See 13.4(a).

"Concursus Proceeding" is the Louisiana term for what federal law calls "interpleader"—a court battle over funds where multiple parties claim a right to the funds. C.C.P. art. 4651.

"Declinatory Exceptions" are Louisiana procedural objections that raise matters such as lack of subject matter jurisdiction, venue, and personal jurisdiction. C.C.P. art. 925. These objections can be waived if not timely raised. C.C.P. art. 928.

"Dilatory Exceptions" are Louisiana procedural objections that slow the process of a lawsuit, such as prematurity and vagueness. C.C.P. art. 926. These objections can be waived if not timely raised. C.C.P. art. 928.

"Executory Process" means Louisiana's expedited foreclosure procedure. See Section 38.1(b).

"Fluctuating Line of Credit Loan" means a loan that operates like a credit card. The debtor may borrow money, pay it back, and borrow more, as long as the maximum outstanding at any time does not exceed the maximum limit set by creditor. See Section 13.3(b) and 13.4(a).

"Future Advance Mortgage" means a mortgage that may secure funds to be lent in the future. See Section 13.3.

"Hand Note" means evidence of advances in a collateral mortgage package. See Section 13.4(a).

"In Rem Mortgage" means a mortgage for which the debtor has no individual personal liability. See Section 12.11.

"Lien" is the common law term for the civilian concept of a "privilege." See Chapter 28.

"Lien Claimant" means those entitled to a material's lien, and in this book it specifically is used to refer to those who are entitled to claim a Private Works Act privilege. See Section 37.1.

"Marshalling of Assets" means ordering the seizure and sale of assets in a way that maximizes the return for all creditors who have a security interest in those assets. See Section 11.1(a).

"Material Defect" means a defect in the title to immovable property such that litigation may be necessary to revolve that defect. See Section 23.1.

"Materialmen's Lien" means a right claimed by workers and others who improve immovable property. See Chapter 37.

"Multiple Indebtedness Mortgage" is not defined in Louisiana statutes, but it is used by lawyers to refer to a mortgage granted under C.C. art. 3298 to secure more than one debt, to secure future advances, or to secure a fluctuating line-of-credit loan.

"Notice of Lis Pendens" means notice of a pending lawsuit involving immovable property. See Section 20.8(c).

"Paraph" refers to a stamp that a notary puts on a note to tie it to a mortgage. See Section 12.4(c).

"Personal Security" is defined in C.C. art. 3137.

"Prescription" is the Louisiana term for the statute of limitations.

"Privilege" is a statutory right given to a creditor which gives the creditor a right to seize and sell property. At the sheriff's sale, the creditor obtains a claim the proceeds of the sale; that claim is superior to the rights of unsecured creditors. See Chapter 28.

"PWA" means the Louisiana Private Works Act, R.S. 9:4801 *et seq.*; see Chapter 37.

"Quit Claim Deed" means a sale made without any warranty. See Section 21.5(e).

"Real Security" is defined in C.C. art. 3137.

"R.S." means the Louisiana Revised Statutes. Instead of citations in this book being "LSA-R.S. X:X" all citations are given as "R.S. X:X."

"Security Device" means the lawful causes of preference available to Louisiana creditors to secure loans. See Section 1.3.

"Third Parties" is the term used in this Précis to refer to what the Civil Code denotes as "third persons." See Section 19.4.

"Third Party Possessor," as used in this book, refers to "third possessors" as defined in C.C. art. 3315 et seq. and as discussed in Chapter 21.

"Title Examination" is the process of collecting all pertinent documents relating to a tract of immovable property. See Section 23.1.

"Title Insurance" is an insurance policy issued by a company which agrees to pay up to the policy value if the title to immovable property has a material defect. See Section 23.1.

"Title Opinion" is the process of reviewing the papers and documents obtained in a title examination to ascertain the status of title to immovable property and to evaluate whether the title contains a material defect. See Section 23.1.

"UCC9" refers to Louisiana's version of article 9 of the Uniform Commercial Code, R.S. 10:9-101 *et seq.*

"Writ of Fieri Facias (writ of fi.fa.)" is the Louisiana mechanism by which a judgment creditor seizes property of a judgment debtor. C.C.P. arts. 2291 *et seq.*

Notes on Editorial Conventions Used in This Book

Direct quotations from Louisiana statutes, Civil Code articles, and Code of Civil Procedure articles have been italicized.

References to the Louisiana Civil Code are set forth as C.C. art ___.

References to the Louisiana Code of Civil Procedure are set forth as C.C.P. art ___.

References to the Louisiana Revised Statutes are set forth as R.S. ___.

References to article 9 of Louisiana's version of the Uniform Commercial Code (R.S. 10:1-101 *et seq.*) are set forth as UCC9.

Almost no cases have been cited by name in the text. At the end of this book there is an index, section by section, giving the citation of key cases.

Acknowledgments

A number of people were instrumental in the creation of the first edition of this book. Professor Alain Levasseur (retired) of the Paul H. Hebert Law Center at Louisiana State University gave me the impetus to write this book. Attorney Brook Thibodeaux carefully read each page and cross checked the statutory references as well as making many corrections in the original manuscript for the first edition. Many helpful comments were received from attorneys Sam Bacot, Keith Colvin, Marshall Grodner, Jay O'Brien, Jamie Seymour, and Susan Tyler, who each read portions of the original manuscript for the first edition, and from Dustin Cooper, Katilyn Hollowell, and Jade Shaffer, who each read portions of the manuscript for this revision. Any errors in this book, however, whether by way of statements or omissions, are entirely my own. Debbie Cothell, with her usual skill and expertise, reformatted the manuscript.

Most importantly, both the first edition and this revision would not have been possible without the encouragement, assistance, and support of my wife, Ayan; her insightful and excellent suggestions for clarification, additions, and improvements were invaluable.

About the Author

Mr. Rubin, who practices full time with the firm of McGlinchey Stafford, PLLC, taught the "Security Devices" course at the LSU Law School for more than three decades, has also taught at the Tulane Law School and the Southern University Law School, and has written and lectured extensively about Louisiana real estate and finance issues. He has served as president of the American College of Real Estate Lawyers, the Louisiana State Bar Association, and the Bar Association of the U.S. Fifth Circuit Court of Appeals. For more than thirty years he has served on the Louisiana Law Institute's Security Devices Committee, and he is a member of the American Law Institute, the American College of Appellate Lawyers, the American College of Commercial Finance Attorneys, and the American College of Mortgage Attorneys, and is a Commissioner of the Uniform Law Comission.

Louisiana Law of
Security Devices

Chapter 1

An Overview of Louisiana Security Devices

1.1. Louisiana Personal Rights and Real Rights Have Different Meanings Than in Common Law

When the Louisiana Civil Code and Louisiana courts speak of "personal" and "real" rights, they are using distinctly civilian concepts that have no relationship to common law phraseology.

In common law, a "real" right generally refers to a right in immovable property, and "personal property" generally refers to those items that Louisiana would characterize as movable property.

In contrast to common law usage, a Louisiana "personal right" is a personal claim against the obligated party (the *obligor*); this means that the creditor has a right to sue the obligated party for specific performance. A Louisiana "real right" gives a creditor a right of pursuit of an asset. That asset may be movable or immovable. If there is a real right in an asset, the asset can be seized and sold to satisfy the obligation, and the creditor has the right to receive money from the sale. The concept of "real rights" is not limited to immovable property.

1.2. Louisiana Contracts Normally Impose Personal Rights; Secured Claims Are the Exception, Not the Rule

The basic Louisiana rules about securing loans begin with the concept that all obligations are essentially personal unless a contract or statute provides otherwise. All assets of the debtor may be pursued to satisfy the debtor's personal liability.

Three Civil Code articles enacted in 2014 state the general principles of personal liability, equal treatment of creditors unless there is a preference authorized or established by law, and the ability of parties to contractually limit personal liability. These provisions are C.C. arts. 3183, 3184, and 3185.

1.2(a). C.C. art. 3133, Liability of an obligor for his obligations

C.C. art. 3133 provides: "*Whoever is personally bound for an obligation is obligated to fulfill it out of all of his property, movable and immovable, present and future.*" This article is subject to exceptions established by law. Those exceptions are dealt with in Chapter 35, below, but in general they include certain exemptions from seizure and sale contained in the Louisiana Constitution for "homesteads" and in La. R.S. 13:3881.

1.2(b). C.C. art. 3134, Ratable treatment of creditors

C.C. art. 3134 states: "*In the absence of a preference authorized or established by legislation, an obligor's property is available to all his creditors for the satisfaction of his obligations, and the proceeds of its sale are distributed ratably among them.*"

This article does not mean that an unsecured creditor gets the proceeds of any type of sale. There are distinctions to be made between non-judicial sales and judicial sales, and one must also take into account the role of unsecured creditors and secured creditors.

In general, the ratable distribution of sales proceeds only occurs when there is a judicial sale that the unsecured creditor(s) provoked or into which they intervened.

1.2(b)(1). Example #1

Debtor has three unsecured creditors, X, Y, and Z, and no secured creditors. Debtor sells a tract of land to Buyer. Unsecured creditors X, Y, and Z have no claim to the proceeds of the sale because this is a voluntary sale by Debtor and not a judicial sale.

Debtor will retain the proceeds of the sale to Buyer. Unsecured creditors X, Y, and Z will have to file a lawsuit to collect from Debtor.

1.2(b)(2). Example #2

Debtor has three unsecured creditors, X, Y, and Z. Debtor owns a tract of land on which secured creditor M holds a $100,000 mortgage. Debtor sells the tract of land to Buyer for $150,000 and uses $100,000 to pay off the mortgage that M holds.

Unsecured creditors X, Y, and Z have no claim to the $100,000 because secured creditor M, by virtue of the mortgage, holds a "preference authorized ... by legislation" (see Chapter 11, below), while unsecured creditors X, Y, and Z do not.

Unsecured creditors X, Y, and Z have no claim to the $50,000 remaining from the $150,000 sale price after the payment of M's $100,000 mortgage. The reason is that this is a voluntary sale by Debtor, not a judicial sale. Debtor will retain the $50,000; unsecured creditors X, Y, and Z will have to file a lawsuit to collect from Debtor.

1.2(b)(3). Example #3

Debtor has three unsecured creditors, X, Y, and Z. Debtor owns a tract of land on which secured creditor M holds a $100,000 mortgage. Debtor has defaulted on the payment of the note that the mortgage secures. M institutes foreclosure proceedings against the property. Unsecured creditors X, Y, and Z do not intervene in the lawsuit. A judicial sale of the mortgaged property is held following a judgment that M obtains against Debtor. The judicial sale brings $150,000.

From the proceeds of the judicial sale, M will receive $100,000 because M is a secured creditor and is entitled to a preference on the sale's proceeds. Debtor, as owner of the property, will receive the remaining $50,000. Unsecured creditors X, Y, and Z will receive nothing from the judicial sale because they did not intervene into the lawsuit to assert their claims; however, they still retain their unsecured claims against Debtor.

1.2(c). C.C. art. 3135, Limitations on recourse

C.C. art. 3135 states: "*A written contract may provide that the obligee's recourse against the obligor is limited to particular property or to a specified class or kind of property.*" This provision, which was added in the 2014 revisions to the Civil Code, permits the parties to contractually agree to limit any creditor's claim to certain types of property.

Therefore, even though under C.C. art. 3133 a debtor is obligated to use all property, movable and immovable, to satisfy creditors, a debtor may enter into a written contract with a specific creditor to limit that creditor's rights. Under C.C. art. 3135, this written contact may supersede other rights an unsecured creditor might receive through judicial process.

1.2(c)(1). Example #4

Debtor owes money to Creditor1 and Creditor2; each loan is unsecured.

Debtor and Creditor1 agree in writing that Creditor1 will never have a right to collect its claim by seeking recourse against Debtor's motorcycle, coin collection, and the farm that Debtor inherited.

Debtor defaults on payment of the loans to both Creditor1 and Creditor2. Each files a suit and each obtains a personal judgment against Debtor.

Creditor1 attempts to use a writ of fieri facias to seize the motorcycle and coin collection. Creditor1 also records the judgment in the mortgage records of the parish where the inherited farm is located and attempts to assert a judicial mortgage against the property. For more on writs of fieri facias, see C.C.P. arts. 2291–2299. For more on judicial mortgages, see Chapter 17, below.

In these instances, Debtor may assert a defense that the written contract with Creditor1 pursuant to C.C. art. 3135 limits Creditor1's "*recourse*" to these items, essentially making them exempt from any claims by Creditor1. Under C.C. art. 3135, Debtor has a basis to file a suit to erase the judicial mortgage in favor of Creditor1 from the parish mortgage records insofar as the judicial mortgage affects the farm.

On the other hand, because Debtor has no such written contract of limitation with Creditor2, Creditor2 may attempt to seize and sell the motorcycle and coin collection and assert a judicial mortgage against the inherited property.

1.3. An Overview of the Types of Louisiana Security Devices

There are four aspects of a Louisiana security device.

First, security is always an accessory right; it secures the performance of a principal obligation. Because security is accessory to the principal obligation, under C.C. art. 3136, it is *"transferred with the obligation without a special provision to that effect."*

Second, as C.C. art. 3136 states, security is always *"established by legislation or contract."* Those established by contract are sometimes referred to as consensual, because they require an agreement of the parties. Other security interests, such as privileges and liens, are nonconsensual; they are established by legislation without any action or consent of the parties. See Section 1.3(a) and Chapter 28, below.

Third, under C.C. art. 3137, security is either personal or real.

Fourth, "security" does not transfer ownership of the item to the creditor; unless provided by special legislation, the creditor's remedy to exercise rights in the security is to seize it judicially, sell it at a judicial sale, and obtain a privilege on the sale's proceeds. Moreover, C.C. art. 3140 prohibits clauses in contracts that, in advance of a default, transfer ownership of security to a creditor when a default occurs in the future. Such contractual provisions are *"absolutely null."*

1.3(a). Consensual and Non-Consensual Louisiana Security Devices

Consensual security devices are those created by a contract in which a party voluntarily gives the creditor a specific right to seize and sell that party's asset (or, in the case of a surety, to sue the surety).

A non-consensual security device is one imposed by a statute. This is sometimes referred to as a security device "imposed by operation of law." A non-consensual security device does not depend upon the contractual intent of a party but rather arises regardless of whether the debtor specifically intended to give a security device or whether the creditor intended to obtain a security device. Non-consensual security devices exist because a statute says that they exist, even if neither the creditor nor debtor knew at the time of entering into an agreement or relationship that a security device was available. Louisiana privileges ("liens" in common law parlance) are non-consensual security devices. See Chapter 28, below.

1.3(b). Personal Security Devices and Real Security Devices

C.C. art. 3137 defines personal and real security devices.

A personal security device gives the creditor a right to sue someone. Suretyship is the only Louisiana personal security device, and it is always consensual. Louisiana does not permit a nonconsensual suretyship.

A real security device gives the creditor a right to seize and sell the assets of the one giving the security interest. The person giving the real security need not be the debtor, but the real security is always an accessory right securing a principal obligation. For example, a mother might grant a mortgage on her property to secure a bank loan to her daughter.

Every security device in Louisiana, except suretyship, is a real security device.

1.3(c). General Security Devices and Special Security Devices

Louisiana real security devices are general when they affect either all classes of all assets of a debtor or when they affect all of certain classes of assets (such as all immovable property or all movable property). Louisiana security devices are specific when they affect a specific asset or a specific group of assets.

1.3(d). A Selective and Non-Exclusive Listing of Louisiana Security Devices

Louisiana law permits five main kinds of security devices (although there are many others allowed under special statutes). The five are: suretyship, pledge, mortgage, privilege, and those permitted by Louisiana's version of the Uniform Commercial Code.

The following charts show how various Louisiana security devices can be categorized:

TYPE OF SECURITY DEVICE	CONSENSUAL	NON-CONSENSUAL
Suretyship	X	
Conventional Mortgage	X	
Legal Mortgage		X
Judicial Mortgage		X
Privileges		X
UCC9 Security Interest	X	
Private Works Act		X
Public Works Act		X
Federal and State Tax Liens		X

TYPE OF SECURITY INTEREST	ONLY A PERSONAL RIGHT	AFFECTS ONLY IMMOVABLES	AFFECTS ONLY MOVABLES	AFFECTS BOTH IMMOVABLES AND MOVABLES
Suretyship	X			
Conventional Mortgage		X		
Legal Mortgage		X		
Judicial Mortgage		X		
Privilege				X
UCC 9 Security Interest			X	
Private Works Act		X		
Public Works Act		X		

Chapter 2

An Overview of Suretyship

2.1. The Requirements of Suretyship

2.1(a). The Civil Code Suretyship Provisions

The Louisiana law of suretyship has always been based on statutes—the articles in the Civil Code. It has been decades since the Louisiana legislature adopted extensive revisions to the Civil Code provisions concerning suretyship in the late 1980s, but some courts today continue to cite cases decided under the prior law and utilize language and concepts developed in those cases.

Those who seek to rely upon jurisprudence decided under Civil Code provisions that existed prior to the extensive amendments of the 1980s must be cautious and should ascertain whether the principles upon which they seek to rely have been legislatively altered. This is because, in many cases, the revisions in the 1980s changed the text of previous Civil Code articles and legislatively overturned prior jurisprudence. A complete understanding of Louisiana suretyship rules therefore must focus first on the language of the Civil Code and the Official Comments of the Louisiana Law Institute, for courts find that these Official Comments furnish persuasive authority in interpreting the law.

2.1(b). Definition of a Surety

Louisiana suretyship law is controlled by the Civil Code. Common law concepts of suretyship and guarantee play no role in Louisiana, and the American Law Institute's Restatement of the Law (3d) of Suretyship is not a reference applicable to Louisiana or utilized by Louisiana Courts.

C.C. art. 3035 defines suretyship as "*an accessory contract by which a person binds himself to a creditor to fulfill the obligation of another upon the failure of the latter to do so.*" Accessory contracts are those "*made to provide security for the performance of an obligation*" (C.C. art. 1913).

Louisiana suretyship law is traceable to the French and Spanish rules that existed prior to the 1803 French Napoleonic Code, although Louisiana's Civil Code articles often track the language of the Napoleonic Code. Louisiana courts frequently look to French commentators at the time of Napoleon to ascertain the principles that underpin the Civil Code articles.

Planiol, the French legal commentator, noted that there are five characteristics of suretyship: it is unilateral, gratuitous, accessory, consensual, and express.

Suretyship is unilateral because the surety has an obligation to the creditor; the creditor need not provide anything to the surety in exchange for a binding contract.

Suretyship is gratuitous because Louisiana has never required consideration for a contract of suretyship. The Louisiana concept of cause sufficient to satisfy any intent for a donation is a sufficient basis for suretyship. A surety need not receive anything in exchange from the debtor or creditor for granting the contract of suretyship; the spirit of liberality that supports any donation in Louisiana is a sufficient basis to grant a contract of suretyship.

Suretyship, states C.C. art. 3055, is "*an accessory contract,*" which is the phase used by Planiol. As Planiol explains, suretyship "can only be understood by the existence of a principal obligation which the surety guarantees." Suretyship is accessory because it depends upon the validity of a primary obligation between the creditor and debtor; if that primary obligation is extinguished, the creditor cannot enforce the accessory obligation of suretyship (see C.C. art. 1892).

Suretyship is consensual because nothing compels a surety to grant the contract of suretyship. Suretyship is never involuntary; it requires specific contractual action by the surety.

Suretyship is express (C.C. art. 3038) because it cannot be implied or assumed. A contract of suretyship exists only if an express contract of suretyship is entered into, in writing, by the surety.

The current Civil Code articles and jurisprudence reflect the same suretyship criteria and analysis that Planiol used more than 200 years ago.

2.1(c). The Parties Involved in a Suretyship Relationship

There are at least three parties involved whenever a contract of suretyship is entered into: the surety, the creditor, and what C.C. art. 3037 calls the "*principal obligor.*" From now on, this book will refer to the principal obligor as the debtor.

The fact that three parties are involved means that there are three separate relationships that must be considered: the creditor-debtor relationship; the creditor-surety relationship; and the surety-debtor relationship. Each relationship is subject to different Civil Code articles. The following diagram can be helpful in keeping in mind the various relationships:

Diagram 2.1(c)(1)

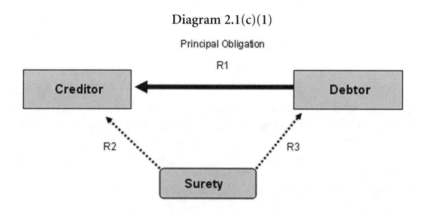

Throughout the rest of this book "R1" will refer to the relationship between the creditor and debtor, "R2" will refer to the relationship between the creditor and surety, and "R3" will refer to the relationship between the surety and debtor. Diagrams will be used because understanding each relationship and how they interact and affect each other can become complex, and a diagram may aid in untangling the web of legal obligations.

If there is more than one surety, each additional surety has a relationship with every other surety as well as with the creditor and debtor. The relationships when two sureties are involved are:

Diagram 2.1(c)(2)

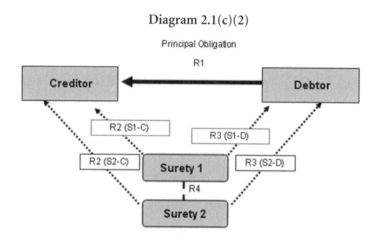

As this diagram shows, there is only one principal obligation (R1), the relationship between the debtor and creditor. The creditor, however, has a separate relationship (R2) with each surety. Likewise, each surety has a separate relationship with the debtor (R3). Finally, the two sureties have a relationship with each other (R4).

The relationships when three sureties are involved are:

Diagram 2.1(c)(3)

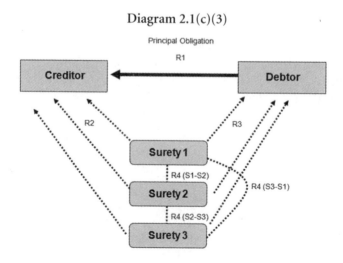

As this diagram shows, when three sureties are involved there still is only one principal obligation (R1), the relationship between the debtor and creditor. The creditor, however, has a separate relationship (R2) with each surety. Likewise, each surety has a separate relationship with the debtor (R3). Finally, each surety has a relationship with every other surety (R4).

2.1(d). Analyzing a Louisiana Suretyship Contract

To properly analyze a Louisiana suretyship contract, one should consider eight issues:

- Has a contract of suretyship been formed?
- What type of suretyship is involved (commercial, legal, or ordinary)?
- What obligations does the suretyship secure?
- What is the surety's obligation to the creditor?
- If there is more than one surety, what is the relationship between or among them?
- What are the implications of the creditor's release of the debtor, another surety, or collateral that secures the principal obligation?
- How may a suretyship be terminated by the surety?
- What statutory rights do sureties possess that may be contractually waived?

The remaining portion of this Chapter, along with Chapters 3 through 9 of this Précis, analyzes each of these issues.

2.1(e). The Formation of a Contract of Suretyship

The Civil Code sets forth specific rules concerning the formation of a suretyship contract. The general principle is that the contract of suretyship must be express and in writing; however, a complete understanding of these two seemingly simple requirements mandate an analysis not merely of the Civil Code suretyship articles but also of the obligations articles.

2.1(f). A Contract of Suretyship Must Be Express and in Writing

Suretyship can be formed only by an express written contract signed by the surety. The concept of a written contract is so important that it is emphasized in two separate sections of the Civil Code.

C.C. art. 3038, in the suretyship section of the Civil Code, states that suretyship "*must be express and in writing.*" Note the dual requirement. It is not sufficient that a contract of suretyship be in writing; it must also be "*express.*"

The requirement of specificity in the writing is further explained in C.C. art. 1847, providing that that oral testimony "*is inadmissible*" to prove "*a promise to pay the debt of a third person.*"

2.1(g). Only the Suretyship Contract Must Be in Writing

The suretyship contract concerns the relationship between the creditor and the surety (R2):

Diagram 2.1(g)(1)

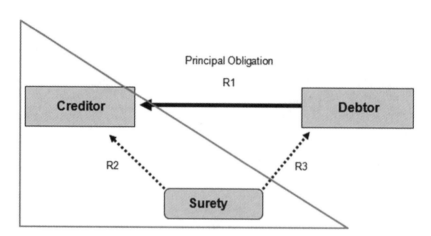

It is only the suretyship relationship (R2) that must be in writing. Because suretyship is gratuitous and unilateral, there is no requirement that either the debtor or the creditor sign the suretyship contract. No witnesses are required to make the suretyship contract valid. There is no requirement that the suretyship contract be created by an authentic act (an act signed in the presence of a notary and two witnesses, C.C. art. 1833).

The principal obligation, the creditor-debtor relationship (R1), is not required to be in writing in order for it to support a valid contract of suretyship if no other provision of Louisiana law requires this relationship (R1) to be in writing. Many principal obligations under Louisiana law can consist of oral contracts or obligations where no writing is required.

Likewise, the surety-debtor relationship (R3) need not be in writing. Although often debtors and sureties enter into contracts regarding this R3 relationship, if they fail to do so, the Civil Code contains the default rules on this relationship. This is in contrast to the creditor-surety relationship (R2); if this relationship is not in writing, there is no contract of suretyship.

2.1(h). The Express Language That Is Sufficient to Create a Contract of Suretyship

Under Louisiana law, oral testimony (called "parol evidence" in Louisiana terminology) cannot be used to prove the promise to pay "*the debt of a third person*" (C.C. art. 1847). This Civil Code article applies to suretyship, where the surety is making a promise to the creditor to pay the debt of a third person (the debtor). This is the reason why C.C. art. 3038 requires that a contract of suretyship be "*express and in writing*." The agreement by the surety to pay the debtor's obligations must be clear, explicit, and in writing.

There are many Louisiana courts that have rendered rulings on whether a contract contains sufficient language to create a suretyship obligation. The gist of the holdings is that, to constitute a valid suretyship agreement, the written document signed by the surety must contain a personal obligation of the surety to pay if the debtor does not pay or perform an obligation — in essence, "if he doesn't pay, I will." The following chart is a list of clauses in contracts that have been held by courts to be either sufficient or insufficient to constitute a suretyship agreement:

LANGUAGE of Contract	RESULT
Please assist X, a bill sent to me for funds he may need will be honored by me.	Suretyship
X is honest. If I had the money I'd lend it to him.	No Suretyship
X is honest and will pay his debts. If he should not, we will be responsible.	Suretyship
If Creditor will sell sugar to Debtor, I will bring back either the sugar or the money.	Suretyship
This letter will be your guarantee.	Suretyship
We will take all steps as are necessary to assure you that X will pay you.	No Suretyship

2.1(i). No Consideration Is Needed for a Suretyship Contract

No "consideration" (as that term is used in common law) is needed for a contract of suretyship, since one may become a surety gratuitously. As long as there is civilian "cause" for the contract, the suretyship is valid. Nonetheless, many drafters of suretyship contracts insert a clause on consideration, not because consideration is needed in Louisiana, but rather because the contract may have to be enforced in another state, and non-Louisiana courts often have a difficult time understanding civilian "cause."

2.1(j). Suretyship Requires No Formal Acceptance

Suretyship can be formed only by a written contract signed by the surety. Neither the creditor nor the debtor need sign the contract of suretyship; the only one who must sign is the surety.

C.C. art. 3039 dispenses with any formal act of acceptance of the suretyship contract by the creditor. Because a suretyship is unilateral, once a surety enters into a suretyship contract, the surety will be bound until (i) the surety takes some action to terminate the suretyship contract (R2) or (ii) until the principal obligation which the suretyship secures (R1) is no longer a viable obligation (see Chapter 8, below, on termination of suretyship).

2.1(k). A Contract of Suretyship Does Not Require Witnesses or an Authentic Act

The contract of suretyship needs to be signed only by the surety (see Section 2.1(j), above). No special form is required for a contract of suretyship. A suretyship need not be witnessed to be valid. A suretyship need not be in authentic form (signed in the presence of a notary public and two witnesses) to be valid.

Louisiana jurisprudence has recognized that a suretyship contract can be created merely by a surety's letter sent to the creditor, as long as the letter contains an express undertaking to personally pay the obligations of the debtor. The creditor's acceptance of the suretyship contained in the letter is presumed (see Section 2.1(j), above).

2.2. Characterizing a Suretyship as Commercial, Legal, or Ordinary

Louisiana law recognizes three types of suretyship contracts: commercial; legal; and ordinary (C.C. art. 3041). Different rules apply to each type of surety.

The proper characterization of the suretyship contract is important in a number of contexts, including but not limited to: the impact of the release of collateral; the impact of the release of another surety; the types of variations in a suretyship contract which are permitted; and whether the suretyship contract is interpreted strictly in favor of the surety.

The definitions of commercial, legal, and ordinary sureties are found in C.C. arts. 3042–3044. There are specific definitions of commercial and legal sureties; an "ordinary" surety is a default category that applies if the suretyship is neither commercial nor legal.

2.2(a). The Commercial Suretyship

Determining whether a contract of suretyship is a "commercial" suretyship requires looking at who the surety and debtor are as well as the cause of both the creditor-debtor relationship (R1) and the surety-debtor relationship (R3).

Diagram 2.2(a)

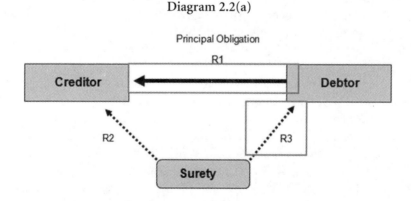

C.C. art. 3042 lists the circumstances giving rise to a commercial suretyship contract; they can be summarized as:

- The debtor or surety is a business entity (such as a corporation or partnership);

- The debtor and surety are individuals (not business entities),
  - but the creditor-debtor relationship (R1) involves a business transaction;
  - or the surety-debtor relationship (R3) involves a business transaction;
- Or the surety is in the business of being a surety.

If a suretyship fits any of C.C. 3042's criteria, then it is a commercial suretyship.

The specific language of C.C. art. 3042 should be carefully scrutinized. A commercial suretyship can arise if: *"(1) The surety is engaged in a surety business; (2) The principal obligor or the surety is a business corporation, partnership, or other business entity; (3) The principal obligation arises out of a commercial transaction of the principal obligor; or (4) The suretyship arises out of a commercial transaction of the surety."*

The first criterion (the *"surety is engaged in a surety business"*) is self-explanatory.

The second criterion means that a commercial suretyship will always arise if either the debtor or the surety is a legal entity (as opposed to a private individual).

The third criterion means that even if the debtor and surety are private individuals and not business entities, if the principal obligation (R1) involves a business transaction, then a commercial suretyship arises. If a parent agrees to guarantee his daughter's bank loan that she obtained so that she can open her own law practice, then the parent has entered into a commercial suretyship agreement, because the principal obligation (the creditor's loan to the daughter for a business purpose) triggers a commercial suretyship under C.C. art. 3042.

The fourth criterion looks solely at the relationship between the surety and the debtor (R3). If that relationship arises out of a commercial transaction of the surety, then the contract is a commercial suretyship, even if both debtor and surety are individuals and even if the creditor/debtor relationship (R1) has nothing to do with business. For example, in both of the following situations, a commercial suretyship will arise: (i) a parent guarantees the loan for her son's new car, which the son plans to use only for personal use, but the son agrees to give the parent 20% interest in the son's new business in exchange for the guarantee of the car loan; or (ii) a relative guarantees the loan for her cousin's medical education, and the cousin agrees to pay the relative $500/year as long as the loan is outstanding.

2.2(b). The Legal Suretyship

C.C. art. 3043 defines a legal suretyship as one *"given pursuant to legislation, administrative act or regulation or court order."*

Legal suretyship arises when a statute or court order requires a person or entity to guarantee the debts of another. Statutory or judicial requirements to furnish "bonds" are requirements to furnish a legal surety. The following are examples of legal suretyships:

- A suspensive appeal bond (C.C.P. art. 2124);
- A bond given by a criminal defendant (C.Cr.P. art. 311, 312);
- A bond given to obtain an injunction (C.C.P. art. 3160); or
- A bond given under the Private Works Act (R.S. 9:4812, see Section 37.8(d), below).

2.2(c). The Ordinary Suretyship

C.C. art. 3044 defines an ordinary suretyship as one *"that is neither a commercial suretyship nor a legal suretyship."*

Ordinary suretyship, therefore, is a residual category. One must first determine if the suretyship contract fits the definition of either a commercial or legal suretyship. Only if the suretyship contract is neither commercial nor legal can the relationship be characterized as an ordinary suretyship.

Only ordinary sureties get a special reading of their suretyship contract in their favor, for C.C. art 3044 states that an *"ordinary suretyship must be strictly construed in favor of the surety."*

Examples of ordinary suretyship include the following if they are in writing and signed by the surety:

- I guarantee my daughter's purchase of a new car.

- I guarantee my brother's credit card.

- I guarantee my friend's credit purchase of a new computer that she plans to use solely for her personal (and not business) use.

2.3. What Obligations a Suretyship May Secure

C.C. art. 3036 states that suretyship *"may be established for any lawful obligation."* This means that suretyship may secure any principal obligation recognized by Louisiana law. The principal obligation is the relationship between the creditor and the debtor ("R1"):

Diagram 2.3

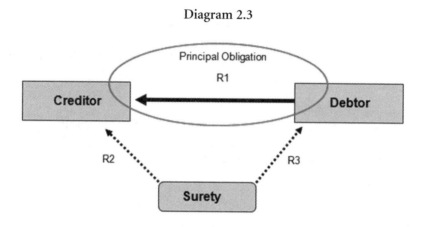

A suretyship may secure a contractual obligation of the debtor, whether that contractual obligation is to pay money or perform a task. A suretyship also may secure potential tort liability of the debtor.

The following are examples of the kinds of principal obligations that a suretyship may secure:

- A note signed by the debtor;
- A line-of-credit loan obtained by the debtor (such as a credit card, under which the debtor may charge items and make repayments and continue to make charges as long as the total upper limit is not reached);
- A debtor's agreement to properly and timely construct a house or building;
- The debtor's obligation to faithfully perform his or her job; or
- The debtor's tort liability if the debtor converts or steals monies belonging to others.

The principal obligation may be subject to a term or condition, may presently exist, or may arise in the future. Therefore, one may become a surety today for an obligation that may not arise until later.

2.4. Suretyship May Be Limited in Scope and Time

Because suretyship (R2) is an accessory obligation to the principal obligation (R1), it cannot be broader in scope than the principal obligation. If it were broader or more expansive than the principal obligation, or if it placed more obligations on the surety than on the debtor, it would no longer be an accessory contract of suretyship but something else and would not be subject to the suretyship rules.

C.C. art. 3040 provides that a suretyship "*may be qualified, conditioned, or limited in any lawful manner.*" Therefore, a suretyship may be: shorter in time than the principal obligation; smaller in dollar liability than the principal obligation; or subject to its own suspensive conditions that would allow the suretyship to terminate even though the principal obligation is outstanding.

The following are examples of valid limitations of a written suretyship obligation (R2) that are narrower in scope than a specific debtor's principal obligation (R1):

- "I guarantee all of Debtor's debts to you, but this guarantee will cease one year from today."
- "I guarantee all of Debtor's debts to you, but only up to the amount of $1,000."
- "I guarantee all of Debtor's debts to you, but only until such time as she is placed on the approved credit list."
- "I guarantee all of Debtor's initial purchases of merchandise from you."

Chapter 3

Suretyship:
The Relationship between the
Creditor and the Surety

3.1. A Surety Is Liable 100% to the Creditor: There Is No Division or Discussion

C.C. art. 3045 provides that once a surety has entered into a suretyship agreement, that surety is fully bound to the creditor for the entire scope of the obligation covered by the suretyship contract (R2). It does not matter whether the debtor has the capacity to pay and refuses to do so. Likewise, it does not matter whether there is one surety or whether there are fifty sureties; each surety is fully liable to the creditor for 100% of the described obligation.

C.C. art. 3045 abolished the dilatory exception of discussion (C.C.P. art. 926). Discussion was the former right of a surety to point out property of the debtor that could satisfy the obligation that the surety was obligated to pay (C.C.P. arts. 5151 *et seq.*).

The result of the statutory elimination of the surety's former ability to claim discussion is that, if the principal obligation (R1) is due and owing, the creditor may seek to collect it from the surety without first suing the debtor. If the contract expressly provides for discussion, however, the surety may claim it (C.C. art. 5152).

C.C. art. 3045 also abolished the affirmative defense of division (C.C.P. art. 1005). Division was a right a surety had when there were multiple sureties for the same obligation. When division was the law, any one of the many sureties could refuse the creditor's demand that the one surety pay 100% of the obligation. By timely claiming division, the surety could compel the creditor to take into account the virile share of all sureties and collect from the surety claiming division only his or her virile share. For the current law of virile shares, see Section 5.2, below.

The result of the statutory elimination of the surety's former ability to claim division is that, if the principal obligation (R1) is due and owing, the creditor may seek to enforce the suretyship contract from any one of the sureties without dividing the debt among the sureties.

3.2. A Surety May Assert All of the Debtor's Defenses against the Creditor Except Lack of Capacity

La. C.C. art. 3046 states that a surety *"may assert against the creditor any defense to the principal obligation that the principal obligor could assert except lack of capacity or discharge in bankruptcy of the principal obligor."* This means that almost all defenses the debtor possesses that would prevent the creditor from collecting the debt can be used by the surety to prevent the creditor from collecting the debt from the surety. Therefore, a surety can assert defenses such as prescription, peremption, usury, accord and satisfaction, and illegality of the principal obligation.

One of the problems a surety may have, however, is that the surety may not be aware of all the defenses that the debtor may possess at the time the creditor calls upon the surety for payment. This issue is explored further in Section 3.3, below. There are two defenses, however, that the surety cannot assert against the creditor in any circumstance, and these are detailed in C.C. art. 3046.

First, a surety may not assert the debtor's lack of capacity. Therefore, a surety cannot prevent the creditor from collecting the debt from the surety even if the debtor is a minor, an improperly formed corporation, or a partnership where the partnership articles prevented the partnership from borrowing money. The rationale why a surety may not raise the lack of capacity defense is that the surety, who voluntarily entered into the suretyship contract, was best situated prior to entering into the contract to ascertain the debtor's capacity.

Second, a surety may not assert either the debtor's bankruptcy or the debtor's bankruptcy discharge as a defense. The "automatic stay" that arises in bankruptcy (11 U.S.C. §362) and which halts all collection actions against a debtor does not apply to the surety. A creditor may pursue the surety even if the debtor is in a bankruptcy proceeding. Likewise, while a bankruptcy discharge prevents a creditor from further pursuing the debtor, C.C. art. 3045 provides that the surety remain fully liable to the creditor.

3.3. A Surety's Rights Concerning a Creditor When the Creditor Calls upon the Surety to Pay the Debt

The rights of a surety are limited when a creditor calls upon a surety to pay the debt. If the principal obligation is due, the surety cannot seek a delay until the creditor tries to collect from the debtor and cannot seek to compel the creditor to pursue other sureties for some or all of the debt (see Section 3.1 above).

A surety who pays the creditor is entitled to legal subrogation (C.C. arts. 1829, 3048), for the surety has paid a debt owed *"for others."* Therefore, a surety who pays the creditor may collect from the debtor whatever the creditor could collect (see Section 4.3, below).

If a surety simply pays the debt without asking the debtor first whether the debtor possesses the kind of defenses that a surety can raise (see 3.2, above), and if the debtor possessed a valid defense to payment, the surety will be unable to collect the money paid from the debtor by subrogation (C.C. art. 3051). This is because legal subrogation places the surety in the creditor's position, but if the debtor had a defense against the creditor and the surety fails to notify the debtor of the creditor's demand, then the debtor can raise that same defense against the surety who is suing in subrogation.

If the surety has paid and the debtor has a defense, however, the surety is not without a remedy. If a creditor has collected from the surety when the debtor possessed the kind of defense a surety could raise, then the creditor has been unjustly enriched. In such instances, the surety can sue the creditor to recover the money paid (C.C. art. 3050).

3.4. "Continuing Guarantees"

Because suretyship is a contract, the surety and creditor may define the scope of the surety's obligation. Sometimes the suretyship is limited in time (see Section 2.4, above). Sometimes the suretyship is limited to a specific loan that the debtor incurred. Sometimes, the surety's liability is limited to a specific dollar amount.

Often, however, creditors insist that sureties guaranty the performance of any and all obligations that the debtor may owe to the creditor for past debts, current loans, and future debts. These kinds of suretyship agreements are called "continuing guarantees," because the surety's obligation is for an unlimited amount of time and for any and all past, present and future obligations of the debtor. A continuing guarantee will be in force and effect until the surety takes affirmative steps to cancel the continuing guarantee (see Section 8.4, below).

3.5. "Solidary Sureties" and C.C. Art. 3037

3.5(a). The History of "Solidary Sureties"

Even before 1988, when division and discussion were available by statute to sureties, these rights could be waived, either in the suretyship contract or in litigation by a failure of the surety to timely and properly raise discussion as a dilatory exception or division as an affirmative defense (see Section 3.1, above).

Before the 1988 Civil Code revisions, a common method for creditors to cause sureties to waive both division and discussion was to have the suretyship contract styled as an *in solido* obligation. Sometimes the language would create a solidary relationship among the sureties, which would result in a waiver of the plea of division (for solidary obligors do not have the right of division), as shown by the next diagram:

Diagram 3.5(a)(1)

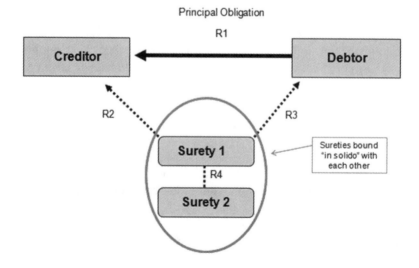

Sometimes the language would create a solidary relationship not only among the sureties, but also among all sureties and the debtor, resulting in a waiver of both division and discussion (for solidary obligors do not have the right of discussion):

Diagram 3.5(a)(2)

The reason that solidary obligors do not have the right of division or discussion is that a solidary obligation is a primary obligation, not an accessory one. A true solidary obligation does not create (as does a suretyship contract) multiple relationships; there is but a single relationship with multiple primary obligors (C.C. art. 1794). Thus, using the examples in the diagrams above, in a true solidary relationship, the diagram would become:

Diagram 3.5(a)(3)

Principal Obligation

Debtors bound
"in solido"

Two key pre-1988 Louisiana Supreme Court cases, *Boutte* and *Aiavolasiti*, created jurisprudential rules governing suretyship contracts when those contracts contained language of solidarity. In both cases: (a) the contract was styled a "continuing guarantee"; (b) the contract contained language binding the sureties solidarily with each other and with the debtor; (c) the creditor drafted the contract; and (d) the creditor knew which person or entity was getting the money and that the sureties were shareholders of the corporate entity.

Nonetheless, in *Boutte* the Court held that the language of solidarity allowed the creditor to view all the parties as solidary obligors (Diagram 3.5(a)(3)) rather than as sureties bound for a principal obligor (Diagram 2.1(c)(3), Section 2.1(c), above).

In *Boutte*, a creditor was allowed to release the debtor and still pursue a surety because the court treated the entire surety/debtor relationship as a solidary obligation in relation to the creditor even though the creditor drafted the contract; therefore, the court concluded that a creditor could release one solidary obligor and pursue a remaining solidary obligor. *Aiavolasiti* held that even though *Boutte* had permitted a creditor to treat the debtor and sureties as solidary obligors, as among the sureties and the debtor, the rules of suretyship (not solidary obligations) must be applied.

Boutte elevated the form of the contract over its substance, allowing a creditor to treat as a primary obligor someone whom the creditor knew was a surety, even though: (a) the contract was written by the creditor; (b) the face of the contract revealed that, despite the solidary terminology, the purpose of the contract was to guarantee the debts of another, and (c) the creditor had knowledge that the shareholder had signed the contract to guarantee performance of another. *Aiavolasiti* recognized that the contractual solidary language inserted by the creditor into a "continuing guarantee" form did not alter the true relationship of the debtor and sureties. As to that relationship, the Supreme Court applied suretyship law. Nevertheless, the court in *Aiavolasiti* allowed creditors to maintain the fiction that, as to the creditor, the relationship among the sureties and debtor was solidary.

In 1988, these jurisprudential rules were changed by the adoption of current C.C. art. 3037. Art. 3037 overruled the result and the analysis of *Boutte*.

3.5(b). C.C. art. 3037 Resolves All Disputes Concerning "Solidary Sureties"

In Louisiana, the phrase "solidary surety" should have no meaning today because C.C. art. 3037 provides the mechanism to resolve all legal issues when a document contains language of solidarity and the signators may or may not be sureties.

C.C. art. 3037 consists of two paragraphs, and each deals with a different situation. The first paragraph states that one "*who ostensibly binds himself as a principal obligor to satisfy the present or future obligations of another is nonetheless considered a surety if the principal cause of the contract with the creditor is to guarantee performance of such obligations.*" This means that even although a contract contains language of solidarity (such as phrases in which the parties bind themselves "in solido"), one must look at the entirety of the document. If a reasonable person reading the entire document could ascertain that the purpose of the contract is to guarantee performance of another, then the creditor and all who attempt to enforce the contract cannot use the rules of solidarity against the signators. Rather, the creditor and others who attempt to enforce the contract must treat as sureties all those who sign to guarantee performance. Important questions to ask when examining such a contract include:

- Is it obvious from the face of the contract that the money is being loaned not to those who signed the contract but to another person or entity? If so, C.C. art. 3037 requires treating as sureties those who sign the contract.
- Is it obvious from the face of the contract that the money is being loaned to only one of the parties signing the contract? If so, C.C. art. 3037 requires treating all the others who sign the contract as sureties.
- Does the contract contain language that those who sign are agreeing to pay in the event that the party receiving the money or loan does not? If so, C.C. art. 3037 requires treating these persons as sureties.

- Does the title of the contract assist in interpreting its meaning (for example, is it entitled "Continuing Guarantee")? If one can ascertain from the title of the document that, along with the rest of the language of the document, the contract evidences an accessory obligation, then C.C. art. 3037 requires that those who sign this accessory obligation must be treated as sureties.

The second paragraph of C.C. art. 3037 states: "*A creditor in whose favor a surety and principal obligor are bound together as principal obligors in solido may presume they are equally concerned in the matter until he clearly knows of their true relationship.*" This second paragraph applies if one cannot determine from the face of the document that it reflects an accessory obligation; therefore, this provision of C.C. art. 3037 applies only if the first paragraph does not.

For example, if a contract contains language of solidarity but it is apparent from the entirety of the document that the real intent of the signators was to be sureties, then the first paragraph of C.C. art. 3037 mandates that they be treated as sureties and there is no need to look at the second paragraph of that article. On the other hand, if an examination of the four corners of the contract does not reveal that its "principal cause" is suretyship, then the creditor is entitled to treat the signators as solidary obligors "*until he clearly knows of their true relationship.*"

There are two obvious implications of this second paragraph of C.C. art. 3037. The first is that usually the original creditor, who drafted the contract, knows of the true relationship of the parties. This means that the original creditor cannot hide behind the language and must treat the signators as sureties if the creditor was aware that was their true relationship to the debtor. Second, if the creditor sells or transfers the debt to a third party, this third party will be able to treat the signators as solidary obligors until "*he clearly knows of their true relationship.*"

Chapter 4

Suretyship:
The Relationship between the
Debtor and the Surety

4.1. The Formation of the Surety/Debtor
Relationship

The following chart is repeated here for ease of reference (see the explanation of the chart in Section 2.1(c), above).

Diagram 2.1(c)(1)

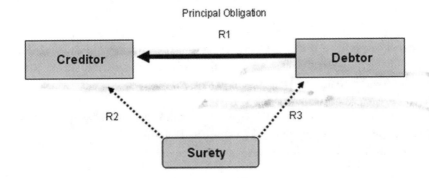

While the surety/creditor obligation must be in writing (R2), no special contract is required for the surety/debtor relationship (R3). That relationship need not be in writing. If there is no specific agreement between the surety and debtor concerning their relationship, the Civil Code provides the default rules. The debtor and surety, however, may always enter into a written contract defining their relationship and the rights and obligations of the parties.

4.2. An Overview of the Surety's Rights Concerning the Debtor

As C.C. art. 3047 states, a surety possess three rights against the debtor—subrogation, reimbursement, and the right to require security.

Each of these is a separate right, and each is subject to different rules, explained in more detail in the next three sections.

4.3. The Surety's Right of Subrogation against the Debtor

4.3(a). A Surety's Subrogation Rights Constitute Legal Subrogation

C.C. art. 1825 defines subrogation as "*the substitution of one person to the rights of another.*" C.C. art. 1829 defines legal subrogation as the legal right received by one has who had paid a debt owed "*for others.*"

A surety is bound to make payment when the debtor does not; the surety is bound "for others" under C.C. art. 1829. Therefore, the surety is entitled to legal subrogation against the debtor. This is made explicit in C.C. art. 3048, which provides that a "*surety who pays the principal obligation is subrogated by operation of law to the rights of the creditor.*"

When subrogation occurs, the surety "steps into the shoes" of the creditor and can enforce all rights that the creditor had against the surety.

The following diagram illustrates legal subrogation:

Diagram 4.3(a)(1)

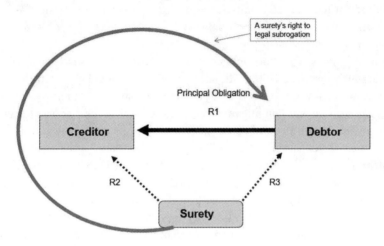

4.3(b). A Surety's Subrogation Rights May Be Contractually Limited

A surety who pays the creditor is entitled to collect that amount from the debtor by asserting the creditor's rights through subrogation.

The surety's legal ability to claim subrogation occurs whenever the surety pays the creditor anything on the principal obligation, whether the payment is for all or only a part of the debt. Creditors, however, often do not want sureties to be engaging in collection efforts against the debtor until the creditor has been paid in full. Creditors often build a clause into the suretyship contract requiring that the surety refrain from using the surety's subrogation rights against the debtor until after the creditor collects all that it is owed. This kind of clause is permissible, for C.C. art. 3040 allows a suretyship contract to "*be qualified, conditioned, or limited in any lawful manner.*"

4.3(c). The Limit on a Surety's Subrogation Rights and the Potential for a Surety to Seek Attorney's Fees and Interest from the Debtor

C.C. art. 1830 limits legal subrogation to the amount paid. In essence, there is a cap on the amount a claimant may receive in subrogation when legal subrogation occurs. The claimant may not recover more by way of contract; once it is determined that the claimant is entitled to legal subrogation, all the claimant may receive is money equal to the "*extent of the performance rendered to the original obligee*" (C.C. art. 1830).

This cap on subrogation rights can be a hardship for a surety who wishes to voluntarily pay the creditor. The surety may not want to be sued by the creditor and may not want to receive the publicity of a lawsuit or to incur the extra costs a lawsuit imposes on litigants. Yet, if the surety voluntarily pays the creditor to avoid these untoward consequences, the surety suffers when the surety attempts to collect from the debtor. This is because a claim by the surety against the debtor at this point may involve a lawsuit. If C.C. art. 1830 caps the surety's recovery at just what the surety paid the creditor, the surety who sues the debtor in legal subrogation may not be able to collect anything beyond legal interest and may not be able to collect attorneys' fees. On the other hand, if the creditor had sued the debtor and if the principal obligation contained clauses granting interest and attorney's fees, the creditor could collect both the contractual interest and the attorney's fees.

C.C. art. 3052 provides protection for the surety. It expressly grants to the surety, who sues a debtor in subrogation, the right to collect attorney's fees and interest from the debtor if the creditor could have collected attorney's fees and interest from the debtor. C.C. art. 3052, therefore, is an exception to the cap on legal subrogation created by C.C. art. 1830.

C.C. art. 3052 only applies if the principal obligation (R1) contains provisions for attorney's fees and interest. If no such provisions are in the principal obligation, the recovery cap of C.C. art. 1830 will apply to bar the surety from collecting attorney's fees and interest from the debtor through legal subrogation.

There is nothing, however, that prevents a debtor and surety from entering into a written contract (R3) defining their relationship and granting to the surety both attorney's fees and interest if the surety pays the creditor. Such an agreement does not violate the C.C. art. 1830 cap on legal subrogation, because now the surety is not seeking attorney's fees and interest through subrogation. Rather, because the agreement is directly with the debtor (R3), this agreement is not dependent upon subrogation rights; instead, it is an aspect of the surety's reimbursement rights (see Sections 4.4, below).

4.4. The Surety's Right of Reimbursement against the Debtor

4.4(a). The Right of Reimbursement

In addition to the right of subrogation, the surety also has the right of reimbursement (C.C. arts. 3049–3050). Reimbursement includes not just the right of a surety to recover from the debtor what the surety has paid the creditor, but it also allows the surety to recover from the debtor even if subrogation is unavailable.

Subrogation is shown in Diagram 4.3(a)(1), above. Reimbursement is shown in the diagram below:

Diagram 4.4(a)(1)

As can be seen, the right of reimbursement is a direct right of the surety against the debtor.

4.4(b). Why a Surety Needs Reimbursement in Addition to Subrogation

One might question why a surety needs reimbursement if a surety already has the right of subrogation. The answer is that reimbursement is an additional right that augments a surety's ability to get repaid even if subrogation does not apply.

Because subrogation allows the surety to collect only to the extent that the creditor could collect, there are defenses that the debtor could assert against the creditor and anyone claiming in subrogation. Reimbursement, however, permits a surety to collect from the debtor what the surety paid to the creditor even if the debtor had possessed a defense that would have prevented the creditor from collecting from the debtor.

For a surety to be entitled to reimbursement even when the debtor had a defense to the creditor, the surety must first inform the debtor that the surety is about to pay the debtor's obligation. C.C. art. 3050 states that a "*surety who in good faith pays the creditor when the principal obligation is extinguished, or when the principal obligor had the means of defeating it, is nevertheless entitled to reimbursement from the principal obligor if the surety made a reasonable effort to notify the principal obligor that the creditor was insisting on payment or if the principal obligor was apprised that the creditor was insisting on payment.*"

If the surety has not asked the debtor about possible defenses before paying the creditor, however, then the surety's rights of both subrogation and reimbursement are eliminated, for C.C. art. 3051 provides that a "*surety may not recover from the principal obligor, by way of subrogation or reimbursement, the amount paid the creditor if the principal obligor also pays the creditor for want of being warned by the surety of the previous payment.*"

From these articles the following principles emerge:

- If the debtor does not have a defense to the debt, the surety who pays may obtain either subrogation or reimbursement.
- If the debtor did have a defense to the debt that the surety could have raised against the creditor (see Section 3.2, above), and if the surety prior to payment told the debtor that the surety was going to pay, and if the debtor did not tell the surety of the defense, then the surety may obtain reimbursement.
- If the debtor did have a defense to the debt that the surety may raise against the creditor (see Section 3.2, above), and if the surety prior to payment did not tell the debtor that the surety was going to pay, the surety may not pursue the debtor either in reimbursement or in subrogation, but the surety may have a claim of unjust enrichment against the creditor (see the discussion at Section 3.3, above).

4.5. The Surety's Right to Require Security from the Debtor

A surety may require security from the debtor to secure the right of reimbursement. The word "security" in C.C. art. 3053, must be read in conjunction with C.C. arts. 3136–3137, which define "security." See Section 1.3(b), above.

There are four separate situations in which a surety may demand security; each one operates independently of the others.

4.5(a). The Right of Security Is Triggered in Four Separate Situations

"Security" under Louisiana law is always an accessory obligation. C.C. art. 3136. The principal obligation that security under C.C. art. 3053 secures is the debtor's reimbursement obligations to the surety (R3).

Diagram 4.5(a)(1)

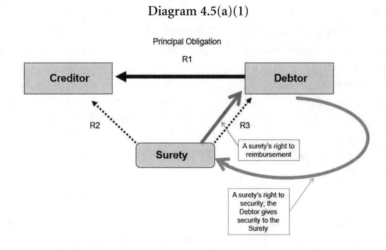

Security can be in many forms, including: an escrow of money; a mortgage on the debtor's property; a security interest under Louisiana's version of the Uniform Commercial Code in assets of the debtor; real security; or a suretyship given by a third party to secure the debtor's reimbursement obligation.

C.C. art. 3053 defines four separate situations giving the surety the right to require that the debtor provide security before the surety pays the creditor: *"(1) The surety is sued by the creditor; (2) The principal obligor is insolvent, unless the principal obligation is such that its performance does not require his solvency; (3) The principal obligor fails to perform an act promised in return for the suretyship; or (4) The principal obligation is due or would be due but for an extension of its term not consented to by the surety."*

The first two triggering events under C.C. art. 3053 are self-explanatory.

The third triggering event (failure of the debtor to perform *"an act promised in return for the suretyship"*) refers to (a) an unfulfilled promise the debtor made to the surety that induced the surety to sign the suretyship agreement, and (b) the performance required by this promise was due on or before the time the surety invokes the security claim.

The fourth triggering event (when the debt is *"due or would be due but for an extension of its term not consented to by the surety"*) applies only when the suretyship is for a specific debt or a specific series of debts with a definite term. As an example, this fourth item would be triggered if a surety guarantees a note due February 1, 2025, and the creditor and debtor later agree (without the surety's consent) to extend the maturity date to March 1, 2030.

The fourth triggering event would not apply if the surety, in the suretyship contract, consented to any and all extensions of the maturity date that might occur in the future, or if (in a later agreement) the surety consented to this particular extension. Creditors often build into suretyship contracts a clause by which the surety consents to all future changes in the principal obligation or debt, including changes in due date and changes in the interest rate.

4.5(b). The Surety's Rights if the Debtor Does Not Provide the Security

C.C. art. 3054 gives the surety a right to sue a debtor who does not voluntarily provide security when requested. The relief that the surety gets in this suit, however, is limited to requiring the debtor to put money into the court registry.

C.C. art. 3054 states: *"If, within ten days after the delivery of a written demand for the security, the principal obligor fails to provide the required security or fails to secure the discharge of the surety, the surety has an action to require the principal obligor to deposit into the registry of the court funds sufficient to satisfy the surety's obligation to the creditor as a pledge for the principal obligor's duty to reimburse the surety."*

As a practical matter, at the point that any of these triggering events occur, it is unlikely that the debtor will possess unencumbered assets that can be given to the surety as security. The cautious surety, who wants to receive security to secure the right of reimbursement, would be advised to obtain this security prior to or simultaneously with signing the suretyship agreement.

Chapter 5

Suretyship:
The Relationship among
Sureties

5.1. An Overview of the Surety/Surety Relationship

C.C. arts. 3055–3057 apply when there is more than one surety and deal with two interrelated areas: virile share and contribution. While each surety is fully liable to the creditor, regardless of how many sureties there are (see Section 3.1, above), among themselves sureties may have differing percentages of liability—this is euphemistically referred to as the surety's virile share. "Contribution" refers to the right possessed by a surety who has paid the creditor to collect some of that money from a co-surety; the extent of contribution depends upon each surety's virile share.

In the following diagram, the surety/surety relationship is shown as R4:

Diagram 5.1(1)

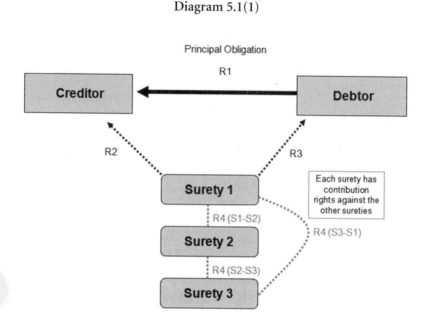

5.2. Calculating the Surety's Virile Share

C.C. art. 3055 provides the default rules for determining each surety's virile share, but nothing prevents the sureties from contractually agreeing otherwise.

C.C. art. 3055 requires an initial determination whether the parties had entered into an agreement about their virile shares. If there is an agreement, it must be enforced. The agreement need not be in writing; Louisiana State Law Institute Comment (b) points out that parol evidence is admissible to prove the virile share agreement.

If no agreement had been made among the sureties, C.C. art. 3055 requires a determination whether the sureties *"contemplated that he who bound himself first would bear the entire burden of the obligation regardless of others who thereafter bind themselves independently and in reliance upon the obligation of the former."*

Although C.C. art. 3055 begins with language about a presumption—that sureties *"are presumed to share the burden of the principal obligation"* by heads—analytically, the presumption is a fall-back position. The presumption applies only after one has analyzed whether there is an agreement among the sureties about their virile share and whether there was "contemplation" that the first surety to sign would "*bear the entire burden.*" In other words, one should use the by-heads presumption of virile-share liability only after investigating and eliminating the possibility of either an agreement among the sureties or a contemplation that they would be liable in the order in which they signed.

Therefore, if there is a contract with three sureties, it is analytically incorrect to assume that each surety's virile share is 1/3. Rather, one must go through the analysis and inquire whether there is an agreement among the sureties (which could be shown by a written contract or even by parol evidence) or whether the sureties contemplated that they would be liable in the order in which they signed the document creating the suretyship. Extrinsic evidence of the agreement or contemplation may be possible.

For example, if the debtor is a corporation with 100 shares of stock and the three sureties who sign a continuing guarantee own, respectively, 80, 15, and 5 shares of the stock, it may be that each contemplated that the virile share would equate with their stock ownership. It should be remembered, however, that a virile share determination has no impact on the creditor's rights, because each surety is liable to the creditor "*for the full performance of the obligation.*" C.C. art. 3045 (see the discussion in Section 3.1, above).

Thus, in this example, even though the sureties may have contemplated or agreed that Surety #1, who owned 80% of the stock, has a virile share of 80%, nonetheless the creditor may collect 100% of the obligation from any of the sureties.

Cautious individuals who are about to become sureties, or who are about to become joint investors in an enterprise where a surety agreement may be required by an existing or future creditor, should consider entering into written contracts with the other sureties detailing the virile share each is to bear as against the others.

5.3. Reallocation of a Surety's Virile Share in the Event of Insolvency

C.C. art. 3056 requires a reallocation of the virile share calculation in the event one of the sureties becomes insolvent. C.C. art. 3056 places the risk of a surety's insolvency on the other sureties.

For example, if there were 100 sureties, each with a 1% virile share, and all but two become bankrupt, the remaining two sureties would have a virile share of 50% each.

5.4. Limitations on a Surety's Right of Contribution

A surety's right of contribution is a form of legal subrogation. C.C. art. 3056 states that "*a surety who pays the creditor may proceed directly or by way of subrogation*" to obtain contribution, and C.C. art. 1829 provides that legal subrogation occurs when one pays a debt "*he owes with others or for others.*" Therefore, every time a surety pays the creditor, the surety is entitled to legal subrogation against both the debtor (see Section 4.3, above) and against the other sureties.

The Civil Code does not require that the surety pay the entire debt in order to obtain contribution. Theoretically, if a surety paid the creditor $1,500 on a $100,000 debt, and if that $1,500 exceeded the surety's virile share (see Section 5.2, above), the surety would be entitled to contribution from the co-sureties. Many creditors, aware of this issue and not wanting the surety to compete with the creditor for payments from the co-sureties, place in suretyship agreements a contractual obligation of the surety not to pursue contribution rights against the co-sureties until the entire obligation to the creditor has been satisfied. This kind of clause is permissible. C.C. art. 3040 allows a suretyship contract to "*be qualified, conditioned, or limited in any lawful manner.*"

The legal subrogation that a surety receives through contribution raises two issues: (a) whether a surety may collect from a co-surety everything that was paid to the creditor, just as the surety can do when the surety pursues legal subrogation against the debtor (see Section 4.3, above); and (b) whether a surety may collect attorney's fees and interest from a co-surety.

5.4(a). A Surety's Contribution Rights Are Limited to Amounts Paid in Excess of That Surety's Virile Share

C.C. art. 3057 limits the amount a surety may collect from a co-surety in contribution. It states that a "*surety who pays the creditor more than his share may recover the excess from his co-sureties in proportion to the amount of the obligation that each is to bear as to him.*"

In order to calculate a surety's right of contribution against a co-surety under C.C. art. 3057, one must first determine the virile share of the surety who pays and the virile share of each of the other sureties (see Section 5.2, above).

The following three examples will help illustrate how this operates. Each example assumes that: (a) there is a $900,000 obligation for which there are three sureties; (b) an analysis has been performed to determine their virile shares; and (c) this analysis has revealed that the virile share of each is 1/3.

5.4(a)1. Example #1

Surety #1 pays $200,000 and the creditor grants Surety #1 (and only Surety #1) a complete release.

Surety #1 will get no contribution from Surety #2 and Surety #3. This is because Surety #1's virile share is 1/3 (1/3 × $900,000 = $300,000), and Surety #1 has not paid more than that virile share.

5.4(a)2. Example #2

Surety #1 pays $500,000 and the creditor grants Surety #1 (and only Surety #1) a complete release. Surety #1 has paid $200,000 more that his virile share.

C.C. art. 3056 permits Surety #1 to "*recover from his co-sureties the share of the principal obligation each is to bear.*" Because the analysis performed on the surety's obligations has determined that each surety's virile share is 1/3, Surety #1 may collect the amount in excess ($200,000) of Surety #1's virile share from either Surety #2 or Surety #3.

5.4(a)3. Example #3

Surety #1 pays $700,000 and the creditor grants Surety #1 (and only Surety #1) a complete release. Now, Surety #1 has paid $400,000 more than his virile share.

Because each of the other sureties' virile share is also 1/3, it may be uncertain what Surety #1 can collect from Surety #2 and Surety #3.

The express language of C.C. art. 3056 appears to permit Surety #1 to collect the $400,000 contribution amount from either Surety #2 or Surety #3, because C.C. art. 3056 allows the contribution to be obtained for "*the share of the principal obligation each is to bear.*" Under this reading of C.C. art. 3056, the share each surety owes to the creditor is 100% of the obligation without the benefits of division and discussion (see C.C. art. 3045, discussed at Section 3.1, above). Because division has been abolished, the remaining two sureties would not be able to claim division as to Surety #1. If Surety #2 paid the entire $400,000 that Surety #1 seeks in contribution, then Surety #2 could seek $100,000 (the amount in excess of Surety #2's virile share) from Surety #3 in contribution.

On the other hand, some read C.C. art. 3056 as prohibiting Surety #1 from obtaining more than each remaining surety's virile share. Under this rationale, since one knows the virile shares, Surety #1 cannot collect from Surety #2 more than $300,000. The remaining $100,000 of the $400,000 contribution Surety #1 may seek would have to be obtained from Surety #3.

The Louisiana Supreme Court has not rendered a decision on this issue at the time of the publication of this Précis; therefore, cautious sureties may want to enter into a written contract addressing how to resolve this issue.

Chapter 6

Suretyship:
Effects of a Modification of the
Principal Obligation

6.1. The Effects of Modification of the Principal Obligation Depends on the Type of Suretyship and the Consent That the Surety May Have Given

C.C. art. 3062 sets forth the rules that apply when the principal obligation is modified or amended "*in any material manner*" or when there has been a material impairment of real security.

Applying C.C. art. 3062 requires an analysis of the suretyship agreement and of any post-suretyship agreements into which the surety enters. The reason is twofold. First, a surety may waive the advantages that C.C. art. 3062 grants to sureties by consenting to the modifications, amendments, and release or impairment of real security. Many creditors typically build such consents into the contract of suretyship. Second, if no consent has been given, either in the contract of suretyship or at a later point in time, then C.C. art. 3062 requires analyzing the suretyship relationship to determine whether it is a commercial or ordinary suretyship (see Section 2.2, above, and Sections 6.1(a) and 6.1(b), below), because C.C. art. 3062 mandates different outcomes depending upon the type of suretyship.

The following are examples of material modifications or amendments of the principal obligation:

- The suretyship contract secures a specific debt due in one year. Three months after the suretyship contract had been signed, the creditor and debtor entered into a binding agreement extending the payment of the debt from one year to three years. This is a material change because, when the suretyship contract was entered into, the surety reasonably anticipated that the suretyship obligation would terminate after one year, absent a default by the debtor.
- The suretyship contract secures a specific debt bearing 5% per annum interest. After the suretyship contract has been signed, the creditor and debtor enter into a binding agreement raising the interest rate to 8% per annum. This is a material change because, when the suretyship contract was entered into, the surety reasonably anticipated that interest rate on the debt was fixed at 5%; when the interest rate increases, the maximum liability of the surety also increases.

C.C. art. 3062 also applies when there is a material "*impairment of real security*" that secures the principal obligation. An example of a material impairment of real security is when, in addition to the existing suretyship contract, the debtor has given the creditor a mortgage on the debtor's property to secure the principal obligation and, six months after the suretyship contract had been signed, the creditor releases the debtor's mortgage. The following diagram illustrates this situation:

Diagram 6.1(1)

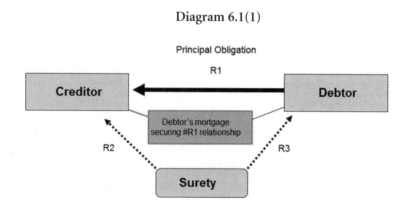

Principal Obligation

R1

Creditor   Debtor

Debtor's mortgage
securing #R1 relationship

R2   R3

Surety

A release of the mortgage does not release the debtor or the principal obligation (see C.C. art. 1891: *"Release of a real security given for the performance of an obligation does not give rise to a presumption of remission of debt."*). Nonetheless, the release of the mortgage does impair the surety's right of subrogation, because if the mortgage had remained in place and the surety had paid the debt to the creditor, the surety could exercise legal subrogation rights (see Section 4.3) against the debtor. The surety's legal subrogation rights would include the right to do what the creditor could do—seize and sell the mortgaged property and obtain a privilege on its sale (see Chapter 11, below). If the mortgage has been released, however, the surety no longer has the option, after paying the debt to the creditor, to seize and sell the mortgaged property as part of the surety's subrogation rights. Thus, the surety's right of subrogation has been impaired.

6.1(a). C.C. art. 3062's Effects on Ordinary Sureties

C.C. art. 3062 provides that, absent consent of the ordinary surety, the ordinary surety is completely released whenever there is a material modification of the principal obligation or a material impairment of real security securing the principal obligation.

The release takes place by operation of law. C.C. art. 3062 states that the *"ordinary suretyship is extinguished."* The surety may assert this defense whenever the creditor seeks to collect from the surety.

6.1(b). C.C. art. 3062's Effects on Commercial Sureties When the Principal Obligation Is for the Payment of Money

C.C. art. 3062 provides that, absent consent of the commercial surety, when the principal obligation is for the payment of money, the commercial surety is released *"to the extent that the surety is prejudiced by the action of the creditor."*

Therefore, when dealing with commercial sureties who have not given prior consent, one must determine *"the extent that the surety is prejudiced by the action of the creditor."* Determining this extent is critical, because unlike an ordinary surety, a commercial surety may get only a partial release despite either a material modification of the principal obligation or impairment of real security.

The following three examples illustrate how this rule operates. Each example assumes that there is a $900,000 obligation by Debtor, a corporation. The $900,000 obligation is represented by a negotiable note. The $900,000 note is due in monthly installments over 10 years, with an interest rate of 5% per annum. The $900,000 note is secured both by a mortgage that Debtor has given on property it owns (see Chapter 11, below) and by the commercial suretyship contract (see Diagram 6.1(1), above). The commercial suretyship contract is restricted to this specific debt, which is described in detail in the commercial suretyship contract. The commercial suretyship contract does not contain any of the consents permitted by C.C. art. 3062.

In these examples, note that Creditor's release of the accessory obligation of mortgage (see Section 11.1, below) does not release the principal obligation (R1) if Creditor does not at the same time expressly cancel the principal obligation. This is because C.C. art. 1891 states that a release "*of a real security given for performance of an obligation does not give rise to a presumption of remission of debt.*"

6.1(b)(1). Example #1

Six months after the suretyship contract has been signed, Creditor enters into a binding agreement with Debtor to extend the time of payment of the $900,000 note from ten years to fifteen years.

This is a material change in the principal obligation, and the commercial surety is released to the extent of the impairment. The impairment is the extension of time; therefore the commercial suretyship is extinguished after the original ten year period expires.

6.1(b)(2). Example #2

Six months after the suretyship contract has been signed, Creditor enters into a binding agreement with Debtor to reduce from ten years to seven years the time of payment of the $900,000 note.

Although this is a material change in the principal obligation, the commercial surety is not released because there is no impairment. When the commercial suretyship was entered into, the commercial surety knew that the obligation could last up to ten years. Now, the note will be due earlier than originally anticipated, and this is a benefit to the surety.

6.1(b)(3). Example #3

Six months after the suretyship contract has been signed, Creditor enters into a binding agreement with Debtor to increase the interest rate on the note from 5% per annum to 11% per annum.

This is a material change in the principal obligation, and the commercial surety is released to the extent of the impairment. The impairment is the increase in interest rate; therefore the commercial surety is not bound for any more than the principal obligation and the original 5% per annum interest rate.

6.1(b)(4). Example #4

Six months after the suretyship contract has been signed, Creditor enters into a binding agreement with Debtor to decrease the interest rate on the note from 5% per annum to 3% per annum.

Although this is a material change in the principal obligation, the commercial surety is not released because there is no impairment. When the commercial suretyship was entered into, the commercial surety knew that the obligation had a 5% per annum interest rate. Now the note will bear less interest than originally anticipated; the surety benefits from this change and cannot claim any release.

6.1(b)(5). Example #5

Six months after the suretyship contract has been signed, Creditor releases the $900,000 mortgage on Debtor's property.

Although this is a material impairment of real security, the extent to which the commercial surety has been released cannot be determined solely from this information. The reason is that the commercial surety is released only to the extent of the impairment. To ascertain the extent of the impairment, one must know the value of the property; however, the value is not measured at the time the mortgage was put in place but rather at the time the mortgage was released.

The fact that the mortgage secures a $900,000 note does not mean that the property was worth $900,000 at the time the mortgage was given and does not mean that the property is worth that today. To determine how this analysis works, assume that the mortgaged property is an area that flooded. Assume that the mortgage was granted in favor of the creditor a year before a flood. At the time the mortgage was entered into, the property was worth $900,000. Assume further, however, that the property was severely damaged by the flood and, at the time of the release of the mortgage, was worth only $350,000.

Under this hypothetical set of facts, C.C. art. 3062 permits the commercial surety to obtain a $350,000 release from liability when Creditor releases the $900,000 mortgage. The reason is that if the commercial surety had paid Creditor the entire $900,000 principal obligation (R1) the day before Creditor released the mortgage, the surety claiming legal subrogation would have been able to realize, at most, only $350,000 from a judicial sale of the property when foreclosing on the $900,000 mortgage (see Chapter 12, below). Therefore, when Creditor voluntarily releases this $900,000 mortgage, the commercial surety remains liable for $550,000 ($900,000 − $350,000).

Chapter 7

Suretyship: Release of One Surety When There Are Multiple Sureties

7.1. Several Civil Code Articles Must Be Considered in Calculating the Effects of Release of One Surety When There Are Multiple Sureties

While C.C. art. 3062 (see Chapter 6, above) addresses what happens when there is a material modification or amendment of a suretyship contract, there is no single corresponding Civil Code article detailing what happens to the remaining sureties when one of them is released from the suretyship contract by the creditor. Determining how to address this situation requires considering a combination of C.C. art. 1892 ("*Remission Granted to Sureties*"), C.C. art. 3055 ("*Liability Among Co-Sureties*"), and C.C. arts. 3057–3058 concerning the right of contribution.

These articles place the burden on the creditor when one of several sureties is completely released. The release may reduce the creditor's rights against the remaining sureties. To determine what occurs when one of several sureties is released requires both ascertaining the virile share of each surety (see Section 5.2, above) and considering how much (if anything) the surety paid the creditor for the complete release. At the same time, one must remember that the analysis of the debtor's obligations to the creditor after the release of a surety differs from the analysis of the effect of that release on other sureties. The next section provides examples of how this works.

7.2. Examples of the Effects of a Creditor's Complete Release of One of Many Sureties

The following three examples deal with situations when one of many sureties is released by the creditor. These examples begin with the same assumptions contained in the examples in Section 5.4, above, but are concerned solely with looking at the creditor's rights against the remaining sureties and the debtor.

Each example below assumes that: (a) there is a $900,000 obligation for which there are three sureties; (b) an analysis has been performed to determine the virile share of each surety; and (c) the analysis has revealed that the virile share of each is 1/3 (see Section 5.2, above). The following diagram illustrates this situation:

Diagram 7.2(1)

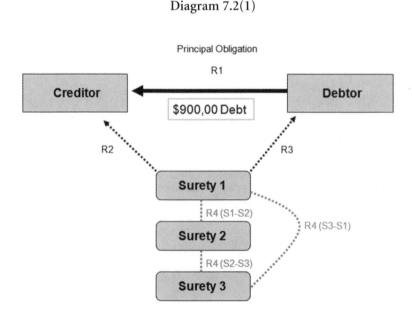

7.2(a). Example #1

Surety #1 pays $300,000 and Creditor grants Surety #1 (and only Surety #1) a complete release.

Debtor's obligation to Creditor is now reduced to $600,000, because Surety #1's $300,000 payment must be applied to the $900,000 principal obligation. As C.C. art. 1892 states: "*[r]emission of debt granted to the sureties does not release the principal obligor*" and "*[i]f the obligee grants a remission of debt to a surety in return for an advantage, that advantage will be imputed to the debt, unless the surety and the obligee agree otherwise.*"

Because the $300,000 payment Surety #1 made equals the amount that has been determined to be Surety #1's virile share, the release of Surety #1 has no impact on the other two sureties, and Creditor may obtain the remaining $600,000 debt from either of them (see C.C. art. 3045). Likewise, Creditor may pursue Debtor for the $600,000 remaining on the principal obligation (R1).

Because Surety #1 has not paid more than Surety #1's virile share, Surety #1 has no right of contribution against the co-sureties (see Section 5.4, above) but does have rights of both subrogation and reimbursement against Debtor (see Sections 4.3 and 4.4 above).

7.2(b). Example #2

Surety #1 pays $400,000 and Creditor grants Surety #1 (and only Surety #1) a complete release.

Debtor's obligation to Creditor is now reduced to $500,000, because the surety's payment must be applied to the $900,000 principal obligation. Creditor may pursue Debtor for the $500,000.

The $400,000 payment Surety #1 made equals more than the amount that has been determined to be Surety #1's virile share; therefore, the release of Surety #1 has no impact on the other two sureties other than to reduce the balance owing, and Creditor may obtain the remaining $500,000 debt from either of them (see C.C. art. 3045).

Because Surety #1 has paid $100,000 more than Surety #1's virile share, Surety #1 has a right of contribution for this $100,000 against the co-sureties (see Section 5.4, above). Surety #1 also has rights of both subrogation and reimbursement against Debtor (see Sections 4.3 and 4.4 above).

7.2(c). Example #3

Surety #1 pays $175,000 and Creditor grants Surety #1 (and only Surety #1) a complete release.

Debtor's obligation to Creditor is now reduced to $725,000, because Surety #1's payment must be applied to the $900,000 principal obligation.

Because Surety #1's $175,000 payment is less than the amount that has been determined to be Surety #1's virile share, the impact of the third paragraph of C.C. art. 1892 must be considered. It states: "*Remission of debt granted to one surety releases the other sureties only to the extent of the contribution the other sureties might have recovered from the surety to whom the remission was granted.*"

This means that Creditor, who has released a surety for less than the surety's virile share, bears the risk of not being able to collect the entire remaining balance of the debt from the other sureties; Creditor is deemed to have released the entire virile share of Surety #1. This is because the "*extent of the contribution the other sureties might have recovered*" from Surety #1 was Surety #1's virile share (see C.C. art. 3057). Therefore, although Surety #1's payment of $175,000 is less than his 1/3 virile share of the $900,000 debt, the effect of the release of Surety #1 is to release the entire 1/3 virile share of Surety #1. Under C.C. art. 1892, Surety #2 and Surety #3 can claim the benefit of this release against Creditor, and thus Creditor can collect only a total of $600,000 from the remaining two sureties. In other words, the Creditor's ability to collect the remainder of the original $900,000 debt from the remaining sureties must be reduced by Surety #1's 1/3 virile share ($900,000 − $300,000 = $600,000).

Remember, however, that although Creditor can collect only $600,000 from either Surety #2 or Surety #3, Creditor can still collect $725,000 from Debtor.

Because Surety #1 has not paid more than Surety #1's virile share, Surety #1 has no right of contribution against the co-sureties (see Section 5.4, above) but does have rights of both subrogation and reimbursement against Debtor (see Sections 4.3 and 4.4 above).

Chapter 8

Suretyship: Extinction or Termination of the Suretyship Contract

8.1. Suretyship Is a Contract; the General Rules on Termination of Contracts Apply

C.C. art. 3058 states that *"the obligations of a surety are extinguished by the different manners in which conventional obligations are extinguished, subject to the following modifications."* These modifications are contained in C.C. arts. 3059–3062.

Suretyship, as in the case with any contact, can be terminated by the consent of the parties—the creditor and surety.

Suretyship may be terminated without the consent of the parties when the principal obligation the suretyship secures is extinguished (C.C. art. 3059 and Section 8.2, below), by prescription (C.C. art. 3060 and Section 8.3, below), or by the death of the surety (C.C. art. 3061 and Section 8.4(c), below).

Suretyship may be terminated in some but not all circumstances by the surety's unilateral notification of the creditor that the surety desires to terminate the arrangement (C.C. art. 3061 and Section 8.4(a), below).

Because suretyship is a contractual obligation (C.C. art. 3035), the rules on vices of consent apply (see C.C. arts. 1948 *et seq.*). For example, a surety who was pressured to sign a contract of suretyship at gunpoint may seek to void the agreement (C.C. arts. 1959 *et seq.*). On the other hand, a surety who signed a suretyship agreement to prevent the creditor from foreclosing on a mortgage on the debtor's house may not void the contract of suretyship for an alleged vice of consent, for under C.C. art. 1962, the *"threat of doing a lawful act or a threat of exercising a right does not constitute duress."*

8.2. Extinction of the Principal Obligation Extinguishes the Contract of Suretyship

Because suretyship is an accessory obligation, C.C. art. 3059 mandates that the *"extinction of the principal obligation extinguishes the suretyship."*

Extinction of the principal obligation can occur in any manner that a conventional obligation is extinguished, such as payment by the debtor.

It should be noted, however, that the mere inability of the creditor to collect the principal obligation because of a personal defense of the debtor (such as minority or bankruptcy) does not extinguish the principal obligation. In such cases, the surety remains liable to the creditor (see Section 3.2, above).

8.3. The Effects of Prescription and Interruption of Prescription on Suretyship

Prescription can affect suretyship in four different ways.

First, the principal obligation can prescribe; in that event, the surety's obligation is extinguished (C.C. art. 3060), because suretyship is an accessory obligation (C.C. art. 3035).

Second, C.C. art. 3054 states that if prescription is interrupted against the debtor, then *"the interruption is effective against his surety."*

Third, if the surety makes a payment or acknowledges the debt, this may, under certain circumstances, interrupt prescription of the principal obligation (see C.C. art. 3060 and Official Louisiana Law Institute Comment (c)).

Finally, under C.C. art. 3060, a *"surety's action for contribution from his co-sureties and his action for reimbursement from the principal obligor prescribe in ten years."* Prescription would not begin to run in this instance, however, until the surety had made a payment to the creditor, for only then would a surety have a claim for contribution against co-sureties (*see* Section 5.4, above) or a claim for reimbursement against the debtor (*see* Section 4.4, above).

8.4. Termination of Suretyship

Termination differs from extinction.

Termination cancels an existing suretyship, but in some circumstances the surety may remain liable for certain pre-existing obligations as well as certain future debts (see Section 8.4(b), below).

Extinction, on the other hand, completely releases the surety from any further obligation (see Section 8.2, above).

8.4(a). Notice of Termination

C.C. art. 3061 begins with the principle that "*a surety may terminate the suretyship by notice to the creditor.*" Louisiana jurisprudence has held that this requires actual notice of an intent to terminate. While neither the statute nor the jurisprudence require written notice of termination, it is always advisable for sureties to give the notice in writing so that they can prove when the notice was given.

Louisiana cases hold that a termination of suretyship does not occur merely because the creditor knows that the surety is no longer in business with the debtor. For example, the jurisprudence has held a termination does not result merely because a creditor is aware that a surety has left town or that a surety who had been a shareholder of the debtor has sold his or her shares.

A termination of suretyship requires that the surety give specific notice to the creditor of the surety's intent to terminate all obligations under the suretyship contract. Creditors frequently place into suretyship contracts the form of notice required and to whom the notice must be given. A creditor running a national operation, for example, may require written notice to an "executive officer" of the enterprise.

8.4(b). Effects of Termination

Even after a notice of termination has been given, a surety is not completely released from all liability. C.C. art. 3061 states that the "*termination does not affect the surety's liability for obligations incurred by the principal obligor, or obligations the creditor is bound to permit the principal obligor to incur at the time the notice is received, nor may it prejudice the creditor or principal obligor who has changed his position in reliance on the suretyship.*"

This means that, even after termination, the surety will be liable for past debts and may be liable for certain future debts.

8.4(b)1. Example #1

Creditor agrees to sell merchandise to Corporation on credit. Creditor agrees to continue selling merchandise as long as Corporation makes timely payments. Surety X, a shareholder and employee of Corporation, signs a continuing guarantee agreeing to pay all of Corporation's debts to the creditor if Corporation fails to do so.

One year after signing the continuing guarantee, Surety X gets a job in another city and sells her shares in Corporation back to Corporation.

Although Creditor may know that Surety X has moved out of town and has sold her shares, nonetheless Surety X remains liable on the continuing guarantee, for Surety X has not given notice of termination to Creditor.

8.4(b)2. Example #2

The facts are the same as in Section 8.4(b)1, Example #1 above, except that Surety Y, another employee and shareholder of Corporation, also has given a continuing guarantee.

One year after signing the continuing guarantee, Surety Y gives a written notice of termination to Creditor.

In this instance, Surety Y remains liable for all unpaid merchandise that Corporation has purchased from Creditor because these are "*obligations incurred*" (C.C. art. 3061) at the time of the termination.

Surety Y also will be liable for merchandise that Creditor had shipped to Corporation at time the notice of termination was received, even if Corporation has not yet received the merchandise. The monies owed for this merchandise are "*obligations that the creditor [was] bound to permit*" at the time of the notice (C.C. art. 3061). By shipping merchandise that has not yet been paid for, Creditor has "*changed his position*" in reliance on the suretyship (C.C. art. 3061).

Surety Y, however, would not be liable for any other future merchandise purchased by Corporation from Creditor.

8.4(b)3. Example #3

Surety Z agreed to pay to Owner of property a sum of money if General Contractor did not properly and timely build Owner's house as designed. Owner had made the suretyship arrangement a condition for entering into the contract with General Contractor. Two weeks after signing the suretyship agreement, Surety Z gives notice of termination to Owner.

In this instance, Surety Z remains liable to Owner until General Contractor's work is completely done, because Owner had changed his position in reliance on the suretyship.

8.4(c). Death of a Surety

Once a creditor knows of the surety's death, this has the "*same effect on a creditor as would a notice of termination received from the surety.*" C.C. art. 3061.

This article also provides for the liability of universal successors: "*A termination resulting from notice of the surety's death does not affect a universal successor of the surety who thereafter unequivocally confirms his willingness to continue to be bound thereby. The confirmation need not be in writing to be enforceable.*"

Chapter 9

Legal Suretyship

9.1. Legal Suretyship: Definition

C.C. art. 3043 defines a legal suretyship as *"one given pursuant to legislation, administrative act or regulation or court order."*

When a statute or court order requires a "bond," this usually refers to a legal suretyship. Examples of legal suretyship include: a suspensive appeal bond (La. C.C.P. art. 2124); a bond required to obtain an injunction (La. C.C.P. art. 3160); bonds for writs of sequestration (La. C.C.P. art. 3574) or attachment (La. C.C.P. art. 3544); and a bond given to allow an arrestee to be released from jail pending trial (La. C. Cr. P. arts. 311–312).

9.2. Requirements of a Legal Suretyship

C.C. art. 3063 states that the Civil Code rules on commercial sureties apply to legal sureties *"except as otherwise provided in this Chapter."* The Civil Code's provisions however, are not the exclusive statutes governing legal suretyships. C.C. art. 3064 states that the Civil Code provisions on legal suretyship *"apply to the extent they are not contrary to special laws governing particular kinds of legal suretyship."*

There are many statutes and regulations detailing the requirements for specific types of legal suretyship. These special statutes and specific laws may add conditions or requirements for a particular type of legal suretyship (C.C. art. 3064).

The Civil Code sets forth, in general terms, who may validly be a legal surety and the parameters of the legal suretyship agreement. Special statutes outside of the Civil Code may add additional requirements.

9.2(a). Qualifications of a Legal Surety

Both business entities and individuals may be legal sureties. C.C. art. 3065 requires that "[l]egal suretyship may be given only by a person authorized to conduct a surety business in Louisiana or by a natural person domiciled in this state who owns property in this state that is subject to seizure and is of sufficient value to satisfy the obligation of the surety."

If a natural person (as opposed to a business entity) desires to be a legal surety, the person's qualifications "must be evidenced by his affidavit and the affidavit of the principal obligor" (C.C. art. 3065). This means that the debtor must take an affirmative action to verify the qualifications of the legal surety. No such actions are required of a debtor when there is a commercial or ordinary suretyship.

Once a legal suretyship has been given, C.C. art. 3065 mandates that the "legal surety may not raise his lack of qualification as a defense to an action on his contract."

9.2(b). The Parameters of a Legal Suretyship Agreement

Except as specifically allowed by specialized statutes, the Civil Code does not permit legal suretyship contracts to limit the statutory or legal requirements that apply. C.C. art. 3066 states that a "legal suretyship is deemed to conform to the requirements of law or order to which it is given, except as provided by Article 3067."

C.C. art. 3067 sets forth permissible variations for legal suretyship contracts: "A surety is not liable for a sum in excess of that expressly stated in his contract. A legal suretyship may contain terms more favorable to the creditor than those required by the law or order pursuant to which it is given, but it may not provide for a time longer than is provided by law for bringing an action against the surety."

In other words, under C.C. arts. 3066 and 3067, even if a legal suretyship contract contains terms at variance with law or court order, that variance is ineffective to limit the surety's liability to the creditor, and the legal suretyship can be enforced to the fullest extent of the law or order, unless one of the limited variations permitted by C.C. art. 3067 exists.

9.3. Testing Whether the Legal Suretyship Meets the Legal Requirements

A legal suretyship is often used to maintain the status quo and to permit the debtor to perform actions or achieve results that would be otherwise be forbidden in the absence of the legal suretyship. For example, a suspensive appeal is permitted only if the judgment debtor provides a legal surety (C.C.P. arts. 2123, 2124). A properly perfected suspensive appeal can cause the erasure of a judicial mortgage created when the judgment was recorded in the mortgage records (see Chapter 17, below). Without a suspensive appeal, the judicial mortgage remains valid and the judgment creditor may execute on the judgment while the devolutive appeal is proceeding. A judgment creditor whose judicial mortgage is cancelled because of a suspensive appeal may be concerned that the legal surety may not be able to satisfy the judgment.

The Code of Civil Procedure provides three ways to "test" the legal suretyship in judicial proceedings. C.C.P. art. 5123 permits *"[a]ny person"* to *"test the sufficiency, solvency of the surety, or validity of a bond furnished as security in a judicial proceeding."*

C.C.P. art. 5123 mandates that the proper procedure is to *"rule the party furnishing the bond into the trial court in which the proceeding was brought to show cause why the bond should not be decreed insufficient or invalid, and why the order, judgment, writ, mandate, or process conditioned on the furnishing of security should not be set aside or dissolved. If the bond is sought to be held invalid on the ground of the insolvency of a surety other than a surety company licensed to do business in this state, the party furnishing the bond shall prove the solvency of the surety on the trial of the rule."*

9.3(a). Testing Whether a Legal Suretyship Meets the Validity Requirements

C.C.P. art. 5123 permits a creditor, in whose favor a legal suretyship has been given, to test the validity of the legal suretyship.

"Validity" in this context refers to whether the legal surety is qualified to be a legal surety (see Section 9.2, above) or whether the form of the document used suffices as a legal suretyship. If the person or entity giving the legal suretyship does not meet the statutory qualifications, the legal suretyship is invalid.

9.3(b). Testing Whether a Legal Suretyship Meets the Sufficiency Requirements

Any interested person (C.C.P. art. 5123), including the judgment creditor in whose favor the legal suretyship is granted, may test the sufficiency of a legal suretyship given in conjunction with a judicial proceeding (C.C.P. arts. 5121–5127). "Sufficiency" in this context refers to whether the legal suretyship bond is in the proper amount.

For example, if a court order requires a suspensive appeal bond of $150,000 but the legal suretyship document reflects that the amount of the bond is only $99,000, the bond can be attacked as being insufficient.

There is a split in the jurisprudence about this "sufficiency" test. Some cases have held that if the amount of the bond is left blank, the bond is invalid on its face and will never suffice as a legal suretyship. Other cases have indicated that it is up to the judgment creditor in a suspensive appeal bond to affirmatively file an attack on the bond with the trial court.

The Louisiana Supreme Court has not spoken definitively on this issue; therefore, cautious creditors will want to affirmatively test the sufficiency of the legal suretyship under C.C.P. art. 5123 *et seq.*

9.3(c). Testing Whether a Legal Suretyship Meets the Solvency Requirements

Any interested person (C.C.P. art. 5123), including the judgment creditor in whose favor the legal suretyship is granted, may test the solvency of a legal suretyship given in conjunction with a judicial proceeding (C.C.P. arts. 5121–5127).

The concept of "solvency" differs from the concept of "validity" (see Section 9.3(a)). A suretyship contract may be valid in form and may have been given by one who possesses all the requirements that allow one to serve as a legal surety, but if the legal surety is insolvent, the legal suretyship itself can be attacked. If insolvency is shown, the legal suretyship is of no effect.

Under C.C. art. 3070, if a "*legal surety ceases to possess required qualifications or becomes insolvent or bankrupt, any interested person may demand*" a replacement legal suretyship.

Under C.C.P. art. 5123, if the legal surety is not a company licensed in the state in a manner that would permit it to serve as a legal surety, the "*party furnishing the bond*" (for example, the judgment debtor in the case of a suspensive appeal) bears the burden of proving the surety's solvency.

For example, if a court order requires a suspensive appeal bond of $20 million dollars, the judgment creditor may wish to challenge the solvency of the legal surety to satisfy the judgment if the case is affirmed on appeal.

9.4. The "Three Strikes and You're Out" Rule for Legal Suretyships

C.C.P. arts. 5123 *et seq.* grant a debtor in a judicial proceeding three separate chances to furnish a legal suretyship that meets all of the requirements of the statutes and any applicable court order.

The debtor has an opportunity to furnish the original legal suretyship. Any interested party may test it (C.C.P. art. 5123), and if the legal suretyship is found wanting, the debtor has four days to furnish a second legal suretyship (C.C.P. art. 5124). Under C.C.P. art. 5124, the furnishing of this second legal suretyship does not release the original legal surety and the second legal suretyship is *"retroactive to the date the original bond was furnished, and maintains in effect the order, judgment, writ, mandate, or process conditioned on the furnishing of security."*

This second legal suretyship also may be tested. If this second legal suretyship is found lacking in validity, sufficiency or solvency, then the debtor has four days to furnish a third legal suretyship (C.C.P. art. 5126). This third legal suretyship also can be tested, but if it is found wanting in sufficiency, solvency or validity, the debtor is not given another opportunity to furnish additional security.

This is the origin of the so-called "three strikes and you're out" rule—a debtor is given only three opportunities to furnish a valid legal suretyship. For example, if a first, second and third suspensive appeal bond are successfully attacked, no suspensive appeal using a bond will be permitted (although the judgment debtor may always provide cash as security under C.C. art. 3068).

9.5. What Happens While the Legal Suretyship Is Being Tested

Although a creditor may attack a legal suretyship for sufficiency, solvency or validity under C.C.P. arts. 5123 *et seq.* (see Section 9.3, above), the attack itself does not invalidate the effect of the bond.

C.C.P. art. 5125 states: "*No appeal, order, judgment, writ, mandate, or process conditioned on the furnishing of security may be dismissed, set aside, or dissolved on the ground that the bond furnished is insufficient or invalid unless the party who furnished it is afforded an opportunity to furnish a new or supplemental bond, as provided in Articles 5124 and 5126.*"

Creditors who are concerned about whether the legal suretyship was given in the proper form, in the proper amount, or by the proper person or entity: (a) must act diligently to ask the court to rule expeditiously on the challenge to the legal suretyship, and (b) should urge the court to set strict time limits for the debtor to furnish a new legal suretyship bond.

For example, a person who obtains a multi-million dollar tort judgment against a corporation may want to vigorously test the validity, sufficiency, and solvency of the corporation's suspensive appeal bond. If the bond cannot be cured after the third try (see Section 9.4, above), the corporate defendant cannot obtain a suspensive appeal, and the judgment creditor can begin to enforce the judgment through writs of seizure while the devolutive appeal is ongoing.

9.6. Cash Instead of a Legal Suretyship

A legal suretyship requires that the debtor find a willing surety. Companies that provide legal suretyships demand a premium for the issuance of the bond. These surety companies usually require that the debtor give them security to ensure that, if the legal surety is called upon to pay, there are assets available to reimburse the legal surety.

The reason that legal sureties often require security from the debtor is that the legal surety anticipates that the likelihood of being called upon to pay the principal obligation may be substantial. In the case of a suspensive appeal bond, for instance, the vast majority of cases are affirmed on appeal by Louisiana appellate courts. Legal sureties who issue suspensive appeal bonds know that (a) the defendant already has lost the judgment at the trial level, and (b) statistically, the chances of defendants overturning results on appeal are not great.

Therefore, legal suretyship businesses not only charge an up-front premium for their services, but they also may demand that collateral be given to secure the surety's right of reimbursement (see Section 4.4, above). A legal surety who is being asked to put up a suspensive appeal bond may require, in addition to the premium for issuance of the bond, a mortgage (see Chapter 11, below) on all of the debtor's immovable property and a UCC 9 security interest (see Chapter 41, below) on the debtor's other assets.

The security given by the debtor to the legal surety secures the debtor's reimbursement obligation to the surety (see Section 4.4, above). The security given by the debtor to the legal surety can be illustrated as follows:

Diagram 9.6(1)

Legal sureties usually require the debtor to both pay a premium to the surety for becoming a legal surety and to furnish security to the legal surety. Obtaining a legal suretyship contract may either be too costly for some judgment debtors or may tie up the judgment debtor's assets during the pendency of the appeal, precluding the judgment debtor from obtaining new loans needed in the daily operations of the judgment debtor's business.

The legislature has recognized the impact on a debtor who wishes to obtain a legal suretyship and has created a special rule permitting any debtor to give a "*pledge*" of funds in lieu of suretyship (C.C. art. 3068). This is done by depositing "*a sum equal to the amount for which he is to furnish security to be held in pledge as security for his obligation*" (C.C. art. 3068).

9.7. Necessity of a Judgment Involving the Legal Surety

C.C. art. 3069 contains two separate rules concerning how a creditor may or may not pursue a legal surety.

The first sentence of C.C. art. 3069 states: "*No judgment shall be rendered against a legal surety unless the creditor obtains judgment against the principal obligor fixing the amount of the latter's liability to the creditor or unless the amount of that liability has otherwise been fixed.*"

The Official Louisiana State Law Institute Comment to this article notes that the "unless" clauses are an exception to the general rule that most sureties can be sued directly when the debtor defaults.

The second sentence of C.C. art. 3069 states that the "*creditor may join the surety and principal obligor in the same action.*" As the Official Louisiana State Law Institute Comment to this article notes, joining both the debtor and the legal surety in the same action "is grounded upon modern procedural notions of judicial efficiency." The comment goes on to warn, however, that "it is not proper, unless authorized by special legislation, to sue the surety alone without joinder of the principal debtor. Such an action is premature, under the first sentence of this Article, until a judgment is obtained against the principal debtor."

The result of these provisions is that a surety can be sued in the same action as the debtor, but execution against the surety under the bond cannot occur before judgment is rendered against the debtor. These provisions also mean that a legal surety cannot be sued in a separate proceeding in which the principal debtor has not been joined unless the surety's liability "*has otherwise been fixed*" (C.C. art. 3069).

9.8. The Ability of a Legal Surety to Obtain a Release during the Existence of the Principal Obligation

Louisiana statutes permit a legal surety, under limited circumstances, to obtain a release from a suretyship bond securing the obligations of an administrator, executor, curator, or tutor.

The legal surety must file a court proceeding alleging that the administrator, executor, curator, or tutor is mismanaging the property and that the legal surety is in danger of being seriously injured by this conduct. The legal proceedings may result in requiring the administrator, executor, curator, or tutor to substitute new security or may result in the removal of the administrator, executor, curator, or tutor (R.S. 9:3911, 3912).

Chapter 10

Pledge

10.1. Historical Background

For almost 150 years, the 1870 version of the Civil Code's pledge articles remained essentially unchanged. In 2014, the Louisiana legislature enacted wholesale amendments to the pledge articles in a bill drafted by the Louisiana State Law Institute.

These changes streamlined rules concerning a pledge of leases and rents of immovable property (Section 10.4, below). They suppressed the outdated concept of antichresis, which was the pledge of immovable property. They recognized that vast swaths of the "old" pledge articles had been superseded in 1990 by the adoption of Louisiana's version of UCC Article 9 (R.S. 10:9-101 *et seq.*, see Chapter 41, below) and eliminated outdated provisions.

The changes also created new rules, including permitting security for loans where the principal obligor has only limited liability (C.C. art. 3135) and validating "negative pledges" (Section 10.5, below).

10.2. An Overview of Pledge

A pledge is a real right that is accessory to the obligation it secures (C.C. arts. 3136 and 3141). Because a pledge is an accessory obligation, it can be enforced only to the extent that the principal obligation remains enforceable.

Because it is a real right, a contract of pledge does not impart personal liability to the pledgee for the principal obligation. *"In the absence of an assumption by the pledgee, the existence of a pledge does not impose upon the pledgee*

75

liability for the pledgor's acts or omissions, nor does it bind the pledgee to perform the pledgor's obligations" (C.C. art. 3167).

The parties to a pledge are prohibited from agreeing that, upon a future default, the pledged item becomes the property of the creditor. Such a provision is *"absolutely null"* (C.C. art. 3040). After the principal obligation is in default, however, the parties can agree that ownership of the pledged item may be transferred to the creditor as a "giving in payment" (C.C. art. 2655).

While a creditor is in possession of a pledged item, the creditor may collect the *"fruits of the thing pledged"* and *"apply them to the secured obligation, even if not yet due"* (C.C. art. 3167).

10.2(a). Delivery of the Pledged Item

A pledge of a corporeal movable is made effective between the parties by delivery of the pledged item to *"the pledgee or a third person who has agreed to hold the thing for the benefit of the pledgee"* (C.C. art. 3149). This reference to corporeal movables may be confusing because, as the official Louisiana State Law Institute comments to C.C. art. 3149 note, under present law, "there may be actually no corporeal movables" subject to pledge, for Louisiana's version of UCC 9 (R.S. 10:9-101 et seq.) seems to preempt the field on how to grant a security interest in corporeal movables. Nonetheless, as this comment goes on to state, the Law Institute left open the possibility that "under present law or under some future change in the law, a particular corporeal movable is insusceptible of encumbrance" under UCC9 "and therefore is properly susceptible of encumbrance by pledge."

For the pledge of anything other than a corporeal movable, delivery is not required, but the pledge is *"effective between the parties only if established by a written contract"* (C.C. art. 3149). The written contract does not need to be witnessed or notarized. The creditor does not have to sign the contract of pledge; the creditor's acceptance is presumed (C.C. art. 3150).

Regardless of what has been pledged, the pledge is never valid against third parties *"until it has become effective between the parties and is established by written contract"* (C.C. art. 3153). Thus, even if any corporeal movable exists that can be pledged, and while such an item could be pledged by the parties merely by delivery, the pledge cannot affect third parties until a written contract has been executed by the pledgor.

There are special rules for the pledge of mineral interests (C.C. art. 3172) and of a lease of immovable property and its rents (see Section 10.4, below).

A creditor holding an item in pledge may refuse to return it to the pledgor until the obligation the pledge secures is extinguished (C.C. art. 3156). A *"con-*

tract of pledge is indivisible, notwithstanding the divisibility of the secured obligations" (C.C. art. 3157). This means that if four items, each worth $250, secure a $1,000 obligation, the party giving the pledge may not pay $250 and demand return of one of the four pledged items. The creditor may retain possession of all the items until the entire $1,000 obligation is extinguished.

The ability of the creditor to retain possession, however, is subject to two exceptions. First, the parties to the pledge may contractually agree to the partial release of pledged items, either before or after a default. Second, the creditor's right of retention is only against the party granting the pledge. As comment (b) to C.C. art. 3156 states, this article "does not alter the long-standing rule that a pledgee may not resist seizure under judicial process, even if instituted by a creditor holding an inferior security right." In case of judicial seizure of the item from the creditor holding it, the remedy is for the creditor to intervene into the lawsuit and assert its rights to the pledge (C.C.P. art. 1092).

10.2(b). The Principal Obligation That a Pledge Secures

A pledge may be given *"to secure the performance of any lawful obligation"* (C.C. art. 3146). It may secure the debts of the pledgor or of a third person (C.C. art. 3148). It may secure the payment of an obligation or it may secure something other than the payment of money; in the latter case, the pledge *"secures the claim of the pledgee for the damages he may suffer from the breach of the obligation"* (C.C. art. 3147).

The parties to a contract of pledge may agree that *"a modification or termination"* of the principal obligation *"or a substitution of a new"* principal obligation *"is a default by the pledgor."* If there is a default or if the principal obligation comes due, the creditor may enforce the pledge and obtain the fruits of the pledge *"to the preference to unsecured creditors of the pledgor"* and to inferior pledgees (C.C. art. 3145).

There are special rules governing the rights of creditors when a pledgee has pledged the same lease or rents to multiple creditors (see Section 10.4(f), below).

10.3. What Can Be Pledged Is Limited

C.C. art. 3142 limits those things that can be pledged to: a *"movable that is not susceptible of encumbrance by a security interest,"* a *"lessor's rights in the lease of an immovable and its rents,"* and things *"made susceptible of pledge by law."*

This list, in the words of the Louisiana State Law Institute comments to this article, is "exclusive."

As a practical matter, the first category—movables that "*are not susceptible of encumbrance by a security interest*"—is a narrow one. As the comments to C.C. art. 3142 note, there are "presently few, if any, corporeal movables that are excluded from coverage" under UCC9 (R.S. 10:9-101 *et seq.*) (see Chapter 41, below). Likewise, these same comments state that the "few incorporeal movables that are excluded" from coverage under UCC9 are "policies of insurance other than life insurance." The special rules concerning the pledge of property insurance policies are contained in R.S. 9:5386 (see Section 15.2, below).

The second category, a "*lessor's rights in the lease of an immovable and its rents*," is discussed in Section 10.4, below. Note, however, that this category does not include the pledge of the rents of movables. Both movables that are being leased and the rents from those leases of movables can be encumbered by a UCC9 security interest. In addition, there is a separate Louisiana Lease of Movables Act (R.S. 9:3301 *et seq.*).

The third category, things "*made susceptible of pledge by law*," permits the legislature to enact statutes that may create specific rules for the pledge of items that do not fit into the first two categories.

10.4. The Pledge of Leases and Rents of Immovable Property

The Civil Code contains specific rules regulating how to pledge a "*lessor's rights in the lease of an immovable and its rents*" (C.C. art. 3142). There are also rules on how to make that pledge effective between the parties and as to third parties. In addition, the Civil Code articles deal with the interrelated rights of the creditor holding the pledge, the landlord, the tenant, and those who may hold an inferior pledge of leases and rents of the same property (see Section 10.4(f), below).

10.4(a). Making the Pledge of Leases and Rental Income from Immovable Property Effective between the Parties and as to Third Parties

A landlord may pledge a lease of immovable property or the rents due the landlord from such properties. A pledge may be of (i) only a single lease, (ii) a part of a lease (C.C. art. 3171), (iii) a lease without the accompanying rents, (iv) the rents without the accompanying lease, or (v) of a lease and its rents. As a practical matter, however, creditors typically demand that the pledge encumber both the lease and its rents. In a commercial building or apartment complex, the creditor typically requires a pledge of all leases and all rents. A landlord can even grant a pledge of leases and rents that are not yet in existence, such as all future leases and rents of the immovable property (C.C. art. 3171).

Likewise, a tenant who executes a sublease becomes a sub-landlord and may pledge the sublease and rents of its subtenant.

No tenant or subtenant may pledge its rights in a lease; the mechanism by which any tenant may encumber its rights concerning the lease is through a mortgage of the tenant's "leasehold" interest (see Section 14.3, below).

It should be reemphasized that the pledge articles apply only to the leases and rents of immovable property. The owner of movable property that is rented may encumber both the movable and the stream of rental income from it under UCC9. Moreover, Louisiana's Lease of Movables Act (R.S. 9:3301 et seq.) deals with the rights of landlords and tenants of movables.

There are three requirements for making the landlord's pledge of leases or rents of immovable property effective between the landlord and creditor.

First, there must be a written contract of pledge (C.C. arts. 3149 and 3168). It need not be witnessed or notarized. As a practical matter, however, because the pledge of leases or rents must be recorded in the mortgage records to affect third persons, creditors typically require that this type of pledge be in authentic form to make it self-proving.

Second, the written contract "*must state precisely the nature and situation of the immovable and its rents*" (C.C. art. 3168). The type of property description required here is the same type of description sufficient for a mortgage (see Section 12.3, below).

Third, the contract of pledge "*must state the amount of the secured obligation or the maximum amount of secured obligations that may be outstanding from time to time*" (C.C. art. 3168). This language is identical to the type of description required for a conventional mortgage. For a more detailed exploration of the description requirements, see Sections 12.4 and 12.4(a), below.

Even if these three requirements are met, the pledge of leases or rents of immovable property is not effective as to third persons until the contract of pledge is recorded in the mortgage records of the parish where the immovable is located (C.C. arts. 3169 and 3338). A contract of pledge of leases and rents may be contained in a mortgage. If that is the case, the pledge becomes effective as to third persons when the mortgage is properly recorded in the parish where the immovable property is located (C.C. art. 3170).

10.4(b). The Length of the Effect on Third Parties of the Pledge of Leases and Rents on Immovables

When the legislature adopted the changes to the pledge articles of the Civil Code, it also amended the articles on the duration of recordation. Third parties are affected by a pledge of leases and rents of immovable property under the same rules that control the effect of mortgages on third parties. (C.C. arts. 3357 *et seq.*)

In essence, if the term of the lease is shorter than nine years, the pledge affects third parties for ten years from the date of the document, not the date of its recordation in the mortgage records (C.C. art. 3357). If the term of the lease is for nine years or more, however, the pledge affects third parties for six years from the expiration of the lease term (C.C. art. 3358). The creditor may extend the effects of recordation by filing an act of reinscription (C.C. arts. 3362–3365). Details of how this works, with examples, can be found in Chapter 20, below.

10.4(c). The Tenant's Obligations When There Has Been a Pledge of the Lease or Rents of an Immovable: The Need for Written Notice

Recordation in the mortgage records of the pledge of leases or rents is critical to affecting third persons (C.C. arts. 3169 and 3338), but a pledge of leases and rents of immovables need not be recorded to affect the tenant of the property. This is because recordation in the mortgage records of the pledge is not sufficient to give the tenant notice of the pledge.

A tenant is not affected by a pledge of rents until a tenant receives actual written notice of the pledge of the lease or rents of the immovable. Until the tenant receives this written notice, the tenant may pay the landlord, even if the creditor has recorded the contract of pledge. This is because C.C. art. 3169 states that a pledge is effective against a tenant only "*from the time he is given written notice of the pledge, regardless of whether the contact establishing the pledge has been recorded.*" Only after receiving this written notice is the tenant obligated to pay the creditor who holds the pledge of the lease or rents.

10.4(d). A Creditor's Rights under a Pledge of Leases and Rents of an Immovable When the Landlord and Tenant Modify or Change the Lease

A creditor who holds a pledge of leases and rents of an immovable cannot assume that, merely by recording the pledge (see Section 10.4(a), above), all future pledged rent will flow to the creditor.

Some creditors attempt to control the stream of rental income by instituting a "lock-box"—a system by which rent is paid either to an agent of the creditor or to a postal box that is in control of the creditor. The creditor than deducts from these funds whatever is owing on the principal obligation the pledge secures and remits the rest to the landlord.

Other creditors, however, permit the landlord to collect rent until there is a default on the obligation that the rent secures; in these instances, the landlord gives a weekly or monthly accounting of rent collections to the creditor.

C.C. arts. 3164 through 3167 create a series of interrelated principles governing the effect on the creditor when the landlord and tenant amend, modify, or substitute a lease of an immovable that has been pledged.

In general, a creditor who does not have a "lock-box" arrangement or who does not notify the tenant of the pledge (see Section 10.4(c), above), bears the risk that the creditor's rights will be affected by the later amendment, modification, or substitution of the lease by the landlord and tenant.

10.4(d)(1). Example #1, Modification of a Lease of Immovable Property

In Year 1, Landlord and Tenant enter into a five year lease that terminates in Year 6. The lease is of a store located on Tract A and requires rentals of $10,000 a month.

In Year 2, Creditor loans Landlord $1 million secured by a written contract of pledge of all of the Landlord's existing leases and rents of Tract A. Creditor promptly records the contract of pledge in the mortgage records of the parish where Tract A is located, but Creditor does not give written notice of the pledge to Tenant.

In Year 3, Landlord and Tenant modify the lease, shortening it by one year, so that it will terminate in Year 5 (not Year 6).

Because the Tenant had not been notified of the pledge by either Creditor or Landlord, the modification is effective against Creditor. Even if Creditor has learned of this modification and then gives written notice to Tenant, Tenant has to remit the rent to Creditor only until the lease terminates in Year 5. Neither Landlord nor Tenant owe Creditor any money for the rents that would have been due in Year 6 (C.C. art. 3167).

On the other hand, if Creditor had an agreement with Landlord that any modification of the lease would be an event of default, then under C.C. art. 3166 Creditor may declare a default in the $1 million loan the pledge secures.

10.4(d)(2). Example #2, Termination of a Lease of Immovable Property

The facts are the same as in Section 10.4(d)1, Example #1, above, except that rather than modifying the lease in Year 3, Landlord and Tenant agree to terminate the lease. Landlord and Tenant are both in good faith in doing this.

Because Tenant had not received written notification of the pledge prior to the termination, the termination is effective against Creditor. Creditor may not collect any rents from Tenant by giving notice now, nor may the Creditor seek to collect the rents from Landlord.

Nonetheless, if Creditor had an agreement with Landlord that termination of the lease would be an event of default, Creditor may declare a default in the $1 million loan the pledge secures.

10.(4)(e). What A Creditor May Do with a Pledge of the Leases and Rents of an Immovable

A creditor who holds a pledge of leases and rents of an immovable may give written notice to the tenant of the pledge and require the tenant to pay the rent to the creditor. This notice may be given at any time, even if there has been no default in the principal obligation that the pledge secures (see C.C. arts. 3159–3161).

While a creditor of the pledge of leases and rents can collect the rents after notice to the tenant, the creditor cannot file suit to sell the pledged lease or rents. Under C.C. art. 3174, a "*pledge of the lessor's rights in the lease of an immovable and its rents does not entitle the pledgee to cause the rights of the lessor to be sold by judicial process. Any clause to the contrary is absolutely null.*"

10.(4)(f). Adjudicating Competing Claims When More Than One Creditor Holds a Pledge of Leases and Rents of the Same Immovable Property

The Civil Code provisions amended in 2014 deal with what happens if two creditors each hold a pledge of the leases and rents of the same immovable property. Adapting a rule from UCC9, C.C. art 3173 permits an inferior creditor whose pledge was recorded second—but who notified the tenant of pledge first—to keep all the rent collected without having to pay it over to the superior creditor as long as the rent is not collected "*more than one month before it is due*" or is not collected "*with actual knowledge that the payment of rent to him violated written directions given to the lessee to pay rent to the holder of the superior pledge.*"

10.4(f)(1). Example #1

On February 1, Superior Creditor loans money to Landlord secured by a pledge of the lease and rents owed by Tenant on Tract A. Superior Creditor records the pledge that same day in the proper parish mortgage records, but Superior Creditor does not notify Tenant of the pledge.

On March 1, Inferior Creditor loans money to Landlord secured by a pledge of the lease and rents owed by Tenant on Tract A. Inferior Creditor both records the pledge that same day in the proper parish mortgage records and gives written notice to Tenant of the pledge. Pursuant to the notice, Tenant pays the rents, as they come due, for April, May, and June to Inferior Creditor.

In July, Superior Creditor becomes aware of the pledge that Inferior Creditor holds and that Tenant is paying rents to Inferior Creditor. Superior Creditor demands that Inferior Creditor pay Superior Creditor the rents for April, May, and June.

In these circumstances, Inferior Creditor does not owe anything to Superior Creditor because, under C.C. art. 3173, a "*pledgee is not bound to account to another pledgee for rent collected*" and none of the exceptions to C.C. art. 3173's general rule apply.

10.4(f)(2). Example #2

On June 1, Bank loans money to Landlord secured by a pledge of the lease and rents owed by Tenant on Tract A. The rent is due on the last day of each month for the next month. Bank records the pledge that same day in the proper parish mortgage records, but Bank does not notify Tenant of the pledge.

On July 1, Savings & Loan loans money to Landlord secured by a pledge of the lease and rents owed by Tenant on Tract A. Savings & Loan both records the pledge that same day in the proper parish mortgage records and gives written notice to Tenant of the pledge. Pursuant to the notice, Tenant pays the rents for August and September to Savings & Loan.

On September 20, Savings & Loan becomes concerned that Bank may be getting ready to give notice to Tenant of Bank's pledge, so Savings & Loan convinces Tenant to pre-pay October, November, and December rent to Savings & Loan.

On September 25, Bank gives written notice of its pledge to Tenant and directs Tenant to send all future rent checks to Bank. Bank also demands that Savings & Loan repay to Bank all the rents that Savings & Loan has collected.

In this situation, Bank gets some of the rents that Savings & Loan has collected, but not all.

Savings & Loan does not have to account to Bank for the rents collected as they came due in August and September, because Bank had not given written notice prior to that time to Tenant. Under C.C. art. 3173, Savings & Loan "*is not bound to account*" for these rents and thus Savings & Loan can keep these monies.

Likewise, Savings & Loan does not have to account to Bank for the Tenant's rent for October. Although Bank notified Tenant before the end of September, the prepayment of October's rent that Savings & Loan received on September 20 was less than "one month before it was due" and was five days before the September 25 written notice to Tenant by Bank.

Savings & Loan, however, must account for and repay to Bank the prepaid rent for both November and December, because the rent for each of these months was paid "*more than one month before it was due*" (C.C. art. 3173). An independent reason under C.C. art. 3173 to require Savings & Loan to account to Bank for these sums is that the rent for these months was paid to Savings & Loan "*with actual knowledge that the payment of rent to him violated written directions given to the lessee to pay rent to the holder of the superior pledge.*"

10.5. A "Negative Pledge" Is Permitted, an "Anti-Pledge" Clause Is Prohibited

A "negative pledge" is a provision in a contract giving the creditor a right to demand immediate repayment of the principal obligation if the debtor grants a pledge on an item over which the creditor has no security interest. A "negative pledge" is not a security interest; a creditor has no rights in assets subject to the negative pledge.

"Negative pledge" clauses are routinely used in commercial documents both in Louisiana and around the country and allow creditors to prevent their borrowers from both dissipating assets and giving other creditors a security interest in them.

The Louisiana State Law Institute comments to C.C. art. 3163 note that nothing in this article prohibits "negative pledge" agreements. On the other hand, C.C. art. 3163 does expressly bar enforcement of what some have called an "anti-pledge" clause. C.C. art. 3163 states that any provision in which a contracting party seeks to prohibit the other party from pledging rights under that contract is "*without effect.*"

10.(5)(a). Example #1

National Tenant insists that Landlord include a special clause in the lease of immovable property that National Tenant is renting from Landlord. The clause prohibits Landlord from pledging the lease or its rents.

C.C. art. 3163 makes this provision unenforceable and "*without effect,*" both as between the parties and as to third parties. This is because it is a "*clause in a contract restricting the pledge of rights of a party to payments that are or will become due under the contract.*"

10.(5)(b). Example #2

Landlord owes money to Creditor on an unsecured basis. Creditor insists on having a "negative pledge" clause in the loan documents. This clause prohibits Landlord from pledging any leases or rents on its property. The loan documents also state that a breach of this "negative pledge" clause will give Creditor a right to accelerate the unsecured loan and demand payment from Landlord.

C.C. art. 3163 does not prohibit this provision. While this clause does not give Creditor any real rights in the Landlord's property, this provision is enforceable. Because Creditor is not a party to the lease, the "negative pledge" provision in the loan documents is not a "*clause in a contract restricting the pledge of the rights of a party to payments that are or will become due under the contract, making the pledge or its enforcement a default under the contract, or providing that the other party is excused from performance or may terminate the contract on account of the pledge.*"

10.6. Pledge and Interruption of Prescription

Although neither the Civil Code provisions enacted in 1870 nor the ones amended in 2014 deal with how a pledge may interrupt prescription of the principal obligation, the jurisprudentially-created rule governing this appears to be unchanged. This rule, emanating from a series of Louisiana Supreme Court decisions, mandates that a pledge interrupts prescription on the principal obligation because the pledge is a "constant acknowledgment" of the validity of the principal obligation.

The cases from which this rule emerged all involved the pledge of life insurance policies, negotiable notes, stock certificates, or corporeal movables. None of these items are subject to the current Civil Code's pledge provisions. In these earlier cases, however, the then-existing articles of the Civil Code included delivery as an aspect of making the pledge effective against third parties. In each instance, there was some physical object that could be delivered to the creditor that either had value in and of itself (like a watch or a piece of jewelry) or that represented a right enforceable by its holder (such as negotiable instruments, bonds, or stock certificates in bearer form).

The result of the "constant acknowledgment" rule is that, as long as a valid pledge exists, the principal obligation will never prescribe. This means that if a principal obligation consists of a negotiable demand note and that obligation is secured by a pledge, the demand note will never prescribe—it will be enforceable a hundred years later, even though the general rule is that a negotiable note prescribes five years from its due date (C.C. art. 3498). On the other hand, the "constant acknowledgment rule" recognized that the subject of the pledge itself (such as a pledged negotiable note) could prescribe. This can occur today in the context of the granting of a security interest in a collateral mortgage note (see Sections 13.5 and 13.6, below).

Most attorneys assume (although the Louisiana Supreme Court has not ruled on this issue) that this interruption of prescription rule applies when a creditor holds a UCC9 possessory security interest (see Chapter 41, below).

It remains to be seen whether courts will hold whether the "constant acknowledgment" rule applies when there has been a pledge of leases and rents of immovables (Section 10.4, above), of mineral interests (C.C. art. 3172), or of policies of property insurance (Section 10.3, above).

10.6(a). Interruption of Prescription, Constant Acknowledgement, and the "Dead Cat" Rule

The "constant acknowledgment" rule was created well before 1990, at a time when the pledge articles controlled security interests in movables, stocks, bonds, and notes. An aspect of this rule dealt with what happened if the item in pledge ceased to have value. This issue appeared in two major Louisiana Supreme Court decisions. In one, there had been the pledge of shares of stock of companies that, after the pledge, had become insolvent and worthless. In the other, there had been the pledge of a negotiable note secured by a mortgage, and prescription had run on the pledged note so that it became unenforceable.

In both cases, the result of the cases was that the pledge of something that had value at the time of the pledge (stock of operating companies and an enforceable negotiable note) interrupted prescription on the principal obligation the pledge secured even if, at a later point in time, the pledged item became valueless. The loss of value of the pledged item did not impact the continued "constant acknowledgement" of the principal obligation. Because of this "constant acknowledgement," the principal obligation never prescribed as long as the creditor (or someone agreeable to both creditor and debtor) held on to possession of the pledged item.

The result of this jurisprudence—that a valid pledge of something valuable that later becomes valueless nevertheless interrupts prescription on the principal obligation—is sometimes called the "dead cat rule." Two illustrations of this rule are given below.

10.6(a)(1). Example #1 of "Constant Acknowledgement" Rule Involving Dead Cats

The "dead cat rule" is a metaphor for the fact that prescription remains interrupted on the principal obligation even if the pledge item loses its value. The metaphor stems from the following example arising in a pre-1990 situation, when the old pledge articles (and not UCC9) controlled how to get a real security interest in items.

Debtor owed Creditor $100, represented by a negotiable note. The $100 note was payable in full 30 days from the date it was given. To secure the $100 note, Debtor pledged to Creditor Debtor's prize Siamese cat. At the time of the pledge, the cat was worth $1,000; however, shortly after Creditor's receipt of the pledged cat, the cat (through no fault of Creditor) died.

Under the "constant acknowledgment rule" if Creditor wrapped the dead cat in plastic and put it in Creditor's safety deposit box, the $100 note will never prescribe. In other words, the fact that the cat ceased to have value at its death neither invalidated the pledge nor stopped the pledge from interrupting prescription on the $100 note.

10.6(a)(2). Example #2 of the "Constant Acknowledgement" Rule

The "constant acknowledgement" rule applies to other things that had value when pledged but which later lose that value, such as the pledge of a negotiable note that later prescribes.

For this example, the facts are the same as in Example #1 (Section 10.6(a)(1)), but what was pledged was not a cat but rather a negotiable, demand note that X owed to Debtor.

Diagram 10.5(a)(2)(1)

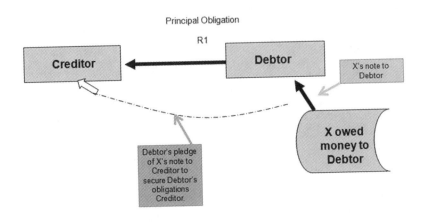

In this instance, the pledge of X's note by Debtor would be a constant acknowledgment of Debtor's $100 note to Creditor; however prescription would continue to run on X's pledged note.

If prescription on X's note was not interrupted (for example, by a payment of interest on the note or by a formal act of acknowledgment), X's note would prescribe and be unenforceable. Yet, this fact will not prevent the pledge of X's note from being a constant acknowledgment of Debtor's $100 note to Creditor.

This situation occurs today when collateral mortgages are used (see Sections 13.5(d) and 13.14, below).

Chapter 11

An Overview of Mortgage

11.1. A Mortgage Is an Accessory, Non-Possessory, Indivisible Real Right

A mortgage is "*a nonpossessory right created over property to secure the performance of an obligation.*" C.C. art. 3278. It is an "*indivisible real right*" (C.C. art. 3280) that is "*accessory to the obligation that its secures*" (C.C. art. 3282).

Because a mortgage is a real right, it does not create personal liability for the mortgagor. Because a mortgage is an accessory obligation, it can be enforced only to the extent that the principal obligation remains enforceable.

11.1(a). A Creditor's Rights under a Mortgage Are Indivisible Real Rights

The indivisible real right of mortgage (C.C. art. 3280) means that every square inch of the property is subject to the mortgage. As the official Louisiana State Law Institute comments to this article state, a "mortgage creditor may not be compelled to execute on only a part of the seized property, nor can the debtor obtain a reduction of the property on the grounds that it is an excessive seizure."

No third party may require "marshalling of assets" under Louisiana law. "Marshalling of assets" is a legal rule applied in some states (but not in Louisiana) that allows courts to order the sale of assets in a fashion that will best benefit all creditors who are secured by those assets.

For example, assume that Debtor has given mortgages to both Creditor A and Creditor B. Creditor A holds a $120,000 first mortgage on Tracts 1 and 2, while Creditor B has no mortgage on Tract 1 but does have a $30,000 second mortgage on Tract 2. Further assume that Tract 1 would bring $120,000 at a sheriff's sale and Tract 2 would bring $30,000 at a sheriff's sale.

Diagram 11.1(a)(1)

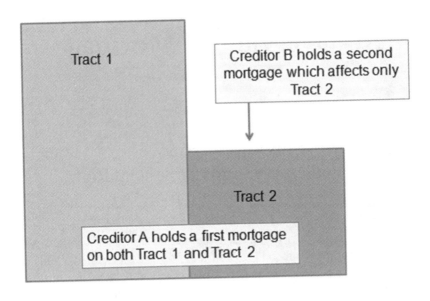

In a state that permitted "marshalling of assets," a court could compel Creditor A to foreclose first on Tract 1; that would allow Creditor A to be paid in full and still leave Creditor B with the ability to foreclose on Tract 2 and be paid in full.

Louisiana, however, prohibits "marshalling of assets" because it is contrary to the "indivisible right" a creditor holds pursuant to a mortgage. Under Louisiana law, Creditor A can decide to foreclose first on Tract 2. This will extinguish Creditor B's second mortgage (C.C.P. art. 2376), and Creditor A will get the entire $30,000. Creditor B is now an unsecured creditor, but Creditor A can still foreclose on Tract 1 to get the balance that is owed under the principal obligation.

While a mortgage may be indivisible, the obligations that the mortgage secures may be divisible, and Louisiana jurisprudence recognizes that an indivisible mortgage frequently secures a divisible debt. R.S. 9:5301 expressly permits a conventional mortgage to secure more than one obligation.

11.1(b). A Debtor Cannot Compel the Order of Sale of Mortgaged Property

Just as an inferior mortgage creditor cannot control the order of sale of mortgaged property when the foreclosure proceeding is instituted by a superior mortgage creditor (see Section 11.1(a), above), a debtor cannot compel that mortgaged property be sold in any particular order. This is because a debtor's right to control the order of sale of certain property under C.C.P. art. 2295 does not apply when the seizing creditor's right is under a mortgage, whether conventional, legal, or judicial.

11.2. A Mortgage Is Limited to Certain Types of Property

C.C. art. 3286 limits mortgages to only specified types of property:

* a "*corporeal immovable with its component parts*";
* a "*usufruct of a corporeal immovable*";
* a "*servitude of right of use with the rights that the holder of the servitude may have in the buildings and other constructions on the land*";
* the "*lessee's rights in a lease of an immovable with his rights in the buildings and other constructions on the immovable*"; and
* property "*made susceptible of conventional mortgage by special law.*"

Because a mortgage is limited to the types of property specified in the Civil Code and "*made susceptible of conventional mortgage by special law,*" parties cannot by agreement create a mortgage on any other type of property unless permitted by the Civil Code or special statutes. C.C. art. 3281 states unequivocally that a mortgage "*may be established only as authorized by legislation.*"

C.C. art. 3291 provides clarification of what property can be mortgaged when the item consists of a corporeal immovable, a servitude of right of use, or a lease. As the official Louisiana Law State Institute comments to C.C. art. 3291 state, sometimes a servitude of right of use or a lease is treated as a movable or as a "distinct immovable." Nonetheless, as the comments explain, these items may be mortgaged "in the absence of a contrary stipulation" contained in the act creating the lease or servitude of right of use.

When a mortgage involves immovable property, servitudes, and leases, the rules of registry apply (C.C. art. 3338 *et seq.* and Chapter 19, below).

11.3. The Civil Code Recognizes Only Three Types of Mortgage

There are three types of mortgages: conventional, legal, and judicial (C.C. arts. 3283–3284). Conventional mortgages are *"established by contract"* (C.C. art. 3284). Legal mortgages secure *"an obligation specified by law that provides for the mortgage"* (C.C. art. 3299). Judicial mortgages secure *"a judgment for the payment of money"* (C.C. art. 3299).

These three types of mortgage (conventional, legal, and judicial) can be further divided into special and general mortgages. Conventional mortgages are always special mortgages; they burden *"only specified property of the mortgagor"* (C.C. art. 3285). Legal and judicial mortgages are always general mortgages; they burden *"all present and future property of the mortgagor"* (C.C. art. 3285).

Although the Civil Code does not subdivide conventional mortgages into other categories, as a practical matter, practitioners and courts recognize three types of conventional mortgages: "ordinary mortgages" (see Section 13.2, below); future advance mortgages (C.C. art. 3298, see Section 13.3, below); and collateral mortgages (see Section 13.4, below).

11.4. A Mortgage Must Be Filed for Registry in the Public Records to Affect Third Parties

An unwritten, oral mortgage is not effective even as between the parties (see Section 12.1, below).

Even though a written mortgage containing all the necessary elements may be effective between the parties, until the written mortgage is filed for registry in the mortgage records of the parish where the property is located, the mortgage does not affect third parties (C.C. are 3338). See Section 19.6, below for a discussion of "filing" and "recordation."

Once a mortgage has been properly recorded, it will affect third parties for as long as the effects of recordation last (see Chapter 20, below). No voluntary sale of immovable property "cancels" a mortgage; the mortgage continues to affect the property no matter who may own it in the future.

For example, assume that Debtor grants a mortgage to Creditor in Year 1, Debtor sells the property in Year 2 to X by a "cash sale," a document that shows the entire purchase price was paid for in cash by X. X sells the property to Y in Year 3 by a "cash sale," and Y sells the property to Z in Year 4 by a "cash sale." In this situation, as long as the effects of recordation last (see Chapter 20, below), the property now owned by Z is still affected by Creditor's mortgage, even though none of the sales made any mention of Creditor's mortgage.

Chapter 12

An Overview of Conventional Mortgages

12.1. Conventional Mortgages Are Created by a Written Contract

Conventional mortgages may be established only by a *"written contract"* (C.C. art. 3287). This means that an oral mortgage is never effective, even as between the mortgagor and the creditor.

12.2. The Three Minimum Requirements of the Contents of a Conventional Mortgage

While a conventional mortgage must be in writing, *"no special words are necessary to establish a conventional mortgage"* (C.C. art. 3287).

The lack of any *"special words"* requirement should not be mistaken to mean that there are no minimum requirements for a conventional mortgage.

To be valid even as between the parties, every document creating a mortgage must contain: (a) a property description of the property being mortgaged (Section 12.3, below); (b) a description of the principal obligation (Section 12.4, below) that the mortgage secures; and (c) the signature of the mortgagor (Section 12.5, below).

12.3. A Conventional Mortgage Must Contain a Property Description

C.C. art. 3288 requires that a conventional mortgage "*must state precisely the nature and situation of each of the immovables or other property over which it is granted.*"

The jurisprudence interpreting this article and its predecessor requires that the property description be the same type of description necessary to transfer title to immovable property. The description must be one that will allow third parties to specifically identify the property from the language contained in the mortgage, in a recorded map to which the mortgage refers, or in another document recorded in the mortgage or conveyance records to which the mortgage specifically refers.

Typically, such descriptions for rural property include: the parish where the property is located; the section, township, and range in the parish where the property is located; the physical boundaries of the property with reference to a plat or map; and a reference to the act of sale (by date and registry number) by which the current mortgagor acquired the property. Often, these descriptions also include information on the ownership of surrounding parcels.

For urban property, such as a subdivision lot, the description typically includes: the parish where the property is located; the recordation information concerning the subdivision plat and the lot number in the subdivision; the section, township and range in the parish where the property is located; the physical boundaries of the property with reference to a plat or map; and a reference to the act of sale (by date and registry number) by which the current mortgagor acquired the property.

Because conventional mortgages are special mortgages, a reference to "all the property I own in X parish" is insufficient, even as between the parties.

If a debtor grants a mortgage on property the debtor does not own at that time, the mortgage is ineffective as to third parties; however, if the debtor later acquires title to the property, the mortgage becomes effective at that point. This is sometimes referred to as the "after-acquired title" doctrine.

12.4. A Conventional Mortgage Must Contain a Description of the Debt the Mortgage Secures

C.C. art. 3288 requires that a conventional mortgage must "*state the amount of the obligation, or the maximum amount of the obligations that may be out-*

standing at any time and from time to time that the mortgage secures."

12.4(a). An Overview of Acceptable Forms of the Description of the Debt Secured by a Conventional Mortgage

The jurisprudence construing C.C. art. 3288 requires that the description of the "amount" of the debt be such that it is either set forth either in dollars or in a formula calculable in dollars. As the official Louisiana State Law Institute's comments to C.C. art. 3288 state, the purpose of this requirement "is to define the limit to which the debtor has encumbered his property."

Thus, any of the following descriptions comply with C.C. art. 3288:

- "This mortgage secures a $1,000 debt."
- "This mortgage secures a note dated February 1, 2018 in the amount of $2,000, bearing interest at the rate of 8% per annum, payable on demand."
- "This mortgage secures a note dated March 1, 2018 in the amount of $300,000, bearing interest at the rate of 5% per annum, payable in 120 equal monthly installments of principal and interest, the first installment being due March 1, 2018 and the final installment being due February 1, 2028."
- "This mortgage secures any and all debts of the mortgagor to mortgagee, up to the principal amount of $400,000, whether such amounts represent past loans, contemporaneous advances, or future advances."

Every debt secured by a conventional mortgage must comply with C.C. art. 3288's requirements that the mortgage must "*state the amount of the obligation, or the maximum amount of the obligations that may be outstanding at any time and from time to time that the mortgage secures.*" If a mortgage secures not only a principal obligation, but also other obligations (such as securing any discretionary advances that the lender may make to pay for insurance or taxes when the mortgagor fails to pay these), each of these other obligations must also be set forth in dollars or in amounts or formulas calculable in dollars. In these instances, any of the following descriptions comply with C.C. art. 3288:

- "Should lender make any advances for taxes or insurance, such advances shall be secured up to an amount equal to 25% of the original principal amount of the note that this mortgage secures."

• "This mortgage secures the lender for up to the principal amount of $100,000 for any advances made by the lender for taxes or insurance, plus interest on such advances at the rate of 8% per annum from the advance until paid."

C.C. art. 3288's requirement of a dollar-calculable debt description is stricter than the requirements for a valid suretyship. A suretyship need not set forth a dollar amount. A valid written contract of suretyship, such as a continuing guarantee (see Section 3.4, above) may secure any and all debts that the debtor may owe to the lender, past, present or future. By contrast, a written mortgage that contains similar language (for example, "This mortgage secures any and all debts that the mortgagor may owe to the lender, past, present or future") is not valid even as between the parties, because it does not set forth a dollar-calculable amount.

12.4(b). Illustrations of Obligations Secured by a Mortgage

Because a mortgage is an accessory obligation, it is important to ascertain which obligation the mortgage secures. The following illustrations aid in an understanding of this.

In Diagram 12.4(b)(1), below, the mortgage given by the debtor secures R1, the debtor's obligation to the creditor.

Diagram 12.4(b)(1)

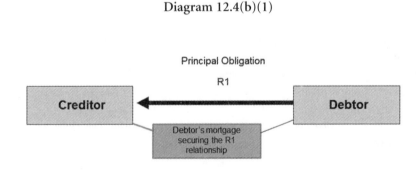

In the next illustration, while the debtor is obligated to the creditor for the principal obligation (R1), the mortgage given by the debtor secures R3, the debtor's obligation to the surety.

Diagram 12.4(b)(2)

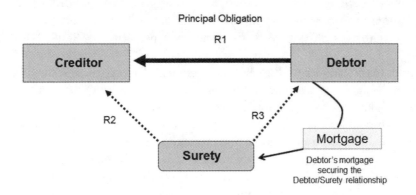

In the final illustration of this section, the mortgage by the third party secures the debtor's obligation to the creditor without imparting personal liability to the third party mortgagor.

Diagram 12.4(b)(3)

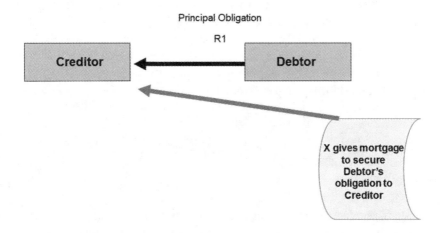

12.4(c). No Necessity of a Note Being Paraphed *Ne Varietur* for Identification with the Act of Mortgage

Most mortgages secure monetary obligations, although mortgages may secure an obligation to perform or an obligation other than one for the payment of money (see Section 12.4(e), below). Many mortgages that secure monetary obligations secure one or more notes described in the mortgage. The only exception to this is a C.C. art. 3298 "future advance" mortgage (see Section 13.3, below).

Prior to the early 1990s, the Civil Code required that every note secured by a mortgage had to be paraphed for identification with the act of mortgage. In Louisiana law, the term "paraph" refers to a notary's signature on a "*ne varietur*" stamp on a note. A "paraph" is derived from a French word meaning a flourish made under a signature to prevent forgery of the signature. The flourish under John Hancock's signature in the Declaration of Independence is an example of a paraph. The phrase "*ne varietur*" is Latin; it can be translated as "it must not be changed" or "it must not be altered."

While a mortgage may describe the note it secures, because the mortgage is recorded in the parish mortgage records and the note is held by the lender, how is one to know whether a specific note relates to a specific mortgage? The notarial paraph was designed to provide an easy way to link the note to the mortgage. The paraph on the mortgage note will indicate which notary notarized the mortgage and the date of the mortgage. Thus, by looking at the paraph and making sure that the date of the mortgage is the same as indicated on the paraphed note, and by making sure that the notary who signed the paraph is the same one who notarized the mortgage, one can better ascertain that this paraphed note is the same one that the mortgage secures.

As used in Louisiana, therefore, a "paraph" refers to the signature of the notary before whom the mortgage was passed; this signature is placed within a "*ne varietur*" clause on the face of the note.

The standard form of a paraph on a note reads:

> NE VARIETUR for identification with an act of
> _____, passed before me this
> _____ day of _____,
> 20_____.
> _____ **Notary Public**

Many years ago, the Louisiana legislature repealed the requirement that notaries paraph notes *ne varietur* for identification with the act of mortgage.

Nothing today prohibits notaries from paraphing notes on their own. Additionally, notaries must paraph the note for identification with the act of mortgage if the parties request it (C.C. art. 3325(A), (B), R.S. 9:5305). As a practical matter, many mortgage notes in Louisiana are still paraphed *ne varietur* for identification with the act of mortgage.

12.4(d). Special Rules on Description of a Past Debt Secured by a Conventional Mortgage as Opposed to a Future Obligation Secured by a Conventional Mortgage

While a conventional mortgage may secure any *"lawful obligation"* (C.C. art. 3293), special care must be taken when a mortgage secures past debts as opposed to contemporaneous loans or future advances.

Louisiana jurisprudence allows a mortgage to secure a note that appears to be for contemporaneous advances but is actually for future advances. No special language is needed in the mortgage to distinguish between contemporaneous loans and future advances (see Section 13.3, below). The jurisprudence, however, requires that if a mortgage is to secure past or pre-existing loans, it must do so specifically.

For example:

- If the mortgage states it "secures a demand note for $100,000," the mortgage may secure a note where the $100,000 was advanced to the debtor at the same time as the $100,000 note and mortgage were executed, or it may secure a loan for up to $100,000 in money to be advanced in the future (see Section 13.3, below). This mortgage, however, will not secure any past loans. The fact that third parties cannot ascertain whether the mortgage secures a contemporaneous loan or a future advance loan has been held to be irrelevant as long as the creditor can prove the intent of the parties to the document.
- If a mortgage states it secures "all previous loans of _____ and all debts up to $30,000," the jurisprudence holds that while this mortgage may validly secure all contemporaneous and future debts up to $30,000, it cannot validly secure any past loans, because the amount of the past loans is left blank.
- If a mortgage states it secures "all previous loans of $15,000 and all debts up to $30,000," the jurisprudence holds that while this mortgage may validly secure all contemporaneous and future debts up to $30,000, it will secure past loans limited to $15,000.

12.4(e). If a Mortgage Secures an Act or a Non-Monetary Obligation, It Still Must State a Dollar Amount

C.C. art. 3293 permits a mortgage to secure performance not merely of monetary obligations, but also of the *"performance of an act."*

C.C. art. 3294 states that a mortgage may secure *"an obligation other than one for the payment of money"* by securing damages suffered from a breach of the contract. For example, a mortgage may provide security to a surety who is issuing a performance bond in a construction contract. The surety in a performance bond promises to pay the owner a set amount of money if the general contractor does not build the building in a timely and appropriate manner (see the discussion of performance bonds at Section 37.9, below).

C.C. art. 3294, however, must be read in conjunction with C.C. art. 3288. Although a mortgage may secure an obligation other than one for the payment of money, the mortgage must describe in dollar terms the damage amounts that the mortgage secures. As the official Louisiana State Law Institute comments to C.C. art. 3288 note, the dollar amount of this non-monetary obligation mortgage does not establish liquidated damages for the contract breach; all it does is set the maximum amount of damages the mortgage secures. The following are examples of mortgages authorized under C.C. art. 3294:

- A mortgage on General Contractor's property securing, up to $100,000, the General Contractor's obligation to Landowner to timely and properly construct the building according the plans on the Landowner's property.
- A mortgage by Roofer, Inc. on the Roofer's Property securing, up to $50,000, the Homeowner for any breach of Roofer, Inc.'s contract to install new shingles on the Homeowner's house.
- A $325,000 mortgage by John Rock on his property securing Concert Promoter, Inc., for any breach of contract by John Rock's band, Rock Band, Inc., to appear at and perform a New Year's Eve concert as called for in a specifically described contract. Note that this example includes securing the obligation of a third party—Rock Band, Inc. This is permitted by C.C. art. 3295 (see Diagram 12.4(b)(3), above).

12.5. A Conventional Mortgage Must Be Signed by the Mortgagor

C.C. art. 3288 requires that a conventional mortgage must "be signed by the mortgagor."

C.C. art. 3288 does not require that the mortgagor's signature be witnessed. It does not require that the mortgagor's signature be notarized. It does not require that the lender sign the mortgage. A mortgage signed only by the mortgagor is valid both as between the parties to the mortgage and as to third parties.

If a mortgage is signed only by the mortgagor and is not in authentic form (in other words, it is not signed in the presence of a notary and two witnesses, C.C. art. 1833), it is not "self-proving." For a document that is not self-proving there is no presumption that the signature is that of the person whose name appears in the document; thus, proof of who signed the document will have to be adduced in court. By contrast, if a mortgage is executed in authentic form, the signature of the mortgagor is presumed valid and the burden of proof the falls upon the mortgagor (or other challenger) to demonstrate that the signature purporting to be the mortgagor's is a forgery.

If a mortgage is not in authentic form, it is not possible to use executory process to seize and sell the property. A lack of authentic form, however, will not prevent a suit by ordinary process to foreclose on the mortgage (see Section 38.1(b), below).

12.6. The Mortgagee's Acceptance Is Presumed; The Mortgagee Need Not Sign the Mortgage

C.C. art. 3289 states that a "*contract of mortgage need not be signed by the mortgagee, whose consent is presumed and whose acceptance may be tacit.*"

Therefore, the lack of a mortgagee's signature on a mortgage is irrelevant to the validity of the mortgage, both between the parties and as to third parties. As the official Louisiana State Law Institute comments to this article explain, this evidentiary presumption may be utilized by the mortgagee in enforcing the mortgage; however, the presumption does not prevent the mortgagor or a third party from "demonstrating that the contract was rejected or the offer lapsed or was revoked before acceptance or even that it occurred at a particular time."

If this presumption of acceptance is challenged, the Law Institute's comments indicate the mortgagor may demonstrate that acceptance was accomplished either "tacitly or verbally." Proof of tacit acceptance is further explored in the Law Institute's comments to C.C. art. 1837.

12.7. Who May Be a Mortgagor: The Power to Mortgage

C.C. art. 3290 describes who may be a mortgagor. A conventional mortgage "*may be established only by a person having the power to alienate the property mortgaged.*"

The word "*property*" in C.C. art. 3290 is a reference to the kinds of property that may be mortgaged under C.C. art. 3286 (see Section 11.2, above).

The following are examples of those with the power to mortgage property:

- An owner may mortgage the owner's property.
- A co-owner may mortgage that particular co-owner's interest in the property, but the co-owner may not mortgage the interest of the other co-owners without their written consent.
- An agent with the written power to sell property is deemed to have the power to mortgage it, but an agent with the written power only to lease property does not have the power to mortgage it.
- A tutor has the power to mortgage property only if expressly authorized to do so by a court order (see C.C.P. art. 4267).

12.8. A Conventional Mortgage of Future Property Is Permitted

While conventional mortgages must specifically describe the property the mortgage secures (C.C. art. 3288; see Section 12.3, above) and may only be given by one with the power to alienate property (C.C. art. 3290, see Section 12.7, above), under certain limited circumstances, C.C. art. 3292 allows a mortgagor to place a mortgage on property that the mortgagor does not yet own.

If a mortgagor attempts to mortgage property that is not yet owned, the mortgage does not become established unless and until the mortgagor acquires ownership of the property. The critical date for "establishing" the mortgage does not relate to the date the mortgage is signed but rather refers to the date of the earliest concurrence of the mortgagor's (a) signing a valid mortgage containing all of the necessary requirements (C.C. art. 3288), and (b) acquiring ownership of the property.

In each of the following examples, the term "Property" refers to a proper, legal description of property that is not owned by the mortgagor at the time the mortgage is signed.

12.8(a). Example #1

On February 1, Debtor gives a mortgage over Property X to Creditor.

On March 1, Creditor records the mortgage in the parish where Property X is located.

On April 1, Debtor acquires ownership of Property X and records the act of sale in the parish conveyance records.

In this case, the mortgage is not established between Debtor and Creditor until April 1, the date Debtor acquires ownership of Property X.

12.8(b). Example #2

On June 1, Debtor gives a mortgage over Property Y to Creditor #2, and Creditor #2 records the mortgage in the parish where Property Y is located.

On July 1, Debtor acquires ownership of Property Y and records the act of sale in the parish conveyance records.

In this case, the mortgage is not established between Debtor and the Creditor #2 until July 1, the date Debtor acquires ownership of Property Y.

12.8(c). Example #3

Seller S owns Property S. Buyer Q is attempting to buy Property S from Seller S, but no written contract has yet been signed and no deal has been struck between them.

On August 1, Buyer Q, who does not yet own Property S, gives a mortgage over Property S to High Finance Company and High Finance records the mortgage that same day in the parish mortgage records.

On September 1, Seller S gives a mortgage over Property S to Big Bank, and Big Bank records that mortgage that same day in the parish mortgage records.

On October 1, Seller S sells Property S to Buyer Q, and the act of sale is recorded in the parish conveyance records.

In this case, the mortgage is not established between Buyer Q and High Finance until October 1, the date of the sale from Seller S to Buyer Q.

It should be observed that, at the time of the October 1 sale, High Finance's August mortgage had been on the public records for longer than Big Bank's September mortgage; nonetheless, as between the two lenders, Big Bank ranks first and High Finance second.

The reason for this result is that High Finance's mortgage was established and ranks only from the earliest concurrence of recordation and ownership (October 1), because Buyer Q did not own the property at the time of granting the mortgage in August to High Finance. On the other hand, Big Bank's mortgage ranks from the date it was recorded (September 1) because its mortgage was given by one who, at the time, had the power of alienation over the property.

12.9. A Mortgage May Secure the Obligations of Any Person or Entity, Even the Obligations of One Who Is Not the Mortgagor

C.C. art. 3295 allows a person to "establish a mortgage over his property to secure the obligations of another." This means that the mortgage may secure the obligation of another to pay a debt (see Diagram 12.4(b)(3), above) or even the obligation of another to perform an act (see Section 12.4(e), above).

Because a mortgage is a real right (C.C. art. 3280) and gives the creditor the ability to seize and sell the property (C.C. art. 3279), it does not impart personal liability to the mortgagor. Whether a mortgagor is personally liable to the creditor is determined by who is the obligor of the principal obligation, not by the fact that a mortgage was given. Therefore, one who gives a mortgage to secure the debt of another does not undertake personal liability to the lender; all the mortgagor does in this instance is encumber property. This is made explicit by the official Louisiana Law Institute comments to C.C. art. 3295: "The right of mortgage does not give rise to personal liability in any case."

Determining which principal obligation the mortgage secures is critical to determining whether the mortgagor is also personally liable or has merely encumbered property without also undertaking personal liability. The following examples help explain these concepts:

12.9(a). Example #1

X gives a $10,000 mortgage to secure Debtor's $10,000 note to Creditor (note that this is similar to Diagram 12.4(b)(3), above).

Diagram 12.9(a)

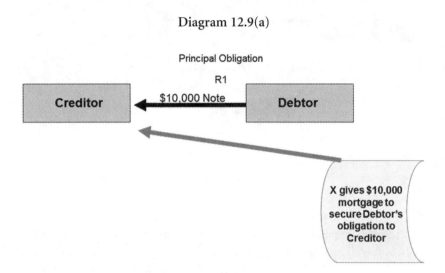

In this case, the principal obligation (R1) is Debtor's $10,000 note. X is not personally liable on Debtor's note, and the fact that X gave a mortgage on X's property to secure Debtor's note does not make X personally liable to Creditor. Creditor has the option of not only suing Debtor on the note, but also foreclosing on X's property. Creditor, however, cannot sue X for a personal judgment. Likewise, if at foreclosure X's property brings only $6,000, Creditor cannot pursue X for the $4,000 deficiency, because X is not personally liable to Creditor.

12.9(b). Example #2

Y gives a $20,000 mortgage to secure Debtor's obligation to reimburse Surety (see Section 4.4, above) should Surety pay Debtor's $20,000 debt to the Creditor.

Diagram 12.9(b)

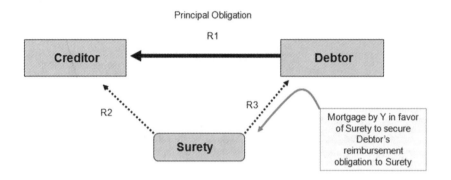

In this case, the principal obligation the mortgage secures is Debtor's reimbursement obligation to Surety (the R3 relationship). Y is not personally liable to Surety. If Surety pays the principal obligation in the amount of $20,000 and Debtor does not reimburse Surety, Surety may foreclose on Y's property. Surety, however, cannot sue Y for a personal judgment. Likewise, if at foreclosure Y's property brings only $12,000, Surety cannot pursue Y for the $8,000 deficiency, because Y is not personally liable to Surety.

Y has no liability whatsoever to Creditor. The principal obligation the mortgage secures does not secure any obligation of either Y or Debtor to Creditor; therefore, Creditor may not foreclose on Y's property.

12.9(c). Example #3

Surety gives a $35,000 mortgage to Creditor to secure both Debtor's $35,000 obligation to Creditor and Surety's suretyship obligation to Creditor contained in a "continuing guarantee" (see Section 3.4, above).

Diagram 12.9(c)

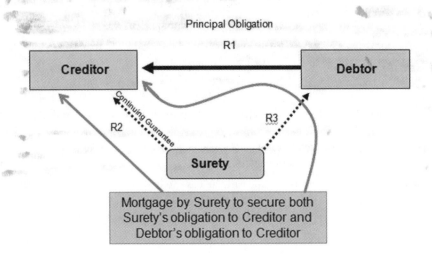

In this case, there are two principal obligations the mortgage secures: the obligation of Debtor to Creditor (R1) and the personal obligation of Surety to Creditor (R2, the continuing guarantee). Surety is personally liable on the R2 relationship because that is the essence of the suretyship agreement.

Creditor may sue Surety directly (see Section 3.4, above), or Creditor may foreclose on Surety's mortgaged property, or both. If the foreclosure on the Surety's property brings only $30,000, Creditor can pursue Surety for the $5,000 deficiency, because Surety is personally liable to the Creditor on the principal obligation that the mortgage secures (the suretyship contract).

12.10. What Defenses a Mortgagor May Raise

C.C. art. 3296 is entitled *"right of mortgagor to raise defenses,"* but the text of the article begins by setting forth the defenses the mortgagor may not raise. C.C. art. 3296 states: *"Neither the mortgagor nor a third person may claim that the mortgage is extinguished or is unenforceable because the obligation the mortgage secures is extinguished or is unenforceable unless the obligor may assert against the mortgagee the extinction or unenforceability of the obligation that the mortgage secures."*

As the official Louisiana State Law Institute comments to C.C. art. 3296 explain, the purpose of this article is to overrule *dicta* contained in cases decided prior to 1991. The essence of C.C. art. 3296 is that (a) if the mortgagor cannot claim that the debt was extinguished, a third person cannot make a claim that the debt was extinguished; and (b) if the mortgage secures the debt of a third person (see Section 12.9(a), above) and that third person cannot claim the debt was extinguished, the mortgagor is likewise forbidden to assert that defense.

C.C. art. 3296 refers to the extinguishment of the debt and the unenforceability of the debt. This means that the principal obligation has ceased to exist. The provisions of C.C. art. 3296, however, do not apply in cases where the principal obligor chooses not to assert the defense, forgets to assert the defense, fails to make an appearance in the case to assert the defense, or where the defense is personal to the principal obligor (such as bankruptcy). The following are examples of the application of C.C. art. 3296:

12.10(a). Example #1

X gives a mortgage to Creditor to secure Debtor's negotiable note to Creditor. Debtor's note has prescribed.

X may assert the defense of prescription when Creditor attempts to foreclose on X's mortgage.

12.10(b). Example #2

Y gives a mortgage to Creditor to secure Debtor's note to Creditor. It turns out that Debtor is illiterate and thought she was signing a receipt for goods delivered by Creditor, not a note obligating Debtor to pay Creditor additional money, much less money bearing interest at a usurious rate.

Y may assert the defenses of usury and of the vice of consent of fraud (C.C. arts. 1948 *et seq.*) when Creditor attempts to foreclose on Y's mortgage.

12.10(c). Example #3

Z gives a mortgage to Creditor to secure Debtor's negotiable note to Creditor. Debtor files for bankruptcy.

While the bankruptcy proceeding prevents Creditor from pursuing Debtor outside of the bankruptcy arena (11 U.S.C. §362), Creditor may foreclose on

Z's property, and Z may not assert Debtor's bankruptcy as a defense. This is because the bankruptcy does not extinguish Debtor's obligation to Creditor or render it unenforceable. The obligation remains, but the type and extent of enforcement against Debtor is controlled by the bankruptcy court.

12.11. "In Rem" or Non-Recourse Mortgages

As has been noted earlier, although a mortgage is a real right (C.C. art. 3280) and gives the creditor the ability to seize and sell the property (C.C. art. 3279), it does not impart personal liability to the mortgagor (see Section 12.9, above).

C.C. art. 3297 allows the parties to a mortgage to agree that the mortgage secures an obligation for which the creditor (a) is not entitled to personally sue the debtor and (b) is not entitled to pursue the debtor for a deficiency judgment (see Chapter 40, below) in the event the judicial sale of the mortgaged property does not bring sufficient funds to pay in full the amounts owed to the creditor. In other words, a mortgage may be written in such a way that the creditor has no right to sue anyone personally for the debt, but instead may only foreclose on the mortgage. This is called a non-recourse mortgage, because the creditor has no personal recourse to sue anyone personally. Another term for this kind of mortgage is an "*in rem*" mortgage.

Prior to the legislative amendments expressly authorizing non-recourse mortgages under C.C. art. 3297, Louisiana lawyers had created *in rem* mortgages even though there was no express statutory authority to do so. The structure employed was a combination of contractual obligations tied to procedural rules. The parties would create a negotiable note signed by the debtor and secured by a mortgage on the debtor's property. The mortgage contained mandatory rules that the creditor had to follow. The mortgage forbade the creditor to sue the debtor directly by ordinary process—a suit that, if successful, would result in an *in personam* judgment against the debtor. Instead, the mortgage required the creditor to first foreclose on the property by executory process without appraisal. This type of foreclosure prevented a creditor from pursuing any deficiency judgment against the debtor (see Chapter 40, below) and thus the creditor was procedurally barred from suing the debtor after the foreclosure proceedings, even if the sale of the property did not bring sufficient funds to pay off the entirety of the debt. Therefore, the result of these contractual provisions in the mortgage was that the debtor could never be sued personally on the debt.

Rather than having to go through these contractual and procedural permutations, C.C. art. 3297 allows the parties, in the mortgage itself, to stipulate that the creditor's ability to collect the debt is limited to the proceeds obtained from the mortgage foreclosure sale. Alternatively, C.C. art. 3297 permits the parties to stipulate that only a portion of the debt be satisfied by a personal suit against the debtor with the remainder of the debt to be satisfied solely from foreclosure on the mortgaged property.

C.C. art. 3297 states: "*The mortgagee's recourse for the satisfaction of an obligation secured by a mortgage may be limited in whole or in part to the property over which the mortgage is established.*"

12.12. No Novation If a Subsequent Owner of the Property Assumes the Mortgage and the Original Mortgagor Is Released

Louisiana statutes recognize that a mortgage remains intact and its rank and priority remain undisturbed if a mortgagor transfers property to one who assumes the mortgage (see Section 19.5, below), even if the original mortgagor is released (C.C. art. 1887 and R.S. 9:5384). The assumption of the principal obligation by the purchaser is recognition that the purchaser is not a "third person" (see Section 21.2, below) to the mortgage and prevents a novation of the principal obligation from occurring.

Chapter 13

The Three Kinds of Conventional Mortgages: Ordinary Mortgages, Collateral Mortgages, and Future Advance Mortgages

13.1. The Three Kinds of Conventional Mortgages

Although the Civil Code does not divide conventional mortgages into different types, real estate lawyers and the jurisprudence use three different phrases to describe conventional mortgages—ordinary mortgages, future advance mortgages, and collateral mortgages. These phrases are a short-hand way of describing types of conventional mortgages that are used in different ways.

13.2. The "Ordinary Mortgage"

"Ordinary mortgage" is the phrase used to refer to a mortgage that secures a single note, with the note representing a loan for money that is given at the same time the mortgage is created. The note is typically paraphed *ne varietur* for identification with the act of mortgage; however, a paraph is not required by law (see Section 12.4(c), above).

The note may be payable on demand or it may be an installment note. An installment note is one payable periodically, such as a note payable on the first of each month. An example of an installment note is a $100,000 thirty-year mortgage for a new home, with a set amount payable each month for the life of the loan.

Each time an installment of the note is paid, it partially extinguishes the obligation of the borrower—that is, from each installment payment sums are applied to both principal and interest. Each payment applied to the principal balance of the note reduces the remaining principal balance. Once the note is fully paid, the obligation that it represents is extinguished. Because a mortgage is an accessory obligation (C.C. art. 3278; see Section 11.1, above), the accessory obligation of the mortgage becomes unenforceable when the principal obligation is extinguished.

13.3. The "Future Advance Mortgage"

Louisiana jurisprudence refers to a "future advance mortgage" in two different contexts. In reviewing cases, one must ascertain the date the case arose, because a pre-1992 "future advance mortgage" may differ significantly from one created after 1992.

The phrase today refers to a mortgage created pursuant to C.C. art. 3298. Under this article, a mortgage may secure either an advance of monies to be made in the future or a fluctuating line of credit.

C.C. art. 3298 was a result of the 1991 amendments to the mortgage articles (Acts 1991, No. 652, § 1) that became effective January 1, 1992. Prior to 1992, the phrase "future advance mortgage" referred only to mortgages that secured an advance of monies to be made in the future; it did not refer to a mortgage that secured a fluctuating line of credit.

13.3(a). The Pre-1992 "Future Advance Mortgage"

Louisiana jurisprudence has long recognized that the note paraphed for identification with the act of mortgage (i) may represent funds contemporaneously advanced at the time the note was made or (ii) may represent sums to be advanced in the future. The jurisprudence acknowledged that a third party examining the public records cannot ascertain, from the language of the mortgage, whether the note it secures represents dollars that had been completely advanced or represented sums yet to be advanced (see Section 13.3(c), below).

Prior to the amendment to C.C. art. 3298, however, the jurisprudence was emphatic that, after the principal amount was fully advanced, the obligations represented by the note had been completely funded; therefore, the mortgage would not secure any further additional advances. In other words, prior to the 1992 amendments to C.C. art. 3298, a "future advance mortgage" could not secure a fluctuating line of credit because, once the principal balance had been advanced, no more sums could be advanced and be secured by the note and mortgage.

13.3(a)(1). Example #1 of the Former "Future Advance Mortgage," Which Never Could Secure a Fluctuating-Line of Credit Loan

Debtor owns a subdivision lot worth $20,000 and wants to borrow $80,000 to construct a home on that lot. Debtor and Creditor agree that the loan will be secured by a mortgage on the property where the home is to be built.

Creditor will not want to advance all the money at the time the note and mortgage are created. The reason is that, at this point in time, no home is built. If Debtor defaults in payment of the note, the only security for the $80,000 loan is a lot worth $20,000. Likewise, Debtor does not necessarily want to have the entire $80,000 advanced at the time the note and mortgage are created, because Debtor does not need all $80,000 immediately and does not want to pay interest on the entire $80,000 from the inception of the loan.

Therefore, Creditor and Debtor agree that Creditor will advance the $80,000 in installments. Each installment is to be advanced only as building progresses on the lot. Some money will be advanced when the slab is poured, another sum will be advanced when the framing is up, yet another sum will be advanced when the roof is completed and the exterior walls are installed, *etc.*

This type of "future advance mortgage" is sometimes referred to as a "construction mortgage," for it is often used for loans to construct buildings.

When this construction loan is first made, before any money is advanced, Debtor executes an $80,000 note and a mortgage. The closing attorney paraphs the $80,000 note "*ne varietur*" for identification with the act of mortgage (see Section 12.4(c), above).

Although no sums have been lent to Debtor at the time Debtor signs the note, Debtor's $80,000 note is not fictitious; it represents the total amount of money that will be advanced in the future. Proof of each advance typically is done either by a separate note representing that specific advance (called a "draw note"), by a receipt signed by Debtor, by a notation on Creditor's records, or by other means. Regardless of how the advances are represented, however, the actual debt that the mortgage secures is the $80,000 note.

Whether or not the entire $80,000 has been advanced, once Debtor starts repaying the loan by repaying principal, the $80,000 note starts to be extinguished. Each repayment of principal partially extinguishes the note. The note is completely extinguished once the entire $80,000 has been advanced and repaid, and once this occurs, Debtor cannot borrow more money pursuant to the $80,000 note, because the note has been extinguished through payment. Because the note represents the principal obligation secured by the accessory contract of mortgage, the mortgage is likewise unenforceable when the note has been completely extinguished though payment.

This extinguishment also occurs in the case of an ordinary mortgage. If a debtor buys a house and executes an $80,000 mortgage for the purchase price, the debtor cannot borrow more money under that note, for the entire amount of the note already has been advanced.

13.3(a)(2). The "Barrel of Money" Method of Analyzing the Former "Future Advance Mortgage" and Any "Future Advance Mortgage" That Does Not Secure a Fluctuating Line of Credit Loan

In the example in Section 13.3(a)(1), above, Debtor cannot borrow some funds under the $80,000 note, pay down a part of the note, and then borrow more money up to $80,000, because each partial payment has extinguished a portion of the principal balance of the note. One way to analyze how much more a borrower can borrow under this type of future advance mortgage is sometimes called the "barrel of money" rule.

The "barrel of money" rule can be illustrated by using the same facts as in Section 13.3(a)(1) Example #1, above. Assume that construction is underway on the property that forms the security for the $80,000 "future advance mortgage." Creditor advances $5,000 when the slab is completed and another $5,000 when the framing is up. Creditor has now advanced $10,000 of the $80,000 note. If Debtor then repays $10,000 of principal, how much more may Creditor advance under the $80,000 note and be secured?

It would be erroneous to give $80,000 as the answer ($80,000 note minus $5,000 advance minus $5,000 advance plus $10,000 repayment). The reason that an answer of $80,000 is in error is because payment of principal on the note (in this case $10,000) extinguishes that portion of the note. In other words, the original $80,000 note has been extinguished to the extent of the $10,000 repayment; therefore, the outstanding principal amount of the note is now

$70,000 and that is all that is available for advances under the note secured by the mortgage.

An easy way to remember this concept is the "barrel-of-money" rule. Under the "barrel-of-money" rule, you imagine that all the money represented by the note (in this example, $80,000) consists of cash nestled inside a barrel. As Debtor needs money, Creditor reaches into the barrel and hands Debtor the funds. If Debtor repays anything to Creditor, that repayment goes into Creditor's back pocket, not back into the barrel. Therefore, at any point in time one can easily determine how much remains to be advanced by looking in the barrel. In other words, one starts by subtracting all advances from the face amount of the note and ignoring repayments to determine how much remains to be advanced. If Creditor advances more than is left in the barrel, the Creditor is unsecured for these additional sums, and the additional sums are not secured by the mortgage.

13.3(b). The C.C. art. 3298 "Future Advance Mortgage" That May Secure a Fluctuating Line of Credit, Sometimes Called a "Multiple-Obligation Mortgage" or "Multiple-Indebtedness Mortgage"

The problem with the pre-1992 "future advance mortgage" is that it could not secure a fluctuating line of credit loan, for the note secured by the mortgage represented sums that would be advanced in the future, and as payments were made on that note the balance due on the note was reduced (see Section 13.3(a), above). Prior to the January 1, 1992, effective date of the amendment to C.C. art. 3298, the only way to secure a fluctuating line of credit with a mortgage was to use a collateral mortgage (see Section 13.4, below).

Current C.C. art. 3298 permits the parties to create a mortgage that secures either monies to be advanced in the future (like the pre-1992 "future advance mortgage," Section 13.3(a), above) or that secures a fluctuating line of credit loan. The C.C. 3298 mortgage may secure many obligations—both current loans and future loans. That is why a mortgage made under C.C. art. 3298 is sometimes referred to as a "multiple obligation mortgage" or "multiple indebtedness mortgage."

C.C. art. 3298 consists of five subparts, (A) through (E), and each deserves detailed attention.

13.3(b)(1). C.C. art. 3298(A): A Mortgage May Secure Future Obligations

C.C. art. 3298(A) provides that a "*mortgage may secure obligations that may arise in the future.*"

This statement reflects the historic rule in Louisiana that a mortgage may secure any lawful obligation (C.C. art. 3293), even one subject to a condition (C.C. art. 3293). Therefore, a C.C. art. 3298 mortgage may be created without any debt owing at the time; it may be created solely to secure loans that will be made in the future.

13.3(b)(2). C.C. art. 3298(B): Retroactive Effect of Advances under a "Future Advance Mortgage"

C.C. art. 3298(B) states: "*As to all obligations, present and future, secured by the mortgage, notwithstanding the nature of such obligations or the date they arise, the mortgage has effect between the parties from the time the mortgage is established and as to third persons from the time the contract of mortgage is filed for registry.*"

This article requires an understanding of the rules of registry (see Chapter 23, below). In essence, C.C. art. 3298(B) means that even if an advance is not made until some point in the future, the mortgage ranks as to third persons from the time of registry; in other words, future advance mortgages get retroactive rank.

For example, consider the situation in Section 13.3(a)(1), Example #1, above, involving an $80,000 construction mortgage. Assume that on February 1, Debtor gives Creditor the $80,000 note secured by a mortgage on Debtor's lot. Creditor records the mortgage in the parish mortgage records on March 1, and Debtor begins construction on the lot the next day. The slab is completed on April 1. On April 2, Creditor advances the first $5,000 of the $80,000 loan to Debtor.

Under this example, and using C.C. art. 3298(B), the mortgage is established between Debtor and Creditor on February 1 ("*the mortgage has effect between the parties from the time the mortgage is established*"). The mortgage begins affecting third parties under C.C. art. 3298(B) on March 1, when it is filed in the parish mortgage records ("*the mortgage has effect ... as to third persons from the time the contract of mortgage is filed for registry*"). Therefore, even though the first advance of monies under the mortgage does not occur until April 1, third persons are affected by the mortgage starting March 1.

This means that if Debtor had placed a second mortgage, an "ordinary mortgage" (see Section 13.2, above) on the property on March 15, the $80,000 "future advance mortgage" would outrank this second mortgage because (regardless of when the sums are advanced on the "future advance mortgage") the "future advance mortgage" began affecting third parties on March 1.

This is why it is said that advances under a "future advance mortgage" are retroactive—meaning that the future advances are secured by the mortgage from the date of registry even though the future advances occur at a later point in time.

13.3(b)(3). C.C. art. 3298(C): No Need for a Note for a "Future Advance Mortgage"

C.C. art. 3298(C) states that a *"promissory note or other evidence of indebtedness secured by a mortgage need not be paraphed for identification with the mortgage and need not recite that it is secured by the mortgage."*

C.C. art. 3298(C) does not prevent the notary from paraphing a note secured by a mortgage. This article simply makes it clear that a paraph is not required (see Section 12.4(c), above).

There can be a problem, however, if a "future advance mortgage" under C.C. art. 3298 that is designed to secure a fluctuating line of credit loan describes only a note as the sole obligation the mortgage secures. This is because payments on the note described in the mortgage—the sole obligation the mortgage secures—will extinguish it, and once the note is extinguished, the accessory contract of mortgage becomes unenforceable (see Section 13.3(a), above).

Therefore, if a creditor wishes to have a C.C. art. 3298 mortgage secure a fluctuating line of credit, the mortgage should not describe the obligation it secures as just a single, specific note. Rather, the description of the obligation should be the line of credit itself, such as "This mortgage secures any and all obligations of the Mortgagor to the Creditor up to the principal limit of $100,000, whether such obligations are past, present or future, and whether such obligations are direct, indirect, or contingent."

The description may go on to state that the word "obligations" includes but is not limited to a particular note; however, in order to secure all future advances it is important to use a phrase such as "including but not limited to" rather than describing but a single note as the obligation secured by the mortgage. The reason one does not want to describe "obligations" as consisting of but a single note is that this eliminates the possibility of a fluctuating line of credit loan, for each payment on the specific note extinguishes that portion of the principal obligation, and once the specific note has been paid off no more money can be advanced (see Section 13.3(a)(2), above).

13.3(b)(4). C.C. art. 3298(D) and (E): Termination of a "Future Advance Mortgage"; Contracting for Reasonable Notice of Termination; and When Payment of a Loan Down to Zero May Not Terminate a "Future Advance Mortgage" That Secures a Fluctuating Line of Credit

C.C. art. 3298(D) and (E) state:

> D. *The mortgage may be terminated by the mortgagor or his successor upon reasonable notice to the mortgagee when an obligation does not exist and neither the mortgagor nor the mortgagee is bound to the other or to a third person to permit an obligation secured by the mortgage to be incurred. Parties may contract with reference to what constitutes reasonable notice.*
>
> E. *The mortgage continues until it is terminated by the mortgagor or his successor in the manner provided in Paragraph D of this Article, or until the mortgage is extinguished in some other lawful manner.*

The usual method to terminate a mortgage that secures a specific note is to mark the note "paid" and then present this paid note for cancellation to the Clerk of Court. Louisiana statutes also permit cancellation through presentation of an "*instrument of release in a form sufficient to bring about the cancellation*" to the Clerk of Court of the parish where the property was located and the mortgage was recorded (R.S. 9:5385). The forms for this are contained in R.S. 9:5166–5167. Also see R.S. 9:5168–5173.

C.C. art. 3298(E) states a future advance mortgage "*continues until it is terminated by the mortgagor or his successor.*" The continuation as to third parties, however, is subject to the rules of inscription and reinscription (see Sections 20.1 and 20.2, below).

C.C. art. 3298(E) eliminates any contention that just because a line of credit loan has been paid down to zero, the mortgage is extinguished. Under C.C. art. 3298(E), as long as the mortgagor has not terminated the "future advance mortgage," the lender may again lend funds after the line of credit loan has been paid down to zero. The new advances will be secured retroactively to the date the mortgage is filed in the parish mortgage records (see Section 13.3(b)(2), above).

As explained in Section 13.3(b)(3), above, however, a "future advance mortgage" securing a fluctuating line of credit loan cannot be structured to secure but a single, specific note. Therefore, C.C. art. 3298(D) and (E) provide the rules for terminating line of credit loans secured by a "future advance mortgage." C.C. art. 3298(D) allows the parties to the mortgage to contract "*what constitutes reasonable notice*" for termination of the mortgage. R.S. 9:5169 governs the procedure for cancelling a "future advance mortgage" securing a fluctuating line of credit loan.

13.3(c). What Third Parties Can and Cannot Ascertain about a "Future Advance Mortgage"

Third parties examining the public records (see Chapter 23, below) cannot necessarily ascertain whether a mortgage stating that it is security for but one specific note secures (i) a note for which monies were advanced when the note was made or (ii) a note that represents monies to be advanced in the future. This is because no "magic" language is required in either the note or the mortgage to permit the mortgage to secure future advances; as long as the mortgage complies with the requirements of C.C. arts. 3288 and 3298, it affects third parties once it is filed for registry in the parish where the property is located (see Section 13.3(b)(2), above).

Therefore, third parties must "assume the worst" (see Section 24.2) when examining any mortgage in the public records that states it secures only a note. Third parties must make the assumption that the note represents sums loaned simultaneously with the granting of the mortgage and that the entire loan is outstanding and unpaid.

The following example illustrates this point. Assume that Mortgage #1, dated March 1, secures a $100,000 note paraphed for identification with the act of mortgage. The mortgage is filed for registry in the proper parish records the same date that it is executed. The face of the mortgage appears to describe a note that is for a contemporaneous loan; however, in fact the parties intend that the note secure advances to be made in the future, and the note represents the sums that will be advanced (see Section 13.3(a)(1), above).

Although the mortgage describes a note that appears to be for a contemporaneous loan, third parties examining the public records cannot ascertain the parties' intent and cannot know whether any money was lent on the day of the note's execution. Likewise, third parties cannot ascertain from the public records whether the note was intended to represent advances to be made in the future. Both pre-1992 jurisprudence and current C.C. art. 3298 permit the mortgage to be treated as a "future advance mortgage" even though the note appears to represent funds advanced contemporaneously with the signing of the note. Under the jurisprudence, all monies advanced in the future under the $100,000 note will be secured by the mortgage, and the mortgage's effective date as to third parties (regardless of the date funds are actually advanced) will be March 1 (see Section 13.3(b)(2), above).

Because third parties cannot ascertain how much has been advanced, the only safe assumption for a third party examining the public records is to assume that the entire $100,000 had been advanced on March 1 and remains unpaid. This is because even if the $100,000 had been advanced in July of that year, the result would be that all advances would have a retroactive rank to March 1, the date the of the mortgage's registry in the mortgage records.

Third parties are not prejudiced by the fact that they cannot ascertain whether this mortgage secures future advances. For example, assume that instead of the $100,000 note representing monies that had been advanced, it represents a contemporaneous advance of the entire amount on March 1, the date the mortgage is executed and then filed for registry in the parish mortgage records. Third parties examining the public records have no way of ascertaining whether any of the $100,000 has been repaid or whether the entire amount remains outstanding. Because third parties cannot know the actual current balance of the note the mortgage secures, the only safe assumption for the third parties is to assume that the entire $100,000 amount remains outstanding and unpaid. This mortgage affects third parties from March 1, the date of its registry.

As can be seen, whether the mortgage secures a note that (as between the parties) is for a contemporaneous advance or for future advances, the effect on third parties is identical. There is no way for third parties to know the outstanding balance of the note secured by the mortgage, so the only safe assumption in examining the mortgage records is to assume that the entire principal balance has remained outstanding and unpaid from the date the mortgage was created.

Today, in fluctuating line of credit loans secured by a "multiple obligations mortgage" or "multiple indebtedness mortgage" created under C.C. art. 3298, the obligations the mortgage secures are often described in broad terms, such as "any and all past, present and future obligations of mortgagor to creditor up to the principal limit of $100,000, including but not limited to mortgagor's $40,000 note dated the same date as this mortgage, bearing interest at the rate of 8% per annum." In an instance such as this, third parties are able to ascertain from the language of the mortgage that it secures future advances; however, third parties cannot ascertain from the public records the outstanding balance of the loans or whether additional advances may be contemplated by the borrower and lender. Therefore, third parties must assume that, because of the retroactive rank of future advances (see Section 13.3(b)(2), above), the entire $100,000 maximum amount of the line of credit remains outstanding and unpaid.

The situation of third parties examining the public records stands in contrast to the litigation involving a mortgage. In litigation, the mortgagee (the creditor under the mortgage) must prove, among other items, the intent of the parties to demonstrate that this was a "future advance mortgage," the outstanding balance of the loan, and all other aspects of the creditor's claim. For examples of the differences between title examination issues and litigation issues, see Chapter 24, below.

13.4. The Collateral Mortgage in General

13.4(a). Overview of the Collateral Mortgage

Prior to the January 1, 1992, effective date of the amendments to C.C. art. 3298, a mortgage could not directly secure a fluctuating line of credit loan (a loan where the debtor may borrow and repay and borrow again, as long as an agreed-upon upper limit of the loan is not exceeded). This is because, before these amendments became effective, mortgages could secure loans for future advances, but once all the funds had been advanced and repaid, no more money that was thereafter loaned could be secured by the mortgage because the principal obligation had been extinguished (see Section 13.3(a)(2), above).

In the early 1800s, there was a need for farmers to be able to use their land to secure fluctuating balance line of credit loans, particularly in the flourishing cotton and sugar cane trade. Although the Civil Code at the time did not allow a mortgage to directly secure fluctuating balance line of credit loans, those Civil Code articles permitted a pledge to secure such loans. Creative lawyers came up with a mechanism to pledge a note to secure a fluctuating balance line of credit loan; this pledged note in turn was secured by a mortgage. This was the basis of what we now refer to as the "collateral mortgage."

Thinking of a "collateral mortgage" primarily as a mortgage often leads to faulty analysis. That is why this Précis will refer to a "collateral mortgage package," because it involves a package of rights, and will distinguish the "collateral mortgage package" from the collateral mortgage itself.

It is far more useful to think of a collateral mortgage package not as a mortgage but rather as "a possessory security interest in a note secured by a mortgage." This concept will help in properly analyzing this unique Louisiana security device, for it reminds us that, first and foremost, what the jurisprudence calls a "collateral mortgage" consists of three different sets of rights or "levels" of rights:

- Level One is the principal obligation.
- Level Two is the security for the principal obligation, the so-called "collateral mortgage note"; a creditor must obtain a perfected UCC 9 secu-

rity interest in the note to be protected. Typically, this collateral mortgage note is a negotiable note due on demand (see Section 13.6, below) and payable to bearer (see Section 13.7, below).

• Level Three is the mortgage that secures the note at Level Two, the so-called "collateral mortgage." It should be emphasized that the collateral mortgage itself secures only Level Two; it does not directly secure the principal obligation, which is Level One.

The following diagram illustrates these three levels:

Diagram 13.4(a)(1)

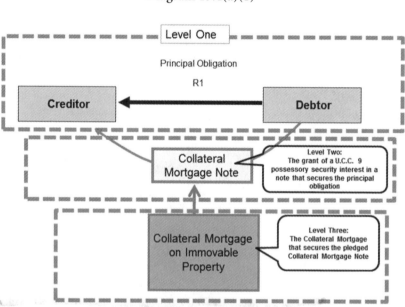

Thus, the mortgage is an accessory obligation to the note at Level Two, while the note at Level Two is an accessory obligation to the principal obligation.

This Précis will use the phrase "collateral mortgage note" to refer to the Level Two note, for this is the common phrase used by real estate attorneys. In the jurisprudence, three phrases are sometimes used for this same note: the "collateral mortgage note"; the "*ne varietur* note"; or the "pledged note."

The term "*ne varietur* note" is used by courts not because the collateral mortgage note is the only kind of note paraphed *ne varietur* for identification with an act of mortgage (see Section 12.4(c), above), but rather because, in a collateral mortgage package, it is this note that is secured by the collateral mortgage, and thus if a paraph is to be done, it is this collateral mortgage note that is paraphed *ne varietur* for identification with the act of collateral mortgage.

Many cases refer to the collateral mortgage note as the "pledged note." This language harks back to the Civil Code articles on pledge that existed prior to 1990, the effective date of the adoption of Louisiana's version of UCC9 (see Chapter 41, below), even though the former pledge articles have not dealt with such matters since 1990. In addition, because the pledge articles of the Civil Code were completely reworked in 2014, using the phrase "pledged note" today is a misnomer.

Two additional definitions may be helpful, particularly when reading cases about collateral mortgages. A "handnote" is the term for notes representing advances on the principal obligation, but the handnotes do not represent the entirety of the principal obligation (see Section 13.13(b), below). A "collateral pledge agreement" was a pre-1990 contract in which the debtor evidenced in writing the debtor's intent concerning what debts or loans were secured by the pledge of the collateral mortgage note. There was no legal requirement for a "collateral pledge agreement" other than for certain financial institutions; however, creditors often required debtors to enter into such agreements so that there would be no dispute in the future about what obligations the pledge of the collateral mortgage note was meant to secure. Since 1990, however, the "collateral pledge agreement" has been replaced by a UCC9 security agreement (see Section 13.5(b), below).

A collateral mortgage is a unique Louisiana creation. Two of the key benefits of a collateral mortgage are that: (a) a collateral mortgage note can be reused by many creditors without being extinguished (see Sections 13.4(d) and 13.13, below), and (b) if structured properly, the principal obligation that a collateral mortgage package secures can never prescribe, although the collateral mortgage note itself may prescribe, rendering the real security represented by the collateral mortgage unenforceable (see Section 13.14, below).

The concepts relating to a collateral mortgage package are difficult to master. Eventually, the collateral mortgage package may become obsolete, because a C.C. art. 3298 mortgage (see Section 13.3(b), above) can accomplish everything that a collateral mortgage can, but without the elaborate complexity and three-level structure of the collateral mortgage package. Currently, however, collateral mortgage packages are still used in a number of ongoing loan transactions.

13.4(b). The History of Collateral Mortgage Packages Prior to 1990

Much of the jurisprudence on collateral mortgage packages evolved prior to 1990. While a detailed historical analysis is beyond the scope of this Précis, understanding the terminology and concepts employed in the jurisprudence may be helpful. Therefore, this Section 13.4(b) describes some of these concepts.

13.4(b)(1). Structuring a Collateral Mortgage Package Prior to 1990 Using a Third-Party Pledgor

Assume that, in 1950, Debtor and Creditor wanted to enter into a $15,000 fluctuating line of credit loan, but Creditor insisted on security for the loan. Debtor did not own any immovable property, but Debtor's rich uncle, Uncle X, agreed to help Debtor obtain the loan with Creditor. Creditor asked Uncle X to sign a continuing guarantee (see Section 3.4, above), but Uncle X refused. Instead, Uncle X offered to execute a $15,000 negotiable note, payable on demand to bearer, and to pledge that note (under the Civil Code pledge articles in existence at that time) to Creditor to secure Debtor's fluctuating line of credit loan. The structure would look like this:

Diagram 13.4(b)(1)(a)

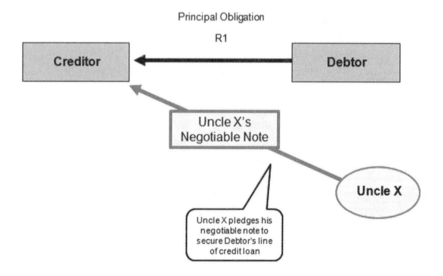

Under this structure, Uncle X's $15,000 note did not represent monies that had been advanced to Uncle X, for the monies were being lent to Debtor on the principal obligation: Uncle X's note is an accessory obligation and no money had been given to Uncle X.

Likewise, Uncle X's $15,000 note did not represent monies in the future that would be advanced to Uncle X, because Uncle X was not borrowing any money from Creditor and never intended to borrow money from Creditor.

Nonetheless, Uncle X's note was not fictitious. It represented a personal obligation of Uncle X, repayable according to its terms. Uncle X's pledge of the note to Creditor gave Creditor all the rights of a pledgee under the pledge articles of the Civil Code as they existed at that time. If Debtor defaulted on his obligations to Creditor under the line of credit loan, Creditor could elect to pursue Debtor directly or sue Uncle X on the pledged note.

Assume, however, that Creditor wanted real security from Uncle X in addition to the personal security represented by Uncle X's pledged note. Assume that Creditor wanted Uncle X to secure the pledged note with a mortgage and Uncle X did so. The structure would look like this:

Diagram 13.4(b)(2)

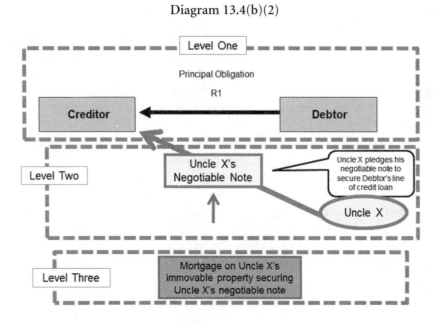

Now, there are three levels to this transaction. There is Level One, the principal obligation consisting of the fluctuating line of credit loan between Creditor and Debtor. There is Level Two, the pledged note of Uncle X, which is an accessory obligation to the principal obligation. Finally, there is Level Three, the mortgage, which is an accessory obligation to the pledged note. Under the former pledge provisions of the Civil Code, the way to affect third parties with a pledge was by delivery of the pledged item (the collateral mortgage note).

It is important to observe that this reflects the same three-level structure described in Section 13.4(a), above. Observe also that both Level Two and Level Three had to be executed in a way that would affect third parties. This structure would not work to protect the Creditor from third party claims and secure the fluctuating line of credit principle obligation unless there was (i) a valid pledge (Level Two) of Uncle X's note, a note designed to secure the fluctuating line of credit, and (ii) Uncle X's mortgage (Level Three) both affected third parties and secured his pledged note.

If Debtor defaulted on the principal obligation, Creditor could pursue Debtor personally on the principal obligation (Level One) or Creditor could foreclose on Uncle X's mortgage (Level Three). Once the mortgaged property was sold at a sheriff's sale (see Chapter 38, below), the mortgage was extinguished and Creditor obtained a privilege on the proceeds of the sale (see Chapter 12, above).

The judicial sales proceeds from the sale of the mortgaged property (Level Three) were used to pay the balance owing on the pledged note (Level Two). Now, instead of holding a note in pledge, Creditor held cash in pledge. The cash held in pledge paid off the pledged note (Level Two) and those funds were applied to pay the principal obligation (Level One). Thus, the money from the foreclosure flowed up from Level Three to Level Two (for Level Three secured Level Two) and from Level Two to Level One, the principal obligation (for Level Two secured Level One). A detailed explanation with numbers can be found the examples in Section 13.9(a), below.

One must be cautious in using this example, because the Louisiana Supreme Court has held that the nature of Uncle X's obligation on the pledged note changes from a personal obligation to an *in rem* obligation when the pledged note is paraphed *ne varietur* for identification with the act of collateral mortgage (see Section 13.12, below). For illustration purposes, however, this example is a starting point in understanding today's structure of a collateral mortgage package.

13.4(b)(2). An Introduction to the Structure of a Collateral Mortgage Package Prior to 1990 with the Debtor as Pledgor

The typical collateral mortgage package, both prior to 1990 and today, does not involve a third-party pledgor, as described in the example in Section 13.4(b), above. The structure after 1990 is set forth in Section 13.5, below.

Prior to 1990, the typical collateral mortgage package consisted of only two parties, the debtor and the creditor. The debtor was the obligor of the principal obligation, the maker of the pledged note, and the mortgagor of the mortgage that secured the pledged note. See Diagram 13.4(a)(1), above.

One might ask why a debtor, prior to 1990, would want to execute a note to be pledged to secure the debtor's own obligation. The reason is the same as one involving the example with Uncle X (Section 13.4(b), above); prior to 1990, it was only by using a pledge of a note that that a debtor could then use a mortgage to secure a fluctuating line of credit loan.

As with the example using Uncle X (Section 13.4(b), above), if a debtor was simultaneously the obligor of the principal obligation, the maker of the collateral mortgage note, and the grantor of the collateral mortgage, the creditor had two main options if the debtor defaulted on the principal obligation (Level One). The creditor could sue the debtor personally on the principal obligation. Alternatively, the creditor could foreclose on the debtor's mortgage (Level Three).

Once the mortgaged property was sold at a sheriff's sale (see Chapter 38, below), the mortgage would be extinguished and the creditor obtained a privilege on the proceeds of the sale. The sales proceeds from the mortgaged property (Level Three, see Diagram 13.4(a)(2), above) were used to pay the balance owing on the pledged note (Level Two). Now, instead of holding a note in pledge, the creditor held cash in pledge. The cash held in pledge which paid off the pledged note (Level Two) was applied to pay the principal obligation (Level One). Thus, the money from the foreclosure flowed up from Level Three to Level Two (for Level Three secured Level Two) and from Level Two to Level One (for Level Two secured Level One). A detailed explanation with numbers can be found the examples in Section 13.9(c), below.

13.4(b)(3). Prior to 1990, a Collateral Mortgage Package Ranked From the Earliest Concurrence of Pledge of the Collateral Mortgage Note and Filing for Registry of the Collateral Mortgage

Prior to 1990, in situations where either the debtor (Section 13.4(c), above) or a third party (Section 13.4(b), above) was the maker and pledgor of both the collateral mortgage note and collateral mortgage, the collateral mortgage package became effective against third parties only if both Level Two (the pledge) and Level Three (the collateral mortgage) were effective against third parties.

Prior to 1990, Level Two (the pledge) was made effective against third parties (or "perfected," to use UCC9 terminology) by delivery of the collateral mortgage note in pledge to the creditor. Under the Civil Code pledge articles in existence prior to 1990, no written document was needed to evidence this pledge of a negotiable note and no written document was needed to evidence the intent of the pledgor concerning what loans or debts were secured by the pledge. Often, however, creditors wanted to have written evidence of the debtor's intent, for proof of intent through written evidence was difficult to overcome; without written evidence, it was merely a battle of testimony and which party a court believed. This written evidence of the debtor's intent was called the "collateral pledge agreement," for it was an agreement detailing the debtor's intent concerning what the collateral secured at the time of the pledge.

Prior to 1990 (and today), Level Three (the collateral mortgage) was made effective as to third parties by filing the mortgage for registry in the mortgage records of the parish where the property was located (see Chapter 20, below).

Therefore, a pre-1990 collateral mortgage package affected third parties only from the earliest concurrence of the pledge of the collateral mortgage note (perfection of Level Two) and the filing for registry of the collateral mortgage (perfection of Level Three).

13.5. The Structure of a Collateral Mortgage Today

As noted in the discussion of the Civil Code pledge provisions (see Section 10.1, above), these provisions were superseded in 1990 by the adoption of

Louisiana's version of Article 9 of the Uniform Commercial Code. The pledge provisions themselves were completely reworked in 2014.

Prior to 1990, a collateral mortgage package was an amalgamation of pledge and mortgage. Today, a collateral mortgage package is an amalgamation of UCC9 security interests and mortgage. The major distinction between the pre-1990 collateral mortgage package and the device today is that rights in the collateral mortgage note are no longer perfected by a pledge but rather by a security interest pursuant to UCC9. The structure of the collateral mortgage package still consists of three levels:

Diagram 13.5(1)

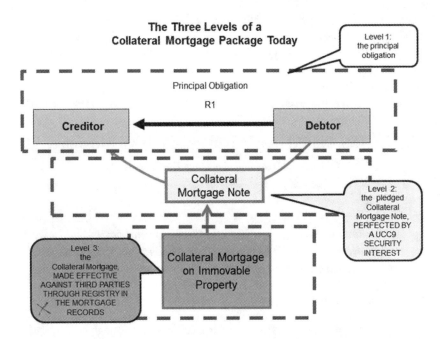

The link connecting the Civil Code mortgage provisions, the rules of collateral mortgage packages, and UCC9 are found in R.S. 9:5550, *et seq.*

Today, a collateral mortgage package ranks against third parties from the earliest concurrence of (i) a perfected security in the collateral mortgage note and (ii) filing for registry of the collateral mortgage. This means that the creditor must use UCC9 to perfect a security interest in the collateral mortgage note (Level Two), and also must use the Civil Code registry rules to make the collateral mortgage (Level Three) effective against third parties.

Under Louisiana's version of UCC9, a security interest in a collateral mortgage note may be perfected only by delivery of the note to the creditor (or to an agent of the creditor) and by "value" being given (see 13.5(b), below).

In addition, the mortgage itself (Level Three) must be made effective against third parties. This requires that the collateral mortgage be filed for recordation in the mortgage records (see Section 11.4, above, and Chapters 19 and 20, below).

13.5(a). R.S. 9:5550: Collateral Mortgage Definitions

R.S. 9:5550 is the link between the Civil Code provisions on collateral mortgage packages and Louisiana's version of UCC9.

R.S. 9:5550 defines a collateral mortgage as "*a mortgage that is given to secure a written obligation, such as a collateral mortgage note, negotiable or nonnegotiable instrument, or other written evidence of debt, that is issued, pledged, or otherwise used as security for another obligation.*" Note the reference to "pledge"; although a security interest in a collateral mortgage note is now controlled by UCC9, the statute still refers to the old, pre-1990 concept of "pledge" (see Section 10.1, above). It is clear, however, that the reference to "pledge" is illustrative only.

13.5(b). R.S. 9:5551(A): When a Collateral Mortgage Becomes Effective as to Third Parties

The provisions of R.S. 9:5551(A)–(C) will be examined separately. R.S. 9:5551(A) provides:

> *A. A collateral mortgage becomes effective as to third parties, subject to the requirements of registry of the collateral mortgage, when a security interest is perfected in the obligation secured by the collateral mortgage in accordance with the provisions of Chapter 9 of the Louisiana Commercial Laws, R.S. 10:9–101 et seq.*

R.S. 9:5551(A) sets forth the rule that a collateral mortgage becomes effective as to third parties at the earliest concurrence of a perfected security interest in the collateral mortgage note (Level Two) and the registry of the mortgage (Level Three) (see Diagram 13.5(1), above). Once this concurrence of events happens, R.S. 9:5551(B) states that the collateral mortgage takes its "*rank and priority*" from that point.

Perfection of a security interest in the collateral mortgage note (Level Two) under UCC9 requires three things.

First, there must be delivery of the collateral note to the creditor or the creditor's agent (R.S. 10:9-313(a)). There is no way to perfect a UCC9 security interest in a collateral mortgage note by filing a financing statement in the UCC9 records (see R.S. 10:9-301(5), R.S. 10:9-310(b)(6), and R.S. 10:9-312(a)). The only way to perfect a security interest in a collateral mortgage note is by delivery to the creditor so that the creditor (or someone designated by the creditor) has possession of the note.

Second, "value" must be given (R.S. 10:9-203). R.S. 10:1-204 defines value as:

Except as otherwise provided in Chapters 3, 4, and 5, a person gives value for rights if the person acquires them:

(1) in return for a binding commitment to extend credit or for the extension of immediately available credit, whether or not drawn upon and whether or not a charge-back is provided for in the event of difficulties in collection;

(2) as security for, or in total or partial satisfaction of, a preexisting claim;

(3) by accepting delivery under a preexisting contract for purchase; or

(4) in return for any consideration sufficient to support a simple contract.

Because creditors seldom have an iron-clad "*binding commitment*" to lend money to borrowers in any and all circumstances, one customary method of making sure that "value" exists for the purposes of UCC9 perfection is for the creditor to advance some small portion of money to the debtor at the same time the collateral mortgage note is delivered to the creditor. Typically, a creditor advances a $100 non-interest bearing loan when the collateral mortgage note is pledged. The creditor holds on to this $100 (holding it as a possessory security interest under R.S. 10:9-313), providing the "value" needed to accomplish perfection of the security interest in the collateral mortgage note.

Third, there must be an agreement by the debtor of what loan(s) are secured by the security interest in the collateral mortgage note. This can be accomplished in a Security Agreement (defined in R.S. 10:9-102(73); also see R.S. 10:9-201 *et seq.*).

There may be a question whether a Security Agreement is required in cases of possessory collateral, such as a collateral mortgage note. Nonetheless, because Louisiana collateral mortgage jurisprudence had indicated that written proof of intent of the debtor at the time of the pledge was helpful, and because a written agreement entered into contemporaneously with the perfection of the security interest helps establish that intent, the typical structure of a collateral mortgage package today includes a Security Agreement. It should be noted that some cases still refer to this written agreement as a "collateral pledge agreement," but because the pledge provisions of the Civil Code have been superseded since 1970, the proper terminology is the UCC phrase "Security Agreement."

It should be emphasized that third parties cannot ascertain whether a creditor has obtained a perfected security interest in the collateral mortgage note because there is nothing recorded in either the UCC9 records or mortgage records about this. Nothing is recorded in the UCC9 records because the only way to perfect a security interest in a collateral mortgage note is to deliver it to the creditor (or one who agrees to hold for the creditor) plus the grant of value. UCC9 expressly states that a security interest in a collateral mortgage note cannot be obtained by filing a Financing Statement in the UCC9 records. Likewise, there is no way to perfect a security interest in the collateral mortgage note by recording something in the parish mortgage records; the only item in a collateral mortgage package that is recorded in the mortgage records is the collateral mortgage (Level Three), not the collateral mortgage note (Level Two).

13.5(c). R.S. 9:5551(B): A Collateral Mortgage Package Properly Perfected Remains Effective Even if the Principal Obligation Is Paid Down to Zero

R.S. 9:5551(B) provides:

> B. A collateral mortgage takes its rank and priority from the time it becomes effective as to third parties. Once it becomes effective, as long as the effects of recordation continues in accordance with Articles 3328 through 3334 of the Civil Code, a collateral mortgage remains effective as to third parties (notwithstanding any intermediate period when the security interest in the secured obligation becomes unperfected) as long as the secured party or his agent or his successor retains possession of the collateral mortgage note or other written obligation, or the obligation secured by the mortgage otherwise remains enforceable according to its terms, by the secured party or his successor.

In this statute, the term "secured obligation" refers to the collateral mortgage note (Level Two).

R.S. 9:5551(B) is designed to deal with the situation where the principal obligation is inadvertently paid down to zero. A perfected UCC9 security interest in the collateral mortgage note requires that there be UCC "value" (see
Section 13.5(b), above). Prior to 1990, however, there was no requirement
that there be a "value" to support a pledge of the collateral mortgage note, because the Civil Code was not concerned with common law consideration; the
Civil Code allows "cause" to be a sufficient basis to support a contract (C.C.
art. 1967).

R.S. 9:5551, enacted in 1990 when Louisiana adopted its version of UCC9,
was designed to protect lenders who (thinking that the pre-1990 law still applied) allowed the principal obligation to be paid down to zero, thereby eliminating value; in the absence of this statute, once value ceased to exist, there
would be no perfection of a security interest in the collateral mortgage note
and the collateral mortgage package (the combination of the collateral mortgage note and the collateral mortgage) would cease being security for the principal obligation.

Therefore, R.S. 9:5551 provides that the collateral mortgage remains effective as to third parties as long as the effects of registry of the collateral mortgage continue (see Chapter 20, below), and as long as the creditor (or his agent)
maintains possession of the collateral mortgage note, despite the fact that the
principal obligation is paid down to zero and "value" ceases. That is what is
meant by the phrase: "*notwithstanding any intermediate period when the security interest in the secured obligation becomes unperfected.*"

The reference in R.S. 9:5551 to C.C. arts. 3328–3334 reflects the failure of
the Legislature to amend R.S. 9:5551 to accommodate amendments to the Civil
Code. C.C. arts. 3328–3334 were the former provisions relating to how long
a mortgage affects third persons on the public records; these statutes were
moved and renumbered C.C. arts. 3357 *et seq.*

13.5(d). R.S. 9:5551(C): A Collateral Mortgage Package Can Be Reused Once the Principal Obligation Is Paid Off or Cancelled

R.S. 9:5551(C) provides:

C. *As long as the effects of registry of the collateral mortgage continue,
in accordance with Articles 3328 through 3334 of the Civil Code, if there
is a termination, remission, or release of possession of the written obligation, a collateral mortgage takes its rank and priority from the time a*

new security interest is perfected in the written obligation, regardless of whether the secured party is the original secured party, his successor, or a new or different secured party.

The *"written obligation"* referenced in this statute is the collateral mortgage note (Level Two).

One of the interesting aspects of a collateral mortgage package, in addition to the constant acknowledgment rule (see Section 10.6, above, and Section 13.14, below), is the fact that a collateral mortgage note can be "pledged" and "repledged" (to use pre-1990 terminology). In other words, the collateral mortgage note can be reused by the debtor time and time again because it does not represent sums that have been advanced or will be advanced.

As long as the collateral mortgage note has not prescribed (see Section 13.14, below), the debtor may grant the same creditor or a new creditor a security interest in the collateral mortgage note to secure new and different obligations. When this happens, the creditor may get a new rank, as to third parties, on the effective date of the collateral mortgage package. This result occurs because a collateral mortgage note (Level Two) does not represent sums that have been advanced or will be advanced, although it is a "real" (as opposed to fictitious) *in rem*, non-recourse note (see Section 13.12, below) that bears interest according to its terms. Therefore, when a debtor has completed all payments of all outstanding agreements on the principal obligation (Level One), the collateral mortgage note remains unpaid and intact (assuming that the collateral mortgage note has not prescribed; if the collateral mortgage has prescribed, the collateral mortgage is unenforceable but prescription remains interrupted on the principal obligation (Level One); see Section 10.6, above).

13.5(d)(1). Example #1

On February 1, Creditor agrees to lend money on a fluctuating line of credit loan to Debtor. On that same day, (i) Debtor executes the principal obligation, a loan agreement representing the lending/borrowing relationship (Level One), (ii) Debtor executes a collateral mortgage note (Level Two) paraphed for identification with an act of collateral mortgage, and (iii) executes a collateral mortgage (Level Three). On the same day, Creditor not only gives value to Debtor, thereby granting Creditor a perfected UCC9 security interest in the collateral mortgage note (Level Two) but also records the collateral mortgage (Level Three) in the parish where the immovable property is located.

By November 1, Debtor has borrowed and repaid the line of credit loan to Creditor and wants to borrow money from Bank, a different lender. On November 2, Creditor cancels the loan agreement and returns to Debtor the collateral mortgage note (Level Two). On November, 3, Debtor delivers the collateral mortgage note (Level Two) to Banker who gives value to Debtor for it, thereby granting Banker a perfected UCC9 security interest in the collateral mortgage note.

In this situation, third parties looking at the mortgage records will not see any changes in the collateral mortgage (Level Three) or the inscription of the collateral mortgage. This leads to two interrelated principles:

- There is no need for any recordation in the public records of anything concerning the new security interest in the collateral mortgage note, because nothing needs to be indicated in the public records about the collateral mortgage note (R.S. 9:5554). Therefore, third parties examining the public records, who always are worried about the "worst case" scenario, will assume that the collateral mortgage affects them from February 1, the date the collateral mortgage was recorded in the mortgage records.
- In litigation, however, Bank must prove its ranking, and that rank will only be from November 3rd. This is because R.S. 9:5551(c) mandates that *"if there is a termination, remission, or release of possession of the written obligation, a collateral mortgage takes its rank and priority from the time a new security interest is perfected in the written obligation, regardless of whether the secured party is the original secured party, his successor, or a new or different secured party."*

Thus, once Debtor and Creditor completed their transaction, Creditor returned the collateral mortgage note to Debtor, and Debtor granted Bank (a new lender) a security interest in the collateral mortgage note, the Bank obtained a new rank in the collateral mortgage package at the earliest concurrence of the perfection of the new security interest and the registry of the collateral mortgage. As to third parties, however, there has been no change in the inscription or recordation information concerning the collateral mortgage. Nonetheless, Bank ranks as to third parties from the time it received a perfected security interest in the collateral mortgage note even though third parties cannot ascertain the "true" ranking date (see Chapter 24, below).

It must be emphasized that this result—permitting Bank to be secured by the collateral mortgage package, albeit with a new ranking date—only occurs if, in the words of R.S. 9:5551(C), *"the effects of registry of the collateral mortgage continue."* This means that the collateral mortgage package will cease to affect third parties if the collateral mortgage (Level Three) has not been timely reinscribed in the mortgage records (see Section 20.2, below) even though the principal obligation may never prescribe because of the constant acknowledgement rule (see Section 10.6, above, and Section 13.14, below) and even if the debtor may have acknowledged the collateral mortgage note (Level Two) so that it does not prescribe.

As is the case with R.S. 9:5551(B) (see Section 13.5(c), above), the references in R.S. 9:5551(C) to C.C. arts. 3328–3334 reflect the failure of the Legislature to amend R.S. 9:5551 to accommodate amendments to the Civil Code. C.C. arts. 3328–3334 were the former provisions relating to how long a mortgage affects third persons on the public records; these statutes were moved and renumbered C.C. arts. 3357 *et seq.*

13.6. Why the Collateral Mortgage Note Should Be Due on Demand

In order for a collateral mortgage package to function as intended, it is important that the collateral mortgage note be due on demand. The reason why can be illustrated by what would happen if the collateral mortgage note contained the same terms and conditions as the principal obligation.

Example #1. On April 1, 2017, Debtor granted Creditor a valid and perfected collateral mortgage package on Debtor's business to secure a $100,000 fluctuating line of credit loan (Level One). The loan agreement called for monthly payments of interest with all principal due at the end of five years. The collateral mortgage note (Level Two) was for $100,000 and was not due for five years, the same period of time that the line of credit will be extant. Debtor granted a collateral mortgage (Level Three) on its store to secure the five-year collateral mortgage note (Level Two). On April 1, 2017, Creditor both recorded the collateral mortgage and granted the first loan under the line of credit to Debtor.

On September 1, 2017 (five months after the inception of the loan), Debtor defaulted on interest payments and Creditor wished to accelerate the loan and foreclose.

Creditor in this instance had a problem. Creditor could not foreclose on the collateral mortgage (Level Three) because the obligation it secured—the collateral mortgage note (Level Two) was not yet due and won't be due until 2022, five years from 2017. Moreover, the default in payments of interest was a default in the principal obligation (Level One); properly structured, a collateral mortgage package's collateral mortgage note should not represent funds that have been advanced or will be advanced (see Section 13.5(d), above), and thus no payments would be due on the collateral mortgage note.

While Creditor may still have decided to sue Debtor personally on the principal obligation (Level I), Creditor would not have been able to foreclose on the collateral mortgage. All Creditor would have been able to do in September of 2017 concerning the security for the loan was to have tried to seize and sell the collateral mortgage note, which in turn was secured by the collateral mortgage. There is an insurmountable obstacle for Creditor at this point. The jurisprudence has firmly held that, as an accessory obligation, the collateral mortgage note cannot be "sold" separately from the principal obligation it secures. Additionally, even if the jurisprudence had permitted the collateral mortgage note to be sold separately, with Creditor retaining the principal obligation, it is unlikely that there would have been many persons who would have wanted to buy a collateral mortgage note at a sheriff's sale when that note (a) was an *in rem* obligation of the debtor (see Section 13.12, below), and (b) did not represent sums that have been advanced or will be advanced, and (c) is not due until 2022. In this hypothetical case (not permitted by the jurisprudence), only in 2022 would the buyer of the collateral mortgage note at the sheriff's sale have the right to foreclose on the property.

Therefore, it is clear that if Creditor wants the right to foreclose on the mortgage that secures the collateral mortgage note, the only way this can occur in all cases is to make the collateral mortgage note due on demand. If the collateral mortgage note is due on demand, it is always "due," and when there is a default in the principal obligation (Level One), the collateral mortgage note (Level Two) is due and foreclosure can begin immediately on the collateral mortgage (Level Three) that secures the collateral mortgage note.

Because the collateral mortgage note should be due on demand, it will prescribe in five years from the date it is signed (C.C. art. 3498). Therefore, it will need to be acknowledged every five years unless payments of principal and interest are made by Debtor or his co-debtors *in solido* on the principal obligation (R.S. 9:5807 and Section 13.14, below).

13.7. Why the Collateral Mortgage Note Should Be Bearer Paper

Not only should a collateral mortgage note be due on demand (see Section 13.6, above), it also should be bearer paper (R.S. 10:3-109). The reasons are twofold.

First, for the purposes of executory process, there is jurisprudence indicating that if a negotiable note is payable to the "order" of a named party, authentic evidence may be necessary to evidence the right of the holder of that note to use executory process. It is unlikely that a transfer of a collateral mortgage note will ever be evidenced by a written instrument, for perfection of a security interest in a collateral mortgage note under UCC9 does not require "filing" in the UCC records and does not require that any document be in authentic form (see Section 13.5, above). Having the collateral mortgage note as bearer paper eliminates any argument about authentic evidence and "order" paper. While there is some question whether that jurisprudence (about authentic acts of transfer being required for order paper) remains valid in light of changes in the Louisiana Code of Civil Procedure (see Section 38.1(c). below), cautious practitioners want to structure the collateral mortgage package in a way that accords with judicial holdings rather than create a document that may lead to future litigation.

Second, bearer paper requires no other documentation for its transfer. This makes the "pledge and repledge" (to use pre-1990 terminology) of a collateral mortgage note easy for both debtors and creditors. Louisiana law recognizes that a collateral mortgage note may be used multiple times by debtors to secure different lenders and different debts and that each new use of the collateral mortgage note may cause the collateral mortgage package to have a different ranking date as to third parties (see Section 13.5(d), above).

Typically, a collateral mortgage note is either payable to "Bearer" or payable to "MYSELF" and then endorsed in blank by the maker; either method results in the note being bearer paper (R.S. 10:3-104 and R.S. 10:3-109).

13.8. Why The Collateral Mortgage Note Is Typically Paraphed *Ne Varietur* for Identification with the Act of Collateral Mortgage

While a paraph is not required on notes secured by mortgages (see Section 12.4(c), above), it is customary to have the collateral mortgage note paraphed *ne varietur* for identification with the act of collateral mortgage. There are two reasons for this.

First, the paraph is helpful to tie the collateral mortgage note, which is payable to bearer on demand (see Sections 13.6 and 13.7, above), to the collateral mortgage.

Second, for the purposes of executory process, a paraphed note is "deemed authentic" (see Section 38.1(c), below). This aids in allowing executory process on a collateral mortgage.

13.9. What Should Be the Principal Amount of the Collateral Mortgage Note?

There is no statute or case mandating how much the collateral mortgage note must be for in relation to the principal obligation. Likewise, no statute or case sets forth what interest rate the collateral mortgage note must bear. Nonetheless, in the almost two hundred years that the collateral mortgage package has been used in Louisiana, certain usual and customary practices have emerged.

Typically, when an attorney creates a collateral mortgage package, the amount of a collateral mortgage note is set at 50% greater than the maximum amount of the anticipated total principal obligation. Stated another way, the amount of the collateral mortgage note is typically 150% of the principal obligation, so that if the maximum principal obligation is anticipated to be $100,000, the collateral mortgage note is for $150,000. Further, a collateral mortgage note typically bears interest at a fixed rate of interest, often set at 12% per annum. The reasons for this are explained in the next two sections.

13.9(a). The Face Amount of the Collateral Mortgage Note (Level Two) Is Typically Set at 150% of the Principal Obligation (Level One)

While a creditor and debtor may agree to an anticipated maximum amount of the principal obligation which the collateral mortgage package secures, that maximum amount may be exceeded from time to time. The face amount of the collateral mortgage note should be large enough to accommodate unexpected increases in the principal obligation, such as increases in the interest rate, additional expenses incurred by the creditor in protecting the property, paying property taxes if the debtor does not, or paying for insurance on the property if the debtor allows the insurance coverage to lapse. A mortgage may also contain a pledge of the mortgagor's property insurance as additional security for the creditor (see Section 15.2, below).

Most commercial loans and most second mortgage "home equity" loans are not made at fixed rates of interest but rather at fluctuating interest rates. These rates, which can change as often as weekly, are often tied to a bank's "prime" rate, a rate related to average rates of U.S. Treasury Notes, or to LIBOR (the London Interbank Offered Rate, which is a rate related to the short-term borrowing of unsecured funds from one bank to another). Borrowers, depending on their credit rating, pay in excess of these rates. For example, a loan may provide for an interest rate of "prime plus 3" meaning that if the prime rate is 6% per annum, the borrower must pay interest at the rate of 9% per annum (6% prime plus 3). It is impossible to know what the interest rate will be in the future over the life of the loan.

Likewise, it may be impossible to know all the instances in which the creditor may have to spend money to protect the property or advance money to the debtor or third parties to cover an emergency situation related to this loan or the total amount of these advances.

To cover all these situations, the creditor wants to be sure that the collateral mortgage package secures the entirety of the principal obligation; the only way to do this is to make sure that the collateral mortgage note is for more than the principal obligation.

13.9(b). The Collateral Mortgage Note Typically Bears Interest at a Fixed (Not Fluctuating) Rate

While there may be a fluctuating interest rate on the principal obligation (Level One) secured by a collateral mortgage package, attorneys creating collateral mortgage packages do not usually want the collateral mortgage note to bear a fluctuating rate of interest. What each creditor desires is that the total amount of principal and accumulated interest on the collateral mortgage at the time of collection or foreclosure exceeds the maximum amount of the principal obligation due at that time. This can be accomplished by using a fixed rate of interest if the principal amount of the collateral mortgage note is properly set (see Section 13.9(a), above).

Having a fixed rate on the collateral mortgage note assists creditors both in using executory process and in making the collateral mortgage package easily transferable from lender to lender.

For executory process, it is helpful to have the amount of the collateral mortgage note calculable on its face with a fixed rate of interest, because the amount of the principal obligation can be proven by an affidavit or verified petition without the need to detail all the weekly interest rate calculations (C.C.P. art. 2637(C) and R.S. 9:5555). This is particularly important for collateral mortgage notes, which can be "pledged and repledged" (to use pre-1990 terminology) and held by multiple creditors. Each creditor wants to set its own interest rate for the principal obligation and does not want to be tied to some other lender's rate on the collateral mortgage note.

Often, creditors use a 12% fixed interest rate for the collateral mortgage note, for 12% per annum interest was the former Civil Code "default" rule on interest that was permissible and not usurious. Today, there are multiple statutes allowing much higher interest rates for mortgages (see, for example, R.S. 9:3500–3509.1), but the 12% per annum interest rate is one that lawyers frequently use in preparing collateral mortgage notes. If properly structured, a collateral mortgage note (that is for 150% of the principal obligation) bearing interest at 12% per annum should usually suffice to cover not only the anticipated maximum amount of the principal obligation, but also any unexpected costs and fees incurred by the creditor as part of the principal obligation or in connection with protection of collateral.

13.9(c). A Collateral Mortgage Package Secures the Creditor to the Lesser of (a) the Principal and Interest Due on the Principal Obligation, or (b) the Principal and Interest Due on the Collateral Mortgage Note

There are two additional advantages to having the collateral mortgage note being 150% of the principal obligation (see Section 13.9(a), above) and having the collateral mortgage note bearing 12% fixed interest (see Section 13.9(b), above).

First, if the amount of the collateral mortgage note is less than the outstanding balance of the principal obligation, the creditor will not be able to obtain a privilege on the proceeds of the sale of the mortgaged property should the amount of those proceeds exceed the amount of the collateral mortgage note.

Second, a foreclosure can occur on property encumbered by a collateral mortgage only if the principal obligation (Level One) is in default and the collateral mortgage note (Level Two) is due (see Section 13.6, above). Upon foreclosure, the mortgaged property that secures the collateral mortgage (Level Three) is sold, extinguishing the collateral mortgage and resulting in cash from the foreclosure sale. The cash from the foreclosure sale is applied to the collateral mortgage note (Level Two), the obligation the collateral mortgage secured. This results in the collateral mortgage note being extinguished by payment, and the cash representing the payoff of the principal and outstanding interest on the collateral mortgage note is applied to the debt (Level One) that the collateral mortgage package secured. Because it is not the collateral mortgage (Level Three) that secures the principal obligation (Level One), and because it is only the collateral mortgage note (Level Two) that secures the principal obligation (Level One), upon foreclosure, a creditor cannot simply take the proceeds from the sale of the immovable property and use them to pay off the principal obligation (Level One). Because the funds from the mortgage foreclosure sale must "flow up" from the collateral mortgage (Level Three) through the collateral mortgage note (Level Two) to the principal obligation (Level One), a foreclosing creditor may not apply to the debt an amount in excess of the principal and outstanding interest on the collateral mortgage note.

The rule that emerges from this analysis is that a creditor is secured by a collateral mortgage package to the lesser of (a) the principal and interest on the principal obligation, or (b) the principal and interest on the collateral mortgage note.

This rule does not mean that the creditor will be unable to recover the full amount of the principal obligation from the debtor as a personal obligation. Rather, the rule means that a creditor may be unsecured for a portion of the debt even if the sale of the mortgaged property brings enough to pay off the principal obligation but is more than the amount of the collateral mortgage note.

The following examples will help explain this situation. In each example, Creditor and Debtor have entered into a fluctuating line of credit agreement (the principal obligation, Level One) secured by a perfected UCC9 security interest in a collateral mortgage note (Level Two), which in turn is secured by a collateral mortgage (Level Three) properly and timely recorded in the parish mortgage records.

In each case, Debtor is in default and Creditor has instituted foreclosure proceedings. In each case, a sheriff's sale has resulted, and the amount that the property brings at that sale is set forth. In each case, this amount is "net" of court costs and sheriff's commissions.

The question in each example is how much of the sheriff's sale proceeds Creditor is entitled to and what amounts (if any) Debtor may be liable for after the distribution of the sale's proceeds.

It may be helpful to keep in mind the structure of a collateral mortgage package (Diagram 13.5(1)) when reading these next examples.

13.9(c)(1). Example #1

The total amount of principal and interest on the principal obligation (Level One) at the time the foreclosure suit is brought is $200,000. The total amount of principal and interest on the collateral mortgage note (Level Two) at the time the foreclosure suit is brought is $200,000. The sheriff's sale of the mortgaged property brings $200,000.

In this situation, the collateral mortgage (Level Three) is extinguished in the sheriff's sale, and the proceeds from the sale are applied to the collateral mortgage note (Level Two). The sheriff's sale proceeds equal exactly the amount of the collateral mortgage note, extinguishing it. Now the proceeds from the payment of the collateral mortgage note (Level Two) are applied to the principal obligation.

In this example, all of the money flows up from the collateral mortgage (Level Three) through the collateral mortgage note (Level Two) to the principal obligation (Level One). Creditor gets the entire $200,000 as a secured creditor and the loan is completely paid off. Debtor owes nothing further to Creditor.

13.9(c)(2). Example #2

The total amount of principal and interest on the principal obligation (Level One) at the time the foreclosure suit is brought is $200,000. The total amount of principal and interest on collateral mortgage note (Level Two) at the time the foreclosure suit is brought is $350,000, because the attorney structuring the transaction made the collateral mortgage note for 150% of the anticipated original maximum amount of the principal obligation (see Section 13.9(a), above). The sheriff's sale of the mortgaged property brings $200,000.

In this situation, the collateral mortgage (Level Three) is extinguished in the sheriff's sale, and the proceeds from the sale are applied to the collateral mortgage note (Level Two). The sheriff's sale proceeds are less than the collateral mortgage note, but the collateral mortgage note is an *in rem* obligation (see Section 13.12, below).

As in Example #1, all of the money flows up from the collateral mortgage (Level Three) through the collateral mortgage note (Level Two) to the principal obligation (Level One). Creditor gets the entire $200,000 as a secured creditor and the loan is completely paid off. Debtor owes nothing further to Creditor.

13.9(c)(3). Example #3

The total amount of principal and interest on the principal obligation (Level One) at the time the foreclosure suit is brought is $200,000. The total amount of principal and interest on collateral mortgage note (Level Two) at the time the foreclosure suit is brought is $125,000. The sheriff's sale of the mortgaged property brings $500,000.

In this situation, the collateral mortgage (Level Three) is extinguished by the sheriff's sale, but the proceeds of the sale exceed both the amount of the collateral mortgage note and the principal obligation.

The problem for Creditor here is that the principal obligation is secured by the collateral mortgage note (Level Two), and that note is for only $125,000. Therefore, that is the only amount of money that may "flow up" from the collateral mortgage to the principal obligation. Thus, from the $500,000 sheriff's sale proceeds, Creditor is secured for only $125,000. Creditor is unsecured for the balance that Debtor owes ($75,000, in other words, 200,000 – 125,000) and is not entitled to that money from the sheriff's sale.

The reason that Creditor does not get more than $125,000 from the foreclosure proceeds as a secured creditor is that the collateral mortgage (Level Three) only secures the collateral mortgage note (Level Two); it does not directly secure the principal obligation (Level One).

The remaining funds from the sheriff's sale ($500,000 – $125,000 = $375,000) must be distributed to secured creditors on the immovable property (if any exist) who are inferior in rank to Creditor and then to Debtor. Creditor must pursue Debtor personally for the unsecured $75,000 deficiency left after the sheriff's sale (see Chapter 40, below).

13.10. Why Determining What Principal Obligation(s) a Collateral Mortgage Package Secures Cannot Be Ascertained by Looking at the Face of the Collateral Mortgage

The question of what principal obligations a collateral mortgage secures cannot be ascertained by looking at the language of the collateral mortgage. The collateral mortgage (Level Three) secures the collateral mortgage note, and the collateral mortgage note is described in the act of collateral mortgage. There is no requirement of filing anything in the public records concerning the granting of a security interest in the collateral mortgage note or the transfer of that note (R.S. 9:5554 and 13.5(b), above).

Therefore, a party looking at the public records where the collateral mortgage is recorded and examining the language of the act of collateral mortgage cannot determine (a) the intent of the parties at the time a security interest is perfected in the collateral mortgage note, (b) when the security interest in the collateral mortgage note was perfected, or (b) the existing (or future) obligations secured by the collateral mortgage note.

In fact, there is no legal requirement that a collateral mortgage contain any special language other than the provisions that apply to all conventional mortgages (see Section 12.2 above). The cases decided in the 1800s that form the basis of Louisiana collateral mortgage package jurisprudence involved mortgages that looked like "ordinary" mortgages (see Section 13.2, above), but courts, by looking at the actions of the parties, the intent of the parties, and the nature of the note paraphed for identification with the act of mortgage, were able to determine that what looked like an "ordinary" mortgage was in fact what we call today a collateral mortgage, a mortgage that secures a note (Level Two) for which there is a security interest given to secure the principal obligation (Level One).

Typically, however, a collateral mortgage is captioned as such and contains the following "boilerplate" clause:

> The above described note is given and this mortgage is granted for the purpose of being used as collateral security by Mortgagor for any indebtedness due the holder of the note, direct or contingent. The note may be issued and pledged by Mortgagor as his interest and convenience may require to secure loans and advances made or to be made or to secure the debt of the maker or of another. Upon payment of said indebtedness, the note may be returned to Mortgagor without extinguishment of the mortgage herein granted to secure the payment thereof, and may again at any time and as many times thereafter as the interest and convenience of Mortgagor may require, be reissued or repledged by Mortgagor as a valid and existing indebtedness in favor of the holder or holders thereof as collateral security for a debt contracted by Mortgagor and this mortgage shall be and remain in full force and effect to secure the note described until that note has been cancelled on its face.

This clause, which describes the mortgagor's intent at the time of the formation of the collateral mortgage, cannot "prove" what the intent of the mortgagor was at the time the creditor perfected a security interest in the collateral mortgage note by receiving it from the maker of that note and giving value for it (see Section 3.5(d), above). Only by ascertaining the mortgagor's intent at the time a creditor perfects a security interest in the collateral mortgage note can one determine what obligations the collateral mortgage note (and thus the collateral mortgage) secures. This is illustrated by the example at Section 13.5(d)(1), above.

Louisiana courts have issued rulings involving situations where the language quoted above was contained in the collateral mortgage, but the debtor was able to prove that the intent at the time of the pledge was to secure a single, specific debt (the principal obligation), not a line of credit or for notes that reworked the original specific debt. In those cases, the creditor was unable to have a secured claim on future advances not contemplated by the debtor at the time of the perfection of a real security interest in the collateral mortgage package.

13.11. Why Determining Who Holds a Collateral Mortgage Note Cannot Be Ascertained by Looking at the Face of the Collateral Mortgage

A collateral mortgage note, properly created, is bearer paper payable on demand (see Sections 13.6 and 13.7, above). A third party examining the public records and reading the description in the collateral mortgage of the bearer collateral mortgage note cannot ascertain who is the current holder of the note.

Typically, however, collateral mortgages contain the following clauses about "future holders":

> Mortgagor declared that Mortgagor is justly and truly indebted unto any future holder or holders of the note described below, appearing through and represented by _____, who appears solely for the purpose of accepting the described note for the use and benefit of any future holder or holders thereof (collectively, "Mortgagee"), domiciled in the Parish of _____, State of Louisiana, whose permanent mailing address is declared to be _____, in the full sum of _____ ($_____) Dollars.

Louisiana statutes explicitly allow collateral mortgages to contain such language. R.S. 9:5550(A) provides: "*A collateral mortgage or collateral chattel mortgage may provide on its face that the mortgage is granted in favor of a designated mortgagee and any future holder or holders of the collateral mortgage note.*"

The "designated mortgagee and any future holder" language in the mortgage, however, does nothing to inform one reading the mortgage who, in fact, is the holder of the bearer collateral mortgage note. This is because the public records do not reveal when a UCC9 security interest was given in the collateral mortgage note (see Section 13.5(b), above), and, because the note is "bearer" paper (see Sections 13.6 and 13.7, above), one cannot ascertain the name of the current holder of the collateral mortgage note.

The reason this "future holder" language has crept into collateral mortgages has nothing to do with the validity of the collateral mortgage; in fact, there is no "magic language" legally required for the creation of a collateral mortgage (see Section 13.10 above). Rather, the reason is historical. Lawyers reading the cases from the 1800s came to the proper conclusion that a collateral mortgage (at that time) required a pledge of the collateral mortgage note, and they were concerned because the Civil Code pledge articles at that time permitted the pledge to affect third parties without written evidence of the pledge or the mortgagor's intention at the time of the pledge. They reasoned that, if they put language about pledge and intent into the collateral mortgage itself, that might suffice to prove delivery and intent. As noted above, however, the language in the body of a collateral mortgage can never prove the intent of the parties at the time of the "pledge" (or, today at the time of the perfection of a security interest) in the collateral mortgage note (see Section 13.5(d)(1), Example #1). Nonetheless, lawyers have adopted this language as "boilerplate" in collateral mortgages, although legally it may have no impact.

13.12. A Collateral Mortgage Note Is an *In Rem* Instrument

The Louisiana Supreme Court has held that a collateral mortgage note is always a non-recourse, *in rem* obligation. *In rem* obligations are further described in Section 12.11, above.

The Supreme Court case arose when a third party pledged a collateral mortgage note to secure the debtor's obligation. While the case involved only a third party who created a collateral mortgage package and used it to secure the obligations of others, most practitioners assume that the rationale of the case extends to all collateral mortgage notes.

The following example illustrates this situation. Debtor has a $100,000 debt with Creditor. To secure this principal obligation (Level One), Debtor's rich Uncle X grants Creditor a security interest in a $150,000 collateral mortgage note secured by a collateral mortgage on Uncle X's property (see Diagram 13.4(b)(2), above). Debtor defaults and Creditor forecloses on Uncle X's mortgage; the mortgaged property brings only $75,000 at the sheriff's sale.

Under the jurisprudence, while Creditor is entitled, as a secured creditor of the collateral mortgage note (in turn, secured by the collateral mortgage) to the entire $75,000 proceeds, Creditor may not pursue Uncle X for the remaining $25,000 of the $100,000 debt, even though the collateral mortgage note is for $150,000. This is because the Supreme Court has held such notes are *in rem* instruments. Creditor, however, may pursue the Debtor for the $25,000 deficiency (see Chapter 40, below).

When, as in Diagram 13.5(1), the maker of principal obligation (Level One) is the same person as the maker of the collateral mortgage note (Level Two) and the collateral mortgage (Level Three), the fact that the collateral mortgage is *in rem* is not a problem for the creditor. The maker of the principal obligation (Level One) is personally liable for all the debt, regardless of the value of the collateral, assuming that the creditor has properly complied with the Louisiana Deficiency Judgment Act (see Chapter 40, below).

13.13. Transferring the Rank of a Mortgage from One Creditor to Another

Just as investors buy and sell properties, mortgage lenders buy and sell their rights in mortgages. Sometimes this is done solely for investment purposes. Other times, however, an original creditor no longer wishes to make additional loans to a borrower, or a new lender is more aggressive and will give better financial terms or extend more credit to the borrower than the original lender. In such instances, the new lender would like to keep the rank of the original creditor.

There are two different analyses that must be employed when Creditor #1 attempts to transfer its rank to Creditor #2. The critical question is what kind of loan is secured by the mortgage:

- If the mortgage secures a note for which all the sums already have been advanced or where the note represents future advances (such as the "barrel of money" situation, see Section 13.3(a)(2), above), one set of issues arise.
- If the mortgage secures a fluctuating line of credit, either as a C.C. art. 3298 mortgage (see Section 13.3(b), above) or as a collateral mortgage (see Section 13.4, above), a different set of issues must be considered.

13.13(a). Transferring the Rank of a Mortgage That Does Not Secure a Fluctuating Line of Credit

When a mortgage secures a note that represents monies which have all been advanced, such as an "ordinary mortgage" (see Section 13.2, above), the only thing the holder of the mortgage note can do is to assign the note to another creditor. The assignment allows the second creditor to assert the first creditor's rights and to be subrogated to the rights of the first creditor (C.C. art. 2642). The assignment of the note also carries with it "accessories" (C.C. art. 2645), such as the mortgage that secures the note.

While this assignment permits Creditor #2 to assert all the rights of Creditor #1, there is nothing that Creditor #2 can do in this situation to advance additional monies to the borrower on a secured basis using the mortgage rank held by Creditor #1. This is because the note represents all sums that have been advanced; since the mortgage is an accessory obligation to only that note, no additional advances can occur which would be secured by the mortgage. Moreover, as the debtor pays off the note, the note is extinguished (see Sections 13.2 and 13.3(a), above).

If the note secured by the mortgage represents sums that will be advanced— but which sums have not all been advanced, such as in a construction mortgage, see Section 13.3(a)(1)—the assignment of the note to Creditor #2 allows Creditor #2 to advance those sums that have not yet been advanced. This type of future advance mortgage, however, will not allow Creditor #2 to advance additional monies beyond the total amount of the note and be secured; Creditor #2 (just as Creditor #1) is in the "barrel of money" situation (see Section 13.3(a)(2)), and this type of note and mortgage will not permit Creditor #2 to use the mortgage to secure a fluctuating line of credit (see Section 13.3(b), above).

13.13(b). Transferring the Rank of a Mortgage That Does Secure a Fluctuating Line of Credit

If a mortgage secures a fluctuating line of credit "future advance mortgage" under C.C. art. 3298 (see Section 13.3(b), above) or if a collateral mortgage package secures a fluctuating line of credit loan (see Sections 13.5(c) and 13.5(d), above), and if a transfer from Creditor #1 to Creditor #2 is properly structured, Creditor #2 may make future advances on a fluctuating line of credit basis and have the same kind of retroactive rank that Creditor #1 would have had if Creditor #1 had continued to make the fluctuating line of credit loans. On the other hand, if the transaction is not properly structured, Creditor #2 will have retroactive rank for all loans outstanding at the point of the assignment from Creditor #1 to Creditor #2, but will have a new rank for all future loans under the line of credit.

If what is to be transferred is a C.C. art. 3298 "future advance" line of credit mortgage, Creditor #1 should assign and transfer to Creditor #2 the entire principal obligation which the mortgage secures. This principal obligation is the agreement between the debtor and Creditor #1 that the mortgage secures a fluctuating line of credit; this often can be ascertained by looking at language of the C.C. art. 3298 "future advance mortgage," which will describe the obligations the mortgage secures. If the mortgage was broadly written, it will cover advances made not only by the original mortgagee (Creditor #1) but also by the mortgagee's "successors and assigns." If the "successors and assigns" language is not contained in the C.C. art. 3298 future advance mortgage, a cautious Creditor #2 may want both Creditor #1 and the debtor to execute a written warranty and representation that it was always their intent, when the C.C. art. 3298 mortgage was created, to secure fluctuating line of credit loans made not merely by Creditor #1 but also by any person or entity that is assigned the principal obligation by Creditor #1.

If what is transferred is a collateral mortgage package (see Section 13.5, above), Creditor #2 does not want to receive an assignment of only the handnotes, for the handnotes do not represent the principal obligation; all the handnotes represent are advances of funds pursuant to the principal obligation (see Section 13.4(a), above). The problem for Creditor #2 receiving an assignment of only the handnotes is that, while this assignment carries with it the accessory collateral mortgage note (see C.C. art. 2645 and the Official Law Institute Comments to that article) and its accessory, the collateral mortgage, all Creditor #2 now has is a right to collect the handnotes. This gives Creditor #2 the ability to have retroactive rank of the collateral mortgage package for these particular handnotes, but it will not give Creditor #2 the ability to advance new funds and have retroactive rank.

The reason for this result is that merely assigning the handnotes does not assign the principal obligation. What is the principal obligation? It is the agreement between Debtor and Creditor #1 that the security interest granted in the collateral mortgage note is intended to secure a fluctuating line of credit (see Section 13.4, above). If the only things assigned are the handnotes and not the entirety of the principal obligation (Creditor #1's and Debtor's agreement to use the collateral mortgage to secure a fluctuating line of credit loan), then while Debtor and Creditor #2 may agree that future loans made by Creditor #2 will be secured by the collateral mortgage package, Creditor #2 will have a new ranking date and will not be able to use Creditor #1's ranking date for these new loans (see Section 13.5(d)(1), Example #1).

To allow Creditor #2 to keep Creditor #1's rank as to third parties for new advances made by Creditor #2 after the transfer, Creditor #1 will have to assign to Creditor #2 the entirety of the principal obligation, not just the handnotes. This "entirety" consists of the agreement between Debtor and Creditor #1 that the collateral mortgage package will be used to secure a fluctuating line of credit, with advances to be made not merely by Creditor #1 but also by any of Creditor #1's successors and assigns.

Because the "entirety" of this principal obligation may consist of an oral agreement between Debtor and Creditor #1, a cautious Creditor #2 may want both Creditor #1 and Debtor to execute a written warranty and representation that: (i) it was always their intent, when the collateral mortgage package was created, to secure fluctuating line of credit loans made not merely by Creditor #1 but also by any person or entity which is assigned the principal obligation by Creditor #1; (ii) the collateral mortgage package had been properly made effective against third parties (see Section 13.5(b), above); (iii) that all previous loans by Creditor #1, as well as any future loans by Creditor #1 or its successors and assigns, had been and will be secured by the collateral mortgage package; and (iv) that Debtor and Creditor #1 at all times have been in good faith.

13.14. The Rules of Prescription Involving a Collateral Mortgage Package

The question of prescription arises in a collateral mortgage package because there is a principal obligation (Level One) and a collateral mortgage note (Level Two). Because of the unique structure of a collateral mortgage, courts have held that as long as possession of the collateral mortgage note (Level Two) remains with the creditor or an appropriate party, the principal obligation (Level One) will never prescribe. On the other hand, prescription can run on the collateral mortgage note. This Section will describe these rules.

One should not confuse, however, the rules relating to prescription on the principal obligation and the collateral mortgage note with the rules on the lapse of inscription of the collateral mortgage. Once a mortgage has been recorded in the public records, the rules of inscription and reinscription apply; these are not rules of prescription but rather rules regulating the length of time a third party is affected by a recorded mortgage. Those rules are contained in C.C. arts. 3357 et seq. and are discussed in Section 20.2, below.

13.14(a). The Constant Acknowledgement Rule as Applied to the Collateral Mortgage Package

Under the provisions of the Louisiana Civil Code pledge articles as they existed prior to the amendments made in 2014, Louisiana courts had developed a "constant acknowledgment" rule (see Section 10.6, above). That rule declared that if there was a pledge of an item (including a collateral mortgage note), the principal obligation that the pledge secured (Level One) would never prescribe, although the collateral mortgage note (Level Two) could prescribe.

Today, perfection of a security interest in a collateral mortgage note requires physical delivery of the note to the creditor or his agent under UCC9 plus the giving of value (see Section 13.5(b), above). Because delivery by the debtor of the collateral mortgage note was required to affect third parties under the old pledge articles and is required today under UCC 9, the constant acknowledgment rule appears to still be applicable to collateral mortgages.

Discerning how the constant acknowledgment rule applies involves remembering that (i) even though the principal obligation (Level One) may never prescribe, (ii) if the collateral mortgage note prescribes (Level Two), then the security for that collateral mortgage note—the collateral mortgage itself (Level Three)—becomes unenforceable, and (iii) even if the collateral mortgage note has not prescribed, the collateral mortgage must be timely reinscribed in order to affect third parties.

13.14(a)(1). Example #1

On June 1, 2010, Debtor borrows $100,000 from Creditor and signs a note for $100,000. The note is payable in one year, with payment in full due June 1, 2011. This principal obligation is secured by Debtor granting a perfected security interest in a collateral mortgage note dated June 1, 2010; the note is a demand instrument payable to bearer (see Sections 13.6 and 13.7, above). The collateral mortgage note, in turn, is paraphed *ne varietur* for identification with an act of collateral mortgage that Creditor records in the proper parish mortgage records on June 2, 2010.

Debtor makes no payments at all on the principal obligation.

Normally, a negotiable note prescribes five years after its due date; therefore, normally, the $100,000 principal obligation would prescribe June 1, 2016 (five years from the due date of 6/1/2011); however, because of the perfected possessory security interest that Creditor holds in the collateral mortgage note, the principal obligation will never prescribe. Creditor can enforce the $100,000 one-year note as a personal obligation of Debtor in 2015, 2030, or even 2130.

On the other hand, the collateral mortgage note can prescribe. It is not a "fictitious" note. While it does not represent a sum of money that has been advanced or will be advanced, it is a non-recourse, *in rem* obligation that bears interest. Prescription will run on the collateral mortgage note five years from the date it was made (because it is due "on demand") and will be unenforceable after June 1, 2015. Once the collateral mortgage note (Level Two) prescribes, the collateral mortgage that secures it (Level Three) becomes unenforceable.

As a result, after June 1, 2015 (the prescriptive date of the collateral mortgage note), Creditor can enforce the principal obligation (the $100,000 note) by suing Debtor but may not foreclose on the collateral mortgage.

It should be pointed out that in this example there are two different prescriptive dates on two different notes. On the principal obligation—the $100,000 note due in one year—prescription would normally run on June 1,

2016, five years from its due date (6/1/2011), but because the constant acknowledgment rule, prescription will never run on the principal obligation as long as a possessory security interest in the collateral mortgage note is held by the creditor.

On the other hand, because the collateral mortgage note is due on demand, prescription will run five years from the date it was made. Since the collateral mortgage note was made on June 1, 2010, prescription on it will run on June 1, 2015.

13.14(b). Interruption of Prescription on the Collateral Mortgage Note

A perfected security interest in a collateral mortgage note interrupts prescription on the principal obligation; however, because the collateral mortgage note itself can prescribe (see Section 13.14(a), above), Louisiana law provides two ways to interrupt prescription on the collateral mortgage note.

First, a creditor may ask the maker of the collateral mortgage note to acknowledge it. Acknowledgement of an obligation interrupts the running of prescription (C.C. art. 3464).

Second, R.S. 9:5807 provides an "automatic" way for prescription to be interrupted. Under this statute, payments of principal or interest on the principal obligation (Level One) will interrupt prescription on the collateral mortgage note (Level Two); however, this statute applies only if the payments are made either (i) by the person who is both the maker of the collateral mortgage and the person who is obligated on the principal obligation (see Section 13.5, Diagram 13.5(1)) or (ii) by that person's "codebtors in solido." The statute does not apply to payments made by someone who is merely a surety.

R.S. 9:5807 contains language that may appear obtuse and cryptic. It states: "*A payment by a debtor of interest or principal of an obligation shall constitute an acknowledgement of all other obligations including promissory notes of such debtor or his codebtors in solido pledged by the debtor or his codebtors in solido to secure the obligation as to which payment is made. In all cases the party claiming an interruption of prescription of such pledged obligation including a promissory note as a result of such acknowledgement shall have the burden of proving all of the elements necessary to establish the same. For purposes of this Section, a 'pledged obligation' shall include any obligation, including a promissory note, in which a security interest has been granted under Chapter 9 of the Louisiana Commercial Laws or the corresponding provisions of the Uniform Commercial Code as adopted in any other state, to the extent applicable.*"

The following is an analysis of the first portion of R.S. 9:5807:

- *"A payment by a debtor of interest or principal of an obligation ..."* This is a reference to the principal obligation (Level One).
- *"shall constitute an acknowledgement of all other obligations including promissory notes of such debtor or his codebtors in solido pledged by the debtor or his codebtors in solido to secure the obligation as to which payment is made."* This reference to *"pledged"* promissory notes refers to the collateral mortgage note (Level Two).
- *"In all cases the party claiming an interruption of prescription of such pledged obligation including a promissory note...."* This is a reference to the collateral mortgage note.
- *"as a result of such acknowledgement shall have the burden of proving all of the elements necessary to establish the same."* In other words, the creditor bears the burden of proof of demonstrating that the payment of principal or interest on the principal obligation interrupted prescription on the collateral mortgage note.
- *"For purposes of this Section, a 'pledged obligation' shall include any obligation, including a promissory note, in which a security interest has been granted under Chapter 9 of the Louisiana Commercial Laws or the corresponding provisions of the Uniform Commercial Code as adopted in any other state, to the extent applicable."* This is a reference to the collateral mortgage note, which today is perfected as to third parties under UCC9 (see Section 13.7(c), below).

13.14(b)(1). Example #2

This example begins with the same facts as Section 13.14(a)(1), Example #1. Debtor had borrowed $100,000 from Creditor and signed a June 1, 2010, note for $100,000 payable in one year. The loan was secured by a collateral mortgage package properly perfected on June 1, 2010.

Unlike Example #1, however, Debtor has continued to make monthly interest payments from July 1, 2010 to the present, but Debtor has never made any principal payments on the $100,000 note and has never signed an act of acknowledgement of the collateral mortgage note. Creditor, because it has been receiving interest payments on the $100,000 note, has not taken any action to demand payment in full, even though the note was due June 1, 2011.

In this situation, as long as the effects of the collateral mortgage continue (see Section 20.2(a), below), every payment by Debtor on the principal obligation serves to acknowledge the collateral mortgage note.

Under R.S. 9:5807, prescription has been interrupted by each monthly payment on the principal obligation by Debtor. Therefore, as long as the effects of registry of the collateral mortgage continue as to third parties (see C.C. arts. 3357 *et seq.* and in Section 20.2, below), Creditor can foreclose on the collateral mortgage if there is a default in the principal obligation.

Likewise, because of the constant acknowledgment rule, the $100,000 note dated June 1, 2010 and due June 1, 2011 will never prescribe as a personal obligation of Debtor.

13.14(b)(2). Example #3

This example begins with the same facts as Section 13.14(a)(1), Example #1 and Section 13.14(b)(1), Example #2: Debtor had borrowed $100,000 from Creditor and signed a June 1, 2010 note for $100,000 payable in one year.

Unlike Examples #1 and #2, however, the loan was secured by a collateral mortgage package given by Debtor's Uncle X and was properly perfected on June 1, 2010 (see Section 13.4(b), Diagram 13.4(b)(2), above). Further, Uncle X signed a "continuing guaranty" stating that he "personally and in solido" guaranteed all monies owed by Debtor.

Further, unlike Example #2, monthly payments of interest on the principal obligation were made by Uncle X, not by Debtor, but Uncle X never signed an act of acknowledgment of his collateral mortgage note.

Uncle X's collateral mortgage note can prescribe even though Uncle X may have paid monthly interest on the principal obligation. Uncle X's payment interrupts prescription on the principal obligation (C.C. art. 3060 and Section 8.3, above). The reason that Uncle X's collateral note can prescribe is that R.S. 9:5807 does not apply. This is because Uncle X is not a "codebtor in solido" with Debtor, despite the language of solidarity in Uncle X's "continuing guaranty." The reason that the language of solidarity in Uncle X's "continuing guaranty" does not make him a solidary obligor with Debtor is because of the first paragraph of C.C. art. 3037; it is obvious from the language of the "continuing guaranty" that the cause of the document is to guaranty payment of a third party, not to undertake a primary obligation (see Section 3.5, above).

Although Uncle X's collateral mortgage note may prescribe, even if Uncle X had not made any payments of principal or interest on the principal obligation (Level One), the pledge of Uncle X's note may constitute a constant acknowledgment of the principal obligation.

Thus, in this situation, whether or not any payments were made by Debtor or Uncle X on the principal obligation, the principal obligation never prescribes; Debtor can be sued personally on it today, or in 2020, or more than a hundred years from now.

It must be remembered, however, that Uncle X's on-demand bearer collateral mortgage note prescribed June 1, 2015 (five years from its due date); when it prescribed, the collateral mortgage became unenforceable. Creditor has lost the real security for the loan; the only option Creditor has left to collect the loan is to sue Debtor personally.

Chapter 14

Conventional Mortgages: Usufructs and Leases

14.1. The Termination of a Usufruct or Lease Extinguishes a Mortgage Encumbering the Usufruct or Lease

C.C. art. 3286 allows a mortgage to be on a usufruct or a lease. Such mortgages present special issues for creditors, because the mortgagee can have no greater rights over the mortgaged property than the mortgagor. Therefore, if the usufruct or lease terminates, the mortgage will terminate (see C.C. art. 3282 and Section 14.2, below).

14.2. Mortgages on Usufructs

A mortgage on a usufruct of a corporeal immovable (C.C. art. 3286) may be given by the usufructuary. A mortgage on the usufructuary's interest burdens the estate only as long as the usufruct is in existence. Thus, if a usufructuary gives a mortgage on the usufructuary's interest (C.C. art. 567), then the mortgage will terminate when the usufruct terminates (C.C. art. 3319 and Section 20.9(a), below).

Under the Civil Code articles on usufruct, however, if there is a danger of termination of the usufruct because the usufructuary is abusing the property, a "*creditor of a usufructuary may intervene and may prevent the termination of the usufruct ... by offering to repair the damages caused by usufructuary and by giving security for the future"* (C.C. art. 625). A creditor of a usufructuary, such as a mortgagor, also may annul a renunciation of the usufruct that operates to the creditor's prejudice (C.C. art. 626).

The naked owner also has the right to give (or not) give a separate mortgage on the naked owner's interest in the property subject to the usufruct. This mortgage may secure any debt the naked owner desires; there is no requirement that it have any relationship to the debts of the usufructuary. If a naked owner gives a mortgage on the naked ownership (C.C. art. 603), then termination of the usufruct will not impact this mortgage, for when the usufruct terminates the naked owner retains the ownership interest. If the mortgage describes a security interest in all of the naked owner's "rights" in the property (and not just the naked ownership interest), then once the usufruct terminates, it is possible that the after-acquired title doctrine (see Section 12.3, above), may extend the mortgage to the entire ownership interest of the former naked owner, now unburdened by the extinguished interest of the usufructuary.

14.3. Mortgages on Leases

This Section 14.3 deals only with the lease of immovables, and it should be emphasized that a mortgage of a lease involves only a lease of immovable property. Leases of movable property cannot be mortgaged. There is a special Louisiana Lease of Movables Act that regulates the rights of lessors and lessees of movable property (R.S. 9:3301 *et seq.*). UCC9 provides a mechanism for securing an interest in movables, the lease of movables, and the rental stream from such leases.

A landlord may not mortgage its interest in a lease of immovable property; however, the landlord may mortgage the entirety of the property or may pledge the lease, the rent, or both (see Section 10.4, above).

A tenant may mortgage its interest in a lease of immovable property. While a tenant's mortgage is commonly called a "leasehold mortgage," this term has no legal meaning in Louisiana, because "leasehold" is purely a common law term.

A tenant's rights pursuant to a lease of an immovable are divisible into the rights of occupancy, use and enjoyment. These rights may be severed from the tenant's obligation to pay rents. For example, a tenant may mortgage only the right of occupancy of the property without mortgaging the obligation to pay rent; in that case, the creditor holding the mortgage has no obligation to the landlord for the rent.

Therefore, designating a mortgage of the tenant's rights as a "leasehold" mortgage, without further description of what is actually being mortgaged, may raise a question of what the tenant has mortgaged and what are the rights and obligations of the "leasehold mortgagor." Sometimes a "leasehold" mortgage is over the entirety of the tenant's rights and obligations, including the obligation to pay rent. Sometimes, however, a creditor may want to have a "leasehold mortgage" on only the tenant's rights of occupancy, use, and enjoyment without imposing on the creditor the obligation to pay the rent. The negotiations about such mortgages are often not just between the tenant and the creditor, but rather among the tenant, creditor, and landlord, for the lease may contain restrictions on the tenant's right to mortgage any interest in the lease without the landlord's prior consent.

Because the term "leasehold mortgage" has no definition under Louisiana law, cautious creditors strive to define the exact meaning of the rights and obligations of the tenant and lender in the "leasehold mortgage" document.

A creditor secured by a "leasehold mortgage" has the rights of any mortgage creditor; the creditor may seize and sell the rights in the tenant's lease that have been mortgaged and obtain a privilege on the proceeds of the sale. Most leases, however, contain clauses allowing the landlord to terminate the lease for many reasons—among them a failure of the tenant to pay rent as well as the attempted seizure and sale of the lease by a secured creditor. If the lease terminates, the "leasehold mortgage" will terminate.

While leases of immovable property need not be recorded as between the parties and need not be recorded to grant the landlord a lessor's privilege on the tenant's movables on the premises (see Section 31.2, below), a lease will not affect third parties unless recorded in the mortgage records of the parish where the leased immovable property is located (C.C. art. 3338). Likewise, a "leasehold mortgage" will not affect third parties unless it is recorded in the mortgage records of the parish where the leased immovable property is located (C.C. art. 3338).

Chapter 15

Special Provisions in Conventional Mortgages

Louisiana statutes and jurisprudence permit contractual clauses in mortgages that grant creditors additional rights beyond merely seizing and selling the mortgaged property. There are also statutes that automatically add clauses or provisions to conventional mortgages by operation of law, even if the parties have not specifically contracted for them in the act of mortgage.

15.1. Keeper Provisions in a Mortgage

If a creditor institutes foreclosure proceedings on mortgaged property, there may be a need for that property to be managed during the pendency of the litigation. This is particularly true if the property is income-producing commercial property, such as an office building with many tenants, a hotel, or a shopping center.

Louisiana statutes allow the parties to mortgages to designate a "keeper" who will control and manage the property once it has been seized by the sheriff (R.S. 9:5136 *et seq.*). The keeper may be a person or entity specified in the mortgage document. Even if the keeper is not specifically identified, a mortgage with a "keeper provision" allows the creditor to name a keeper at the time of the foreclosure (R.S. 9:5136).

The designation of the keeper need not be in the act of mortgage itself; however, if it is in a separate instrument, that instrument must be signed in the presence of a notary and two witnesses (R.S. 9:5136).

The keeper must act as a "prudent administrator" (R.S. 9:5138), must render an accounting to the court (R.S. 9:5138(C)), and may use revenues generated from the property to preserve it, provide "*services*" and "*amenities*" required by any existing leases (R.S. 9:5138(B)), and operate the property until the sheriff's sale is complete.

If the parties have designated a keeper in the mortgage, they may dispense with a bond (a legal suretyship, see Section 9.1, above); however, if the keeper is not designated in the documents and the creditor later decides that one is needed, the keeper must furnish a bond (R.S. 9:5137 and 5139).

The keeper may apply to the court for instructions or authority to act if the keeper believes that "*some action beyond the ordinary course of administration or management of the property is required*" to preserve or protect it (R.S. 9:5140).

The keeper provisions may also be contained in a UCC9 security agreement and may pertain to the assets that the security agreement affects (R.S. 9:5140.2).

There are special (but similar) provisions relating to keepers in the case of mineral mortgages (R.S. 9:5131 *et seq.*).

15.2. A Mortgage May Contain a Pledge of Casualty Insurance on the Property Covered by the Mortgage

R.S. 9:5386 allows a mortgage to contain "*a pledge of the mortgagor's rights under policies of insurance covering the immovable.*" This statute is an example of what the Civil Code pledge provisions describe as things "*made susceptible of pledge by law.*" (C.C. art. 3142; see Section 10.3, above).

Under R.S. 9:5386, a pledge of property insurance contained in a mortgage becomes effective against third parties when the mortgage is recorded; there is no necessity of notice to the insurer to make the pledge effective against third parties. As a practical matter, however, creditors give written notice to the insurer of the pledge to make sure that, in the event of a loss covered by the insurance policy, the insurer deals with the creditor. This is because, under R.S. 9:5386(B), "*until the insurer receives written notice from or on behalf of the mortgagee or the mortgagor*" of the pledge, the insurer may deal directly with its insured and ignore the pledged interest of the creditor, even though a mortgage with a pledge of the insurance policy has been recorded.

The effects of a pledge of an insurance policy against third persons under R.S. 9:5386 continues "*for so long as the mortgage is given the effect of recordation.*" The length of time that a mortgage affects third persons is dealt with in C.C. arts. 3357 *et seq.* (see Sections 20.1 and 20.2, below).

Regardless of whether a mortgage contains a pledge of property insurance, creditors typically insert provisions into mortgages requiring that the debtor maintain casualty insurance on the property. These provisions usually mandate that the contract of insurance contain a "standard," "union," or "New York" clause. These are three different names for the same type of insurance coverage.

This "standard," "union," or "New York" clause assures the creditor that the insurance company will pay the insurance proceeds to the creditor even if the debtor commits an act that would otherwise void the insurance (such as committing arson). In other words, the creditor's rights under a "standard," "union," or "New York" clause are not derivative of the rights of the debtor but instead constitute a separate insurable interest and give the creditor a direct claim against the insurer (see Section 26.2, below).

15.3. Assignment of Certain UCC9 Enforcement Rights

It may be difficult to ascertain at the inception of a transaction whether incorporeal collateral and incorporeal rights are fully encumbered by a UCC9 security interest, are encompassed in a statutory right, or are covered by a mortgage.

R.S. 9:5388 allows the parties to cover both UCC9 and mortgage issues by permitting inclusion of both mortgage and UCC9 security interest clauses in a mortgage. R.S. 9:533 allows "*provisions granting the mortgagee or secured party and its agents the power to carry out and enforce all or any specified portion of the incorporeal rights collaterally assigned or pledged by the mortgagor or on which the mortgagor/debtor has granted a security interest.*"

This clause may be coupled with an irrevocable power of attorney (R.S. 9:5388).

15.4. Security for Funds Advanced to Protect the Property

Even if the parties to a mortgage do not expressly contract for it, R.S. 9:5389(A) provides that every mortgage and UCC9 security interest "*shall secure additional funds that may be advanced by the mortgagee or secured party for the protection, preservation, repair, or recovery of the mortgaged or encum-*

bered property, or the protection and preservation of the mortgagee's mortgage or secured party's security interest." The only way a mortgage or security interest will not include this right is if the parties expressly provide otherwise (R.S. 9:5389(B)). This statute, however, may need to be read in conjunction with the requirement that a mortgage describe the maximum amount of obligations it secures (C.C. art. 3288; see Section 12.4, above).

Any advance made by the creditor under this statutory provision bears interest at the rate provided for in the principal obligation secured by the mortgage (R.S. 9:5389(B)).

Most mortgages and security agreements also contain a clause granting the creditor the option (but not the obligation) to "*purchase insurance or pay taxes on the mortgaged or encumbered property*" should the debtor fail to do so (R.S. 9:5389(A)).

15.5. Additions and Accessions

Just as R.S. 9:5389 automatically includes in every mortgage a provision securing certain advances made by the creditor to protect the property, R.S. 9:5391 automatically adds to every mortgage rights to additions and accessions.

R.S. 9:5391 states: "*A mortgage of immovable property without further action attaches to present and future component parts thereof and accessions thereto, without further description and without the necessity of subsequently amending the mortgage agreement.*" Therefore, if a debtor mortgages an undeveloped tract of land and later constructs a building on it, the building is automatically covered by the mortgage.

15.6. Special Rules Concerning Amendments of Notes Secured by Mortgages

R.S. 9:5390 concerns amendments of notes secured by mortgages.

Often, parties to a mortgage may change the terms of the note after the mortgage documents are signed. For example, in difficult economic times, the creditor may agree to alter the interest rate, extend the length of payments, or alter the payment amount. R.S. 9:5390 provides that when these and similar actions occur, the rank and priority of the mortgage is not affected. Likewise, in good economic times, a creditor may agree to loan modifications to deal with changing conditions.

R.S. 9:5390 also covers the situation where a mortgage expressly secures not merely an original note, but also *"automatically secures payment of a renewal or refinancing note."* In such situations, the rank and priority of the mortgage is not affected by the renewal or refinancing, unless the principal amount increases. If the mortgage does not expressly secure payment of a renewal or refinancing note, however, the payoff of the original note will extinguish the principal obligation that the mortgage secures, thereby rendering the mortgage unenforceable (see Section 13.3(a)(1), above). A properly drafted "future advance mortgage" to secure a fluctuating line of credit or multiple obligations (see Section 13.3(b) above) should not have this problem, because such a mortgage does not secure only a single note (see Section 13.3(b)(3), above). Thus, payment of one note will not extinguish that type of "future advance mortgage."

As R.S. 9:5390(B) makes clear, if a mortgage secures but a single note and the parties agree, after the initial recordation of the mortgage, to increase the principal amount of the note, then there must be recordation of the amendment of the mortgage to affect third parties. In such an event, the statute provides that there is a new rank at that time for the increased principal amount, but the original principal amount that is refinanced maintains its original rank and priority.

15.7. Special Exemptions from Usury Provisions

Louisiana has strict rules against usury. A contract for interest in excess of that permitted by law results in the *"forfeiture of the entire interest so contracted."* R.S. 9:3501. The maximum interest rate on loans secured, in whole or in part, by a mortgage on immovable property, is 12% per annum (R.S. 9:3503; also see R.S. 9:3500(C)).

Despite this strict rule, however, Louisiana has a number of exemptions from and exceptions to the usury provisions. Many of these relate to loans secured by mortgages. The key statutes in this regard are found at R.S. 9:3502 *et seq.*, although there are many other exceptions and exemptions contained in R.S. 9, R.S. 6, and other provisions.

There is no usury ceiling on loans secured by mortgages on immovable property if the loan is guaranteed in whole or in part by the Veteran's Administration or insured by the Federal Housing Administration (R.S. 9:3504(A), R.S. 9:3508). There are exceptions to the usury prohibitions for:

- *"wrap-around"* mortgages (R.S. 9:3504(B)),
- *"graduated payment"* mortgages (R.S. 9:3504(C)),

- *"adjustable rate"* mortgages (R.S. 9:3504(D)),
- certain seller-financed transactions (R.S. 9:3504(E)), and
- certain commercial, business and agricultural loans (R.S. 9:3500(D), 3509, and 3509.1).

15.8. Special Rules for Certain Residential Mortgages

Certain regulated financial institutions (such as banks) may make residential loans under the Louisiana Secure and Fair Enforcement of Residential Mortgage Lending Act (R.S. 6:1081 *et seq.*). The Act regulates those who engage *"directly or indirectly"* (R.S. 6:1084) in residential mortgage lending. The Louisiana Office of Financial Institutions is in charge of these regulations and licensing procedures (R.S. 6:1083). The Act also controls the "rates, fees, charges, and disclosures applicable to residential mortgage loans" (R.S. 6:1095).

A detailed discussion of residential mortgage lending by financial institutions and the regulation of mortgage brokers and loan originators is beyond the scope of this Précis. Likewise, this Précis does not address the kinds and nature of disclosures federal law mandates for consumer loans and residential loans.

Chapter 16

The Legal Mortgage

16.1. Definition of a Legal Mortgage

C.C. art. 3284 states that a legal mortgage "*is established by operation of law*" and C.C. art. 3299 defines a legal mortgage as a mortgage that "*secures an obligation specified by the law that provides for the mortgage.*"

When one looks at the statutes that create legal mortgages, it is apparent that legal mortgages primarily are on property of those who act as fiduciaries of others, and that the legal mortgage secures the fiduciary's obligation to those for whom the fiduciary is acting.

An example of a legal mortgage is the mortgage that arises on the property of a natural tutor (C.C. art. 322).

A legal mortgage, like all other forms of mortgage, is an accessory obligation (C.C. art. 3282). It secures the fiduciary obligations of the mortgagor.

16.2. Legal Mortgages Are General Mortgages

In contrast to a conventional mortgage, which affects only the property specifically described in the mortgage (see Section 12.3, above), a legal mortgage is a general mortgage. A general mortgage is defined in C.C. art. 3303 as affecting "*property that the obligor owns when the mortgage is created and over future property of the obligor when he acquires it.*"

C.C. art. 3302 provides that "*legal mortgages burden all the property of the obligor that is made susceptible of mortgage by Paragraphs 1 through 4 of Article 3286 or that is expressly made subject to judicial or legal mortgage by other law.*" Therefore, legal mortgages impact not only immovable property, but also usufructs, leases of immovable property, servitudes, and component parts of immovables.

Because a legal mortgage affects all the current and future property of the mortgagor, no property description is required. A legal mortgage, once recorded in a parish, is a "blanket mortgage" affecting all current and future-owned property of the mortgagor.

Because no property description is ever given in a legal mortgage, the name of the mortgagor is the basis for determining whose property is affected by the legal mortgage. Therefore, as a practical matter, it is important to use the correct name of the mortgagor on any document creating a legal mortgage.

A legal mortgage will only affect present and future-owned property in the parish where the mortgage is recorded. If one wants to impact all potential property in Louisiana that might be acquired by a mortgagor under any kind of general mortgage, including a legal mortgage, recordation of the document creating the mortgage must be filed in every parish.

As a general mortgage affecting all property currently owned and to be owned in the future by the mortgagor, the existence of a legal mortgage makes it difficult for the mortgagor to get financing.

For example, assume that Homeowner is named and qualified as a natural tutor of a minor. The process of becoming a curator results in a legal mortgage against Homeowner (C.C. art. 322). When Homeowner goes to the bank to get a second mortgage on her home, the bank will be reluctant to make the loan, because the second mortgage will be outranked by the legal mortgage. Likewise, with the legal mortgage in place, it is difficult for Homeowner to get a bank to finance the purchase of a new home, because the minute Homeowner purchases the new home, the legal mortgage attaches to it.

Therefore, because of the difficulties that legal mortgages create, and because it is in society's interest to encourage people to serve as fiduciaries for minors and interdicts, there are statutes permitting the mortgagor to substitute a bond (meaning a legal suretyship, see Chapter 9, above) in lieu of the legal mortgage. For example, C.C.P. art. 4132 allows tutors to use a legal suretyship to secure the tutor's obligations.

16.3. How a Legal Mortgage Is Created

Because legal mortgages arise by operation of law (C.C. art. 3283), each statute establishing a legal mortgage provides for how that mortgage is to be established. Generally, an inventory of the property of the person protected by the mortgage is taken, that inventory is recorded in the mortgage records, and the fiduciary is then formally given the power to act. See, for example, C.C. art. 322.

16.4. Discussion Applies to Legal Mortgages

While discussion (as defined in C.C.P. art. 5151) has been abolished for sureties by the Civil Code (see Section 3.1, above), discussion is still available in the case of legal mortgages as well as judicial mortgages (C.C.P. art. 5151 *et seq.*).

C.C.P. art. 5154 states: "*When a legal or judicial mortgage securing an indebtedness due by a former owner of property is sought to be enforced against the property after its acquisition by a third possessor, the latter may plead discussion to compel the mortgagee to enforce the mortgage against other property affected thereby, which is owned by the mortgagor, or which has been acquired from the mortgagor by a third person after the third possessor acquired his property.*" As a practical matter, however, this situation seldom arises, because most transfers of immovable property occur only after a lawyer or title company has checked the title to the property (see Chapter 23, below). A review of the abstract of title (see Section 23.2, below) will reveal the existence of the legal mortgage, and the buyer will normally require that the legal mortgage be removed by the seller before the sale is consummated. If the buyer is financing the sale with a lender who will secure the loan with a mortgage, the lender will insist that its mortgage not be superseded by the prior legal mortgage and thus will require that the legal mortgage be removed. The seller may remove the legal mortgage by substituting a bond (see Section 16.2, above).

Chapter 17

The Judicial Mortgage

17.1. Definition of a Judicial Mortgage

C.C. art. 3284 states that a judicial mortgage "*is established by law to secure a judgment*." C.C. art. 3299 clarifies that rule by noting that a judicial mortgage "*secures a judgment for the payment of money*."

Judicial mortgages affect only immovable property and property that the Civil Code or special laws state are susceptible of being mortgaged (see C.C. art. 3286 and Section 11.2, above).

A judicial mortgage transforms an unsecured creditor to a secured creditor. For example, consider the situation of a tortfeasor who causes an automobile accident. The injured party may sue the one at fault. That suit seeks a personal judgment against the tortfeasor; the mere fact of the accident does not grant the injured party any claim of real security against the tortfeasor. Once the judgment is obtained and recorded in the mortgage records, however, the injured party (as a judgment creditor) is transformed from an unsecured creditor to a secured creditor with a judicial mortgage over the tortfeasor's immovable property.

17.2. Judicial Mortgages Are General Mortgages

Judicial mortgages, like legal mortgages, are general mortgages and encumber all property of the mortgagor, whether owned at the time of the creation of the judicial mortgage or acquired later (C.C. art. 3302).

See Section 16.2, above concerning the rules of general mortgages. While Section 16.2 refers to legal mortgages, the same rules apply to judicial mortgages, with one exception. Once a judicial mortgage attaches, the only way to remove the judicial mortgage (other than paying it off or having its inscription lapse (see section 20.4, below)) is to file a suspensive appeal of the judgment, post a suspensive appeal bond, and rule the judgment creditor into court to show why the judicial mortgage should not be cancelled (R.S. 13:4434–4435). Unless and until this occurs, however, "a judicial mortgage is not affected or suspended by a suspensive appeal or stay of execution of the judgment" (C.C. art. 3304).

A suspensive appeal bond is a legal suretyship (see Chapter 9, above).

17.3. How a Judicial Mortgage Is Created

Judicial mortgages secure money judgments (C.C. art. 3299). C.C. art. 3300 provides that a *"judicial mortgage is created by filing a judgment with the recorder of mortgages."* Not only must the judgment be filed, but it also must be recorded in the parish mortgage records (see Section 19.7(c), below).

A judgment prescribes in ten years from the date of its signing (C.C. art. 3501). Interruption of prescription occurs only if a timely suit for revival of the judgment is filed (C.C. art. 3501, C.C.P. art. 2031). If the judgment prescribes, the accessory right of the judicial mortgage becomes unenforceable.

The judgment must set forth the name of the judgment creditor and the judgment debtor as well as the dollar amount of the judgment. These items are critical to having a valid judicial mortgage, for no property description is given. No property description is given or needed because the judicial mortgage is a general mortgage (see Section 17.2, above).

17.3(a). Judicial Mortgages Arising from a Judgment of a Louisiana State Court

Judicial mortgages result from money judgments of any Louisiana trial court or appellate court (*cf.* C.C. art. 3299). The only exception to this rule is that judgment for ongoing alimony and child support payments do not create a judicial mortgage; however, judgments for arrearages in child support or alimony do create judicial mortgages if recorded in the mortgage records.

C.C. art. 3305 provides the general rule for creating judicial mortgages when the judgment is from a court of a state other than Louisiana. The provisions of R.S. 13:4241 *et seq.* set forth the procedure for accomplishing this.

C.C. art. 3305 states:

*The filing of an authenticated copy of a judgment of a court of a juris-
diction foreign to this state, such as the United States, another state, or
another country, creates a judicial mortgage only when so provided by
special legislation, or when accompanied by a certified copy of a judgment or order of a Louisiana court recognizing it and ordering it executed according to law.*

*In all other cases the judgment of a court of a jurisdiction foreign to this
state creates a judicial mortgage only when a Louisiana court has rendered a judgment making the foreign judgment the judgment of the
Louisiana court, and the Louisiana judgment has been filed in the same
manner as other judgments.*

17.3(b). Judicial Mortgages Arising from a Judgment of a State Court from a State Other Than Louisiana

Under the Louisiana Enforcement of Foreign Judgments Act (R.S. 13:4241
et seq.), a Louisiana court may recognize a foreign judgment and order it executed. This order, along with the foreign judgment, is then filed in the mortgage records to create the judicial mortgage. The Enforcement of Foreign
Judgments Act also contains provisions concerning the notice a judgment
debtor must receive and the procedures by which a judgment debtor may obtain a stay order.

17.3(c). Judicial Mortgages Arising from a Judgment of a Federal Court

Judgments of certain federal courts may create judicial mortgages.

If the federal court has original jurisdiction in Louisiana, the recording of
the judgment in the mortgage records of any parish creates a judicial mortgage in that parish (R.S. 13:4204).

If the federal court does not have original jurisdiction in Louisiana, the
judgment *"must be registered in accordance with 28 U.S.C. § 1963"* and then
recorded in the parish mortgage records. 28 U.S.C. § 1963 states that a *"judgment in an action for the recovery of money or property entered in any court of
appeals, district court, bankruptcy court, or in the Court of International Trade
may be registered by filing a certified copy of the judgment in any other district
or, with respect to the Court of International Trade, in any judicial district, when
the judgment has become final by appeal or expiration of the time for appeal or*

when ordered by the court that entered the judgment for good cause shown ... A judgment so registered shall have the same effect as a judgment of the district court of the district where registered and may be enforced in like manner."

Louisiana courts have held that the registry of a judgment under 28 U.S.C. §1963 must occur before (and not after) the recordation of the registered federal judgment in the mortgage records to create a valid judicial mortgage.

17.3(d). Judgments from Courts of Foreign Countries

There is no procedure under Louisiana law permitting judgment creditors to create a judicial mortgage by directly recording a judgment rendered by a court from another country. A separate, ordinary lawsuit may be required to validate that judgment and prove jurisdiction. In addition, there are several statutes restricting the scope and impact of certain court judgments rendered by jurisdictions outside of the United States (see, for example, C.C.P. art 2542 concerning foreign defamation judgments and R.S. 9:6000, which protects Louisiana citizens *"from the application of foreign laws"* that are contrary to state or federal constitutional rights).

17.4. Discussion Applies to Judicial Mortgages

Just as discussion (as defined in C.C.P. art. 5151) applies to legal mortgages (see Section 16.4, above), discussion applies to judicial mortgages (C.C.P. art. 5151).

17.5. The Effect of a Judgment against a Deceased Person

C.C. art. 3306 provides that a "judicial mortgage burdens the property of the judgment debtor only and does not burden other property of his heirs or legatees who have accepted his succession."

As the Official Louisiana Law Institute Comments to C.C. art. 3306 note, the purpose of this article accommodates *"the public records doctrine and limits the mortgage enjoyed by the judgment creditor to the property of the decedent that is transmitted to his successors. Such a judgment does not affect the other assets of the heir or legatee."*

17.6. The Effect of a Judicial Mortgage against the State or a Governmental Entity

The Louisiana Supreme Court has held that a party obtaining a judgment against the state or a Louisiana state or local governmental entity may record the judgment; however, the Supreme Court also has held that there is no right for the judgment creditor to execute on the judicial mortgage or attempt to collect on it if the governmental entity ever sells the property.

The Louisiana Supreme Court has held that the only way a litigant may collect on a judgment against a Louisiana state or local governmental entity is to ask that entity to appropriate funds to pay the judgment. If the entity does not appropriate the funds, there is no way for the litigant to judicially compel enforcement and collection of the judgment.

Chapter 18

Mortgages Disguised as Sales, "Due-on-Sale" Clauses, and Issues Involving Bond-for-Deed Contracts

18.1. Mortgages "Disguised" as Sales

Some states have a "deed of trust" theory, where title to immovable property is transferred temporarily to the creditor as security for a debt. In these states, title is transferred to a creditor or to a trustee who is acting for the creditor. The title remains in the transferee's hands until the loan is paid in full, at which point the title is transferred back to the owner/borrower. Louisiana law has always rejected this approach; a mortgage is not a transfer of title but rather a non-possessory, non-ownership interest in property (see Section 11.1, above).

A document that is labeled a "sale" may still be treated as a mortgage under Louisiana law if it is obvious from the face of the document that the sale is to secure an obligation that the seller owes to the buyer. In such an instance, the ostensible "sale" document will not transfer title to the buyer but instead will be considered a mortgage, both as between the parties and as to third parties. This is because, on the face of the "sale" document, the seller is shown to be the debtor and the buyer is shown to be the creditor. The fact that this purported "sale" document has been recorded on the face of the public records does not change the analysis. The Louisiana "public records" doctrine does not create rights where none exist nor does it presumptively validate an item merely because it is recorded in the public records (see Section 19.3, below).

A mortgage-disguised-as-a-sale document must be distinguished from three other situations.

The first situation is a seller-financed credit sale, where the face of the document shows that the buyer has only partially paid the purchase price and remains liable to the seller for the balance due, with the seller retaining a mortgage to secure the loan. On the face of the document, the seller is the creditor and the buyer is the debtor. This type of credit sale is a valid sale and gives rise not only to a mortgage but also to both a vendor's privilege (see Section 31.1, below) and a resolutory condition (see Chapter 22, below).

The second situation is a sale with a right of redemption, which is always a completed sale (subject to the right of redemption) as to third parties, but which may be a mortgage as between the parties (see Section 22.4, below).

The final situation is a cash sale from the seller to the buyer. In this situation, even if the parties intend for it to secure a debt that the seller owes to the buyer, the failure of the act of sale to disclose that any monies remain to be paid from buyer to seller means that third parties, looking at the public registry, may treat this as a completed sale and that the seller has no real security for the transaction. Third parties may rely upon the absence in the public records of any indication that the seller has retained any kind of real security in the property (see Section 33.2, below).

18.2. Bond-for-Deed Contracts

Louisiana historically has not recognized conditional sales; however, there is one statutory exception to this rule—the bond-for-deed contract (R.S. 9:2941 et seq.).

A bond-for-deed contract is a conditional sale of immovable property in which the seller agrees to transfer ownership to the buyer at a point in the future when the buyer has paid all the buyer owes to the seller.

A bond-for-deed contract is not a mortgage, because in a mortgage, the creditor does not receive title to the property as security for the loan (see Section 18.1, above). Rather, in a bond-for-deed contract, the seller/creditor keeps full title to the property pending the buyer's completion of all payments for the property. Under Louisiana law, however, while the bond-for-deed purchaser is not the owner until the final bond-for-deed price is paid, the bond-for-deed purchaser is deemed to be the owner solely for the purposes of the

Louisiana homestead exemption (R.S. 9:2948; see Chapter 25, below on the homestead exemption, especially Section 25.4).

18.2(a). The Advantages of Bond-for-Deed Contracts

Historically, bond-for-deed contracts have been used in two separate instances. First, bond-for-deed contracts have been used when the buyer cannot obtain conventional financing. Second, bond-for-deed contracts have been used in times of rising interest rates when the buyer cannot obtain a loan at a rate as low as the seller's existing mortgage.

If a buyer cannot obtain conventional financing from a mortgage company, bank, or other home-loan lenders, the seller may have to finance the purchase. Some sellers prefer to finance the purchase with a bond-for-deed contract, because if the buyer defaults, the seller does not have to institute foreclosure proceedings but can merely cancel the contract.

For example, assume that in Year 1, Seller enters into a bond-for-deed contract with Buyer; Buyer agrees to pay the purchase price in monthly installments over 20 years. If Buyer defaults at the end of Year 18 (several years before the 20 years has expired), the Seller may cancel the contract and give a 45-day notice to Buyer (R.S. 9:2945). At that point, if Buyer does not voluntarily leave the property, Seller may take legal action to evict Buyer. No foreclosure proceedings are necessary to eliminate Buyer's rights to the property. If the property is worth significantly more in Year 18 than it was in Year 1, Seller keeps all the equity that has accumulated, because the title has been with the seller all along.

Rising interest rates also lead to an increase in bond-for-deed contracts, especially when the buyer cannot obtain as favorable an interest rate as the seller.

For example, assume that, in Year 1, Seller had placed a 5% per annum 30-year first mortgage on the property in favor of Creditor. Further assume that in Year 5, Buyer wants to purchase the property from Seller, but mortgage interest rates are now at 8%. Buyer might like to assume the first mortgage but either (a) Buyer cannot meet the lender's qualification requirements to allow for the sale with assumption of the mortgage (see Section 19.5, below, and C.C.P. art. 2702) or (b) Seller's mortgage allows for the entire mortgage obligation to be immediately due if Seller sells the property, such as in a due-on-sale clause that does not cover bond-for-deed contracts (see Section 18.2(d), below). If Seller and Buyer enter into a bond-for-deed contract, then as to the Creditor, Seller remains owner and mortgage debtor. Seller will use the funds from the monthly bond-for-deed payments to pay off the monthly mortgage indebtedness. In this situation, the bond-for-deed contract allows Seller and

Buyer to keep Seller's first mortgage in place in a situation where otherwise the first mortgage would have to be paid off with the buyer having to come up with both a down-payment to the seller and new, more expensive conventional financing. This bond-for-deed contract example, however, will not work if Seller's first mortgage has a due-on-sale clause that can be triggered by a bond-for-deed contract (see Section 18.2(d), below). Further, the bond-for-deed statute requires that Seller establish an escrow account, because R.S. 9:2943 states: *"All payments by the buyers under bond for deed contracts of property then or thereafter burdened with a mortgage or privilege, shall be made to some bank authorized to do business in this state, which shall have been designated as the escrow agent for all parties interested in the contract. The payments shall be distributed by the escrow agent between the seller and the holder of the mortgage or privilege, in such proportion as the secured obligation shall bear to the purchase price in order to insure the buyer an unencumbered title when all payments have been made as provided in the bond for deed contract."*

18.2(b). The Disadvantages of Bond-for-Deed Contracts

The bond-for-deed purchaser is not the owner of the property until the final installment on the bond-for-deed contract is paid. Additionally, a bond-for-deed contract poses a number of significant risks for the buyer, the biggest of which is that the buyer never builds up an equity interest in the property.

For example, assume that in Year 1, Seller enters into a $100,000 bond-for-deed contract with Buyer; Buyer agrees to pay the purchase price in monthly installments over the next 20 years. Assume that when the bond-for-deed contract's final payment is almost due, the property is now worth $300,000, but Buyer defaults on the second-to-last monthly payment and Seller cancels the entire contract (R.S. 9:2945). In this situation, Buyer loses everything that has been paid to Seller and loses possession of the property. While there may be some accounting due between Buyer and Seller under the jurisprudence concerning the rental value of the property and improvements placed on the property by the bond-for-deed buyer, nonetheless the bond-for-deed buyer has been deprived of any interest in the $200,000 increase in the value of the property.

Had the transaction been done, however, as a credit sale with title transferred from Seller to Buyer and with Seller retaining a mortgage, then Seller would have had to institute foreclosure proceedings on the property and would have been entitled only to a privilege on the proceeds of the sheriff's sale in an amount equal to the unpaid portion of the $100,000 mortgage. If the sheriff's sale brought in more money than the pay-off of the Seller's mortgage note,

Buyer would have been entitled to all the excess funds, assuming that there were no other inferior creditors on the property (see Chapters 39 and 40, below).

Another disadvantage to both a buyer and seller under a bond-for-deed contract is that some courts have indicated that a transaction structured as a lease with an option to purchase may be treated legally as a bond-for-deed contract. These cases have serious implications for sellers and buyers, not only in ownership rights but also in tax implications for both parties. The cases have not dealt with the tax implications, and this remains a developing area of law. Therefore, cautious owners structuring leases with options to purchase should try to carefully craft the documents so that a court will not later construe the transaction as a bond-for-deed contract.

Further, bond-for-deed contracts cause difficulties in the arenas of both insurance and premises liability, for the bond-for-deed "purchaser" does not have title to the property and thus cannot obtain a typical homeowner's insurance policy. Moreover, because the bond-for-deed "seller" retains title to the property, the "seller" may remain liable for actions, inactions, and constructions that give rise to premise liability claims.

18.2(c). The Statutory Requirements of Bond-for-Deed Contracts

Although a bond-for-deed contract is a sale and would typically be filed only in the conveyance records, certain Louisiana statutes make it advantageous for the parties to record the document in both the mortgage and conveyance records. This is because R.S. 9:2941.1 provides that upon "*the recordation in the mortgage and conveyance records of a bond for deed contract as defined in R.S. 9:2941, any sale, contract, counterletter, lease, or mortgage executed by the bond for deed seller, and any lien, privilege, or judgment relating to or purporting to affect immovable property that has not been filed previously for registry or recorded in the mortgage records shall be subject to the rights created by the bond for deed contract.*"

If there is a pre-existing mortgage or privilege on the property being sold, R.S. 9:2942 makes it "*unlawful*" to sell the property "*without first obtaining a written guarantee from the mortgage and privilege holders to release the property upon payment by the buyer of a stipulated mortgage release price, with which agreement the secured notes shall be identified. The agreement shall be recorded in the mortgage records of the parish where the property is situated before any part of the property is offered for sale under bond for deed contracts.*" Further, R.S. 9:2947 makes it a crime (punishable by up to $1,000 or up to six months in prison, or both) for failing to comply with R.S. 9:2942. Louisiana trial and intermediate appellate courts, however, have not strictly enforced the requirements of R.S. 9:2942 and have not held bond-for-deed sales invalid for failure to comply with this statute. Given the structure of Louisiana law which disfavors "lawful causes of preference" (C.C. art. 3183) without strict compliance with statutory provisions, it remains to be seen whether the Louisiana Supreme Court will take a different view of the situation should the issue reach that court.

If there is a pre-existing first mortgage, R.S. 9:2943 requires that payments *"shall be made to some bank authorized to do business in this state, which shall have been designated as the escrow agent for all parties interested in the contract."* This statute also has not been strictly enforced by Louisiana courts, but the Louisiana Supreme Court has not directly ruled on this provision.

18.2(d). Due-on-Sale Clauses and Bond-for-Deed Contracts

A due-on-sale clause is a contractual provision in a mortgage allowing the mortgage lender to accelerate the entire balance due on the principal obligation secured by the mortgage if the debtor sells the property without the lender's prior written consent. This clause is one of the "non-monetary" defaults in a mortgage (see Section 27.1, below), because it allows the mortgage holder to seek immediate repayment of the entire principal balance secured by the loan even if the debtor has not missed a payment.

There are three main reasons that lenders give for inserting due-on-sale clauses in mortgages. First, lenders assert that the loan they made was to a particular borrower based upon that borrower's credit status; the mortgage is additional security. Second, particularly for borrowers who use mortgages to secure monies lent for the purchase price of homes, lenders assert that when a homeowner no longer lives in the house there is a greater likelihood that the loan ultimately will go into default. Third, lenders want to have a chance to evaluate whether the person who is acquiring ownership of their collateral is credit-worthy. Lenders often deem this an important consideration because lenders want to be able to evaluate whether the acquiring party has the capacity to keep the mortgage payments kept current, even though the mortgage continues to affect the property after the sale.

Most "due-on-sale" clauses also contain provisions allowing the lender to accelerate the loan if the borrower allows any other mortgage, lien, privilege, or encumbrance to exist on the property (even if inferior to the lender's mortgage), because lenders assert that if such inferior encumbrances exist, there is a greater likelihood that the loan ultimately will go into default.

A bond-for-deed contract is particularly useful if the seller's existing mortgage contains a due-on-sale clause that is effective only when sales, mortgages, or privileges occur. In such instances, sellers under bond-for-deed contracts take the position that their mortgage lender cannot use the bond-for-deed contract as an excuse to accelerate the loan under the due-on-sale clause because a bond-for-deed contract is not a completed sale but rather an agreement to sell in the future.

Most Louisiana mortgage lenders today insert provisions into their mortgage forms to avoid this problem by expressly making their due-on-sale provisions triggered not merely by sales but also by long-term leases on residential property as well as by bond-for-deed agreements.

Additionally, the jurisprudence has recognized that, under federal statutes and regulations, certain national lenders have the right to accelerate the loan if there is a bond-for-deed contract entered into even if the mortgage's due-on-sale clause does not expressly forbid bond-for-deed contracts.

Chapter 19

The Rules of Registry as They Relate to Mortgages and Certain Privileges on Immovables

19.1. Registry Is Parish Specific

The Louisiana law of registry concerning immovable property requires that certain items be filed for recordation in the parish conveyance or mortgage records (C.C. arts. 3341(4) and 3346–3347). There is no way to file in a single location and affect all immovable property in all parishes.

Therefore, if one wants to create rights in several parcels of immovable property located in several parishes, one must record the original (or certified copies of the original) in each and every parish where the immovable property is located. See Section 19.9, below, concerning properties located in multiple parishes.

19.2. Registry Is Not Needed to Affect the Parties to a Document

Registry in the conveyance or mortgage records is necessary only to affect third parties to documents; no registry is needed to make the document effective between the parties.

Even though a document is effective between the parties, however, without registry third parties are unaffected (see Section 19.4, below, on who is a third party to a document). As a practical matter, a creditor holding a mortgage or privilege on immovable property wants to be sure that the creditor's security interest affects third persons.

Once a document has been recorded, the parties to it "may not contradict the terms of the instrument or statement of fact it contains to the prejudice of a third person who after its recording acquires an interest in or over the immovable to which the instrument relates" (C.C. art. 3342).

19.3. Registry Is Needed to Affect Third Parties

The Louisiana rules of registry exist to create certainty concerning immovable property transactions so that third parties (see Section 19.4, below) who wish to examine the public records can make informed decisions about the title to property and about certain encumbrances that may impact the property.

19.3(a). Third Parties May Ignore Certain Matters That Are Not Contained in the Public Records

The Louisiana public records doctrine is not one of "constructive notice," although many cases use that term. Rather, as the Louisiana Supreme Court has explained and as C.C. art. 3338 makes clear, the Louisiana public records doctrine protects third parties from being affected by certain information concerning immovable property if that information is not contained in the mortgage or conveyance records. Under Louisiana law, actual knowledge is irrelevant; a third party may rely upon the absence of something that, by statute, must be in the public records to affect third parties.

For example, X executes an act of cash sale of immovable property to Y on Day 1, but Y does not file that act of sale for registry until Day 6. In the meantime, on Day 2, X sells the same property to Z and Z promptly records that act of sale on Day 3. Under Louisiana law, Z validly holds title to the property, even if Z knew about the sale from X to Y, because to affect third parties (such as Z), the sale from X to Y had to be filed for registry and at the time Z recorded the act of sale, the sale to Y had not been recorded. The failure of either X or Y to file the sale cannot affect Z's rights.

Thus, Louisiana public records law is different from the laws of many other states. Some states use a theory of "equity" to determine who owns the property in the X/Y/Z situation just described and would look to Z's personal knowledge as a key factor. Louisiana law rejects this "equity" theory as a subjective test and instead looks to the objective test of whether the public records reflect the filing for registry of the appropriate document.

C.C. art. 3338 defines what documents concerning immovable property must be placed on the public records to affect third parties. These include, for immovables: sales, mortgages, and leases, as well as documents that terminate these rights. Additionally, to keep certain mortgages and privileges effective against third parties, there must be timely reinscription of these real rights (C.C. art. 3357 *et seq*; see Chapter 20, below).

19.3(b). The Public Records Are Not Proof of the Validity of What Is Recorded

Recordation of a document in the public records "*is not evidence of the validity of the obligation that the encumbrance secures*" (C.C. art. 3320(C)) or that the instrument itself is valid or genuine (C.C. art. 3341(1)). It does not "*create a presumption as to the capacity or status of the parties*" (C.C. art. 3341(2)). It is effective "*only with respect to immovables located in the parish where the instrument is recorded*" (C.C. art. 3341(4)).

Filing a mortgage or privilege in the public records does not prove that it is effective at all (even as between the parties) and does not prove that the document secures a valid obligation. All recordation does is protect those valid rights that must be recorded to affect third parties; it is up to the holder of the real right (such as a mortgage) to prove at the appropriate time the validity of the debt the mortgage secures and the validity of the mortgage itself.

For example, one examining the public records and finding a collateral mortgage recorded in the mortgage records cannot ascertain whether the collateral mortgage is valid, whether the collateral mortgage note has prescribed, what obligations the security interest in the collateral mortgage note secures, the balance due (if any) on these obligations, or when the current security interest of the collateral mortgage was perfected (see Sections 13.9, 13.10, and 13.11, above). All a third party can ascertain from the public records is that a collateral mortgage is of record and then make certain assumptions about the effect of this recordation. On the other hand, if a third person examines the public records and finds that no collateral mortgage has been filed for registry, the third person will not be impacted by the collateral mortgage, even if the third person has actual knowledge that a collateral mortgage has been executed between a creditor and debtor (C.C. art. 3338).

Likewise, as C.C. art. 3339 recognizes, one examining the public records cannot necessarily ascertain the "*capacity or authority*" of the parties, "*the occurrence of a suspensive or resolutory condition, the exercise of an option or right of first refusal, a tacit acceptance, a termination of rights that depends upon the occurrence of a condition,*" and similar matters. As C.C. 3339 states, these items that pertain to rights in recorded documents "*are effective as to third persons although not evidenced of record.*"

19.3(c). There Is No Need to Record Certain Items

Not everything affecting immovable property has to be recorded to affect third persons. The Louisiana public records doctrine is statutorily based; if a statute does not require recordation, then recordation is not necessary to affect third persons.

On the other hand, there are certain statutes that permit third persons to be affected by items even if they are not in the public records. For example, a funeral privilege affects all movable and immovable property of the decedent even if never filed for registry (C.C. art. 3276, and see Section 29.2, below), and thus third persons are affected by a funeral privilege, even if they have no way of ascertaining from the public records that it exists.

19.4. Who Is a Third Party to a Document

While this Précis has used the phrase "third party," because that is the term most attorneys employ when discussing the issue, the proper phrase under the Civil Code is "third person."

C.C. art. 3343 defines a "third person" as one "*who is not a party to or personally bound by an instrument.*" Witnesses to documents are third persons (even though they have signed the document), because C.C. art. 3343 specifically states that a "*witness to an act is a third person with respect to it.*"

C.C. art. 3343 also provides a mechanism by which someone who did not sign the document can cease being a "third person" and can be treated as a party to the document. That instance is when a person "*by contract, assumes an obligation or is bound by contract to recognize a right.*" Therefore, a buyer of property who "assumes" a mortgage is no longer a third person with respect to that mortgage; thus, registry becomes irrelevant to this "assumer" and the "assumer" is treated for all purposes as a debtor on the obligation that the mortgage secures (see Section 19.5, below).

On the other hand, one who buys property "subject to" a mortgage remains a third person, because the "subject to" purchaser is acknowledging that the seller has informed the buyer that the property is encumbered; the purchaser is not agreeing to be personally bound by the mortgage or the obligation it secures by signing a sale "subject to" a mortgage (see Chapter 21, below, about those who purchase property subject to a mortgage).

19.5. Assumption of Mortgages: The Obligations of One Who Assumes a Mortgage and the Public Records Implications

The usual and customary terminology employed in sales of property with assumption of mortgages is that the buyer "assumes the mortgage" described in the document. This terminology may be a bit confusing for two reasons. First, the mortgage being described is a pre-existing mortgage on the property to which the buyer is not a party. Second, a mortgage is an accessory real right that, by its nature, does not impart personal liability to the maker of the mortgage (C.C. arts. 3278–79).

What the phrase "with assumption of mortgage" means is that the buyer is "*bound to recognize*" the preexisting mortgage as if the buyer were a party to it (C.C. art. 3343). Moreover, the assumption clause means that the buyer has agreed to be obligated on the principal obligation that the mortgage secures (C.C. art. 3282). If the principal obligation is one that imparts personal liability, the obligor has become liable in solido with the principal obligor.

When one purchases property by an act of assumption, the rules of inscription and registry no longer apply to the purchaser, because the purchaser is no longer a "third person" with respect to the mortgage (C.C. art. 3343). Thus, the purchaser who assumes a mortgage cannot claim that inscription has not been made or has lapsed, although third parties may still make these claims.

Additionally, if the holder of the mortgage begins foreclosure proceedings against the property, the defenses available to those who purchased the property with an assumption are far more limited than the defenses available to those who purchased the property without assuming the mortgage (compare C.C.P. arts. 2702 and 2703).

19.6. The Mortgage Records and the Conveyance Records Are Copies of the Original Documents; the Original Documents Are Not Contained in the Mortgage or Conveyance Records

There are three sets of public records affecting immovable property: the originals, the mortgage records, and the conveyance records.

"Filing" is the process of handing to the Clerk of Court a document for recordation in the conveyance or mortgage records. The Clerk is to mark this original document with the time and date of filing (C.C. art. 3348), but this pertains only to documents handed to the clerk at the clerk's office. The jurisprudence has held that handing a document to the Clerk of Court in the courtroom is not a proper location, and the time of handing the document to the clerk in the courtroom is not determinative of its filing date. C.C. art. 3347 states that an *"instrument is filed with a recorder when he accepts it for recordation in his office."*

The failure of the clerk to endorse the document with the time and date of filing is not fatal; under C.C. art. 3349, in such cases *"it is presumed that the instrument was filed with respect to other instruments in the order indicated by their registry numbers...."* Thus, every document filed with the clerk contains a "registry number," which is simply a numerical listing of every document handed to the clerk for filing in the conveyance or mortgage records.

The clerk takes that original document and binds it with all other originals in books. Each book is called a "bundle." Each clerk's office contains hundreds, and sometimes thousands, of books. If one wants to describe an original document, the usual formulation is along the lines of "Original 356, Bundle 899." This means that this particular document can be found in book 899 of the original books ("Bundle 899"), and the document was the 356th document in that bundle. Note that the "356" refers to a document number, not a page number. Remember also that each original bears a registry number.

In addition to binding all the originals into books (bundles), the clerk also makes a copy of each document and inserts that copy in the conveyance records or mortgage records, as appropriate. Some documents go into only one record; for example, a cash sale needs to be recorded only in the conveyance records and a conventional mortgage needs to be recorded only in the mortgage records.

Sometimes an original document creates both a conveyance and a security interest. In that case, the document may need to be recorded in both the conveyance and mortgage records. An example of this is given at the end of this Section.

"Recordation" occurs when a document is inscribed in the conveyance or mortgage books. The conveyance books and mortgage books are simply copies of originals filed with the clerk's office. In the early 1800s, these books consisted of handwritten pages where the clerk copied in longhand, word-for-word, information contained in the original. Today, conveyance and mortgage books consist of photocopies or electronic copies of the originals, but in all cases, the conveyance and mortgage books consist of copies and not original documents.

The Clerk of Court creates indices of documents. Each Clerk of Court has staff members who scrutinize each document and determine the names and information that will go in the index of recorded documents. The index is created as a part of the recordation process.

For the conveyance records, there is a "vendor" index and a "vendee" index. For the mortgage records, there is a "mortgagor" and "mortgagee" index. If a document is filed in both locations, the names will appear in all of the indices. For example, assume that there is a "sale with mortgage" from Andy Arnold to Betty Belle. This type of document reflects that Andy has sold property to Betty on credit and has retained a conventional mortgage as security for the unpaid portion of the purchase price. This document not only transfers title and creates a mortgage, it also creates a vendor's privilege (see Section 33.2, below) and a resolutory condition (see Section 22.2, below). To transfer title effective against third parties and to create a resolutory condition effective against third parties, the conveyance must be recorded in the conveyance records. To make the mortgage and vendor's privilege effective against third parties, the document must be recorded in the mortgage records. Therefore, in this example, Andy Arnold will appear as a "vendor" in the conveyance indices and as the "mortgagee" in the mortgage indices. Likewise, Betty Belle will appear as "vendee" in the conveyance indices and as "mortgagor" in the mortgage indices. A title examiner must analyze each index to ascertain the status of the title to immovable property and to ascertain whether there are any recorded encumbrances that affect third parties (see Chapter 23, below).

19.7. Filing vs. Registry of Conveyances and Mortgages Concerning the Effect on Third Parties

19.7(a). An Overview of the Issue

Historically, the Louisiana Constitution made a distinction between the effects of "filing" an act of conveyance or mortgage and the "recordation" of that act. The revision of the Louisiana Constitution in the 1970s attempted to remove that constitutional distinction and the Civil Code was amended extensively after that point in time to deal with registry issues.

C.C. art. 3347 provides that the *"effect of recordation arises when an instrument is filed with the recorder...."* Louisiana jurisprudence that arose prior to the amendments to C.C. art. 3347 made in 2005 had held that as long as a mortgage was "timely" recorded after it had been filed, third parties were affected from the time of filing, not recordation. On the other hand, if the gap between filing and recordation was "untimely," then third parties were affected only once recordation occurred. No court has delineated the precise definitions of what is "timely" or "untimely" filing, but cases have held that recordation within three days of filing was timely and recordation accomplished eighteen months after filing was untimely.

In 2010, the Louisiana Supreme Court rendered an important opinion that, while dealing directly only with judicial mortgages, raises issues concerning the effects of filing and registry for all conveyances and mortgages. In essence, the Supreme Court's opinion may mean, as a practical matter, that those who file acts of conveyances and mortgages with a Clerk of Court may have to verify that the act in fact has been inscribed into the proper conveyance or mortgage record in order to affect third parties.

19.7(b). The Historical Background

Historically, Louisiana had different rules on the effect of recordation of conveyances and mortgages.

For almost 200 years, the rule was that conveyances were effective upon filing, even if the document was never recorded in the conveyance records (for a discussion of the distinction between filing and recordation, see Section 19.6, above). Of course, if a document is never recorded in the conveyance or mortgage records, no index is created and third parties have no way of locating the document; nonetheless, the filing of the conveyance was held to affect third parties. The concept here is the same as if you had no access to electronic searches or any index to any Supreme Court case; even if you couldn't find a case without an index, the holding of that case remains effective.

In contrast, until the 1970s the Louisiana Constitution had required that mortgages be "recorded" to affect third parties. Therefore, if a mortgage was merely filed but never recorded in the mortgage books, it had no effect.

The former constitutional provision (La. Constitution of 1921, art. XIX, § 19) was converted, in the 1970s, into an unnumbered statute (La. Constitution of 1974, art. 14 § 16(A)(15)). Because there was no further constitutional restriction preventing mortgages from being effective upon filing (rather than upon recordation), theoretically any later amended statute could alter the rule of this unnumbered statute and create a new rule on whether a mortgage had to be actually recorded to affect third parties.

19.7(c). Judicial Mortgages Must Be Recorded, Not Just Filed, and Questions Raised by a 2010 Supreme Court Decision Concerning This Issue

In 2010, the Louisiana Supreme Court, in *Hans Wede v. Niche Marketing USA, LLC,* held that to be effective against third parties as a judicial mortgage, a judgment must be recorded in the parish mortgage records; filing the document with the clerk is not sufficient. The case arose when an out-of-state court judgment, made executory in Louisiana (see Section 17.3, above), was filed with the clerk's office. The clerk, by mistake, recorded in judgment the conveyance records and not the mortgage records.

The Court did not discuss the historical constitutional distinction between conveyances and mortgages (see Section 19.7(b), above) but rather rested its decision on a statutory analysis of the Civil Code rules of registry. The Court concluded that while C.C. art. 3347 states that "*the effect of recordation arises when an instrument is filed with the recorder…,*" this is a reference only to the time the effect of recordation begins. The Court held that C.C. art. 3338 controlled where the recordation must occur, pointing to the provision in C.C. art. 3338 that certain written instruments (including mortgages) "*are without effect as to a third person unless the instrument is registered by recording it in the appropriate mortgage or conveyance records.…*" The Court augmented its opinion by quoting from the Louisiana Law Institute's official comments to the 1992 revisions to C.C. art. 3320. Comment (c) contains this sentence, quoted by the court with approval: "Thus, a mortgage recorded in the conveyance records or a sale recorded in the mortgage records, is without effect as to third persons."

Although the case involved a judicial mortgage, the court's reasoning does not appear to be limited to judicial mortgages and may apply to all mortgages and conveyances.

In light of the Supreme Court's reliance on comment (c) to C.C. art. 3320, it would appear that cautious buyers and lenders may want to make sure that documents which they file with the clerk are in fact recorded in the proper conveyance or mortgage book.

Among the questions raised by the Supreme Court's ruling is the relationship between filing and recordation. For example, under the Supreme Court's analysis, a mortgage filed on one day but later recorded in the mortgage books is nonetheless effective from the date of filing (C.C. art. 3347), but the Court's analysis does not address what effect the mortgage would have if a third party purchased the property in the interval between the time of filing of the mortgage with the clerk's office and the clerk's recordation of the mortgage in the mortgage records.

19.8. The Recorder Has the Power to Refuse to Record Certain Documents

C.C. art. 3344 gives the recorder the authority to refuse to accept for filing documents that do not meet certain formalities, such as those not bearing the *"original signature"* of a party or a *"judgment, administrative decree, or other act of a governmental agency that is not properly certified in a manner provided by law."* C.C. art. 3352 contains a list of what instruments filed for registry must contain.

The jurisprudence has held that if the recorder files something that could have been refused because of formality requirements, nonetheless that document may still affect third parties. C.C. arts. 3345, 3352, and 3353 recognize this fact.

C. C. Art. 3345 states that a duplicate *"shall nonetheless have the same effect as recordation of the original instrument."* The Louisiana Code of Evidence (Art. 1003.1) allows introduction into evidence a duplicate that *"is in electronic form or is a reproduction of electronically imaged or stored records, documents, data, or other information."* Louisiana law recognizes that sometimes the only "original" of a document is electronic. The Louisiana Electronic Transactions Act (R.S. 9:2601 *et seq.*) allows for electronic documents with electronic signatures.

C.C. art. 3352(c) provides that the *"recorder shall not refuse to record an instrument because it does not contain the information required by this Article. The omission of that information does not impair the validity of an instrument or the effect given to its recordation."*

While C.C. art. 3352 requires that the *"full name"* of a party to a document be given if it is to be recorded, C.C. 3353 requires that the document is effective against third parties even if the full name is not given, as long as *"the name of a party is not so indefinite, incomplete, or erroneous as to be misleading and the instrument as a whole reasonably alerts a person examining the records that the instrument may be that of the party."*

19.9. Special Civil Code Rules Pertaining to the Mortgage Records

C.C. arts. 3354–3356 contain special rules that apply only to the mortgage records.

C.C. art. 3355 concerns a mortgage affecting properties in multiple parishes. It allows a single mortgage to encumber properties in multiple parishes. In that instance, the original needs to be filed only in one of the parishes where the property is located and certified copies can be filed in the other parishes.

C.C. art. 3356 deals with transfers, amendments, and releases. It is not unusual for one creditor to transfer to another an obligation secured by a mortgage or privilege affecting immovable property. C.C. art. 3356(A) protects the creditor who is receiving the transfer from certain actions by the former creditor. C.C. art. 3356(A) provides that a *"transferee of an obligation secured by a mortgage is not bound by any unrecorded act releasing, amending, or otherwise modifying the mortgage if he is a third person with respect to that unrecorded act."* Although the transferee creditor may have a right to enforce the mortgage fully, C.C. art. 3356(A) is a special rule that supersedes the general principle that recordation is not needed to affect the parties to a mortgage (see Section 19.2, above). As C.C. art. 3356(B) makes clear, it is only recorded acts of the prior creditor that affect the transferee. These provisions, however, must be read in conjunction with R.S. 9:5554 when there is a transfer of an obligation secured by a collateral mortgage package (see Sections 13.4(d)2, 13.11, and 13.13, above).

Chapter 20

The Effect and Ranking of Conventional, Legal, and Judicial Mortgages

20.1. There Are Different Rules That Apply in Determining When Mortgages Begin to Affect Third Parties and When Mortgages Cease Affecting Third Parties

A creditor who holds a mortgage as security for a loan wants to affect third parties to assure both that third parties are aware of the existence of the mortgage and to enable the creditor to extinguish all inferior mortgages, ownership rights, and encumbrances if the creditor must foreclose on the mortgage (C.C.P. art. 2376). Two dates are critical to every holder of a mortgage. First, the date the mortgage begins to affect third parties, and second, the date when the mortgage ceases to affect third parties.

Mortgages begin to affect third parties upon filing and timely recordation of the document creating the mortgage in the mortgage records of the parish where the property is located. See Sections 19.3, 19.4, and 19.7, above, for mortgages in general, and Section 13.5 for the special rules concerning collateral mortgages.

Mortgages cease affecting third parties when the duration of their inscription lapses (see C.C. art. 3357 *et seq.* and Section 20.2, below).

20.2. How Long Are Third Parties Affected by a Recorded Conventional Mortgage?

Once a mortgage begins to affect third parties, the effects of registry do not last forever. Louisiana law requires that creditors reinscribe their mortgages within certain time periods or lose their secured status. The time limits for reinscription depend upon the obligation that the mortgage secures (see Sections 20.8(b), 20.8(c), and 20.8(d) on reinscription).

Additionally, the effects of a conventional mortgage can be extended if the obligation that the mortgage secures is extended by an act filed for registry in the mortgage records (see Section 20.7, below).

20.2(a). The General Rules: The 10-Year Rule and the 6-Year-after-Maturity Rule

C.C. art. 3357 contains the general rule on how long a mortgage affects third parties. It provides that, except *"as otherwise expressly provided by law, the effect of recordation of an instrument creating a mortgage or pledge or evidencing a privilege ceases ten years after the date of the instrument."* The reference to "pledge" was added by amendments effective January 1, 2015, to reflect the changes in Louisiana law concerning granting a real security right in a landlord's right to collect rent from immovable property by pledge (see Section 10.4, above).

It is important to note that C.C. art. 3357 states that the effective date lasts until *"ten years after <u>the date of the instrument</u>."* The date of filing of the instrument is irrelevant to determine when the mortgage ceases to affect third parties. The date of filing (plus timely recordation) is when the mortgage begins to affect third parties, but C.C. art. 3357 is concerned only with when the effects of the registry of the mortgage cease to affect third parties.

C.C. art 3357 begins with the caveat that it applies *"except as otherwise provided by law."* The first exception is contained in C.C. art. 3358.

C.C. 3358 relates to mortgages, pledges of a rental stream on immovable property, and privileges on immovable property when the obligation secured by the real security is due nine years or more from the date of the document. In this case, the effect on third parties lasts until *"six years after the latest maturity date described in the document."* As with C.C. art. 3357, C.C. art. 3358 is unconcerned with when the mortgage, pledge, or privilege, was filed (the time when parties are first affected by the registry of the real security). C.C. art. 3358 is concerned with the date on which real security ceases to affect third parties, not when it begins to affect third parties.

The following chart may be helpful in keeping these general rules in mind. While this chart deals only with mortgages, the same rules apply to a pledge of a rental stream of immovable property and to privileges on immovable property:

The length of time from the date of the execution of the mortgage to the maturity of the obligation that the mortgage	How long does the mortgage affect third parties?	C.C. art.
Less than 9 years	10 years from the date of the document	3357
9 years or more	6 years from the maturity of the obligation that the mortgage	3358

Note that nothing in this chart relates to whether the obligation secured by the mortgage (such as a mortgage note) has prescribed. Third parties cannot ascertain from the mortgage records how much is outstanding on the note (see Sections 13.3(c) and 13.10, above), whether anything has been paid on the note, or whether prescription on the note has been interrupted by payment of principal or interest on the note or by an act of acknowledgment (C.C. art. 3464 and R.S. 9:5807). Third parties examining the public records therefore must assume that prescription has been interrupted and that the entire amount remains outstanding. Third parties, however, are protected by the absence from the public records (see Section 19.3(a), above) of a timely reinscription. Therefore, creditors will want to reinscribe their mortgages timely, for a timely reinscription preserves the rank of that mortgage from its original filing date (see Section 20.8, below).

If litigation ensues, a creditor holding a mortgage will need to prove the validity of the principal obligation, including the fact that this obligation has not prescribed (see Section 24.3).

20.2(a)(1). Example #1

Debtor #1 borrowed $10,000 from Creditor #1 represented by a negotiable promissory note and granted a mortgage on Debtor #1's property to secure the $10,000 note. The note, which is due in monthly installments over five years, was signed and dated January 15, 2011. The mortgage was signed and dated the same day and the note was paraphed *ne varietur* for identification with the Act of Mortgage (see Section 12.4(c), above, on paraphing notes *ne varietur*).

Creditor #1, however, did not file the mortgage for recordation with the Clerk of Court until May 1, 2011; the Clerk of Court recorded the mortgage on the same day it was filed.

In this instance, the mortgage did not begin to affect third parties until May 1, 2011, the date it was filed for registry.

Because the note the mortgage secures was due in less than nine years from the date it was executed, C.C. art. 3357 mandates that its effects cease as to third parties January 15, 2021, which is ten years from the date of the document (January 15, 2011), not ten years from the date of filing in the public records. Third parties cannot ascertain from the public records whether the note has prescribed or whether the obligation has been acknowledged by payment or otherwise, thereby interrupting prescription. Therefore, third parties must "assume the worst" (see Section 24.2, below) and assume that the note has not prescribed. Thus, the only protection third parties have from the effects of this mortgage is the failure of the creditor to timely reinscribe it.

Therefore, the mortgage held by Creditor #1 started to affect third parties on May 1, 2011 and will cease affecting third parties on January 15, 2021. Note that even if the effects of recordation had ceased, the mortgage would remain in effect between the parties (Debtor #1 and Creditor #1) as long as the note has not prescribed.

20.2(a)(2). Example #2

The facts are identical to Section 20.2(a)1, Example #1, above, except that now the note was due not in five years from the date of its execution but rather it was payable in monthly installments over the course of ten years.

In this instance, as in the previous example, the mortgage did not begin to affect third parties until May 1, 2011, the date it was filed for registry.

Because the note the mortgage secures now is due more than nine years from the date it was executed, C.C. art. 3358 mandates that its effects cease as to third parties on January 15, 2027, which is six years from the maturity date on the note (the date of maturity is January 15, 2021). The effect on third parties does not lapse six years from the date of filing of the mortgage in the public records.

Therefore, the mortgage held by Creditor #1 started to affect third parties on May 1, 2011 and will cease affecting third parties on January 15, 2027. Note that even if the effects of recordation had ceased, the mortgage would remain in effect between the parties (Debtor #1 and Creditor #1) as long as the note has not prescribed.

20.2(a)(3). Example #3

On February 1, 2011, Debtor #2 executed a $100,000 fluctuating line of credit agreement with Creditor #2 and secured it with $150,000 collateral mortgage package, consisting of a collateral mortgage note and collateral mortgage of that same date (see Section 13.4, above, on collateral mortgages).

Creditor #2 recorded the collateral mortgage on March 1, 2011.

Debtor #2 has borrowed the entire $100,000 on the line of credit, represented by two handnotes (see Section 13.4, above), one for $25,000 dated March 1, 2011 payable in monthly installments over the course of five years, and one for $75,000 dated April 1, 2011, payable in monthly installments over the course of fifteen years.

When does the collateral mortgage package cease to affect third parties? Don't get confused by this example. The first thing to understand is that, in a collateral mortgage package, the collateral mortgage (Level III) secures the collateral mortgage note (Level II), not the handnotes (Level I), for the handnotes are secured by a pledge of the collateral mortgage note (see the Diagram 13.4(a)(1), above).

It is the collateral mortgage note that is the obligation secured by the mortgage. In a properly constructed collateral mortgage package, the collateral mortgage note is due on demand (see Section 13.6, above).

With this understanding in mind, the answer to the example becomes easier. The collateral mortgage package ceases to affect third parties on February 1, 2021 (ten years from the date of the document, C.C. art. 3357). The reason is that the obligation secured by the collateral mortgage (Level III) is the collateral mortgage note (Level II). Since the collateral mortgage note is due on demand, it is due in less than nine years from the date of the note (for a demand note is due immediately upon being signed). The possessory security interest the creditor has in the collateral mortgage note may prevent the handnotes from prescribing (see Section 13.4, above), and payment of principal or interest on the handnotes may have interrupted prescription on the collateral mortgage note (see R.S. 9:5807 and Section 13.14 above), but third parties cannot ascertain any of this information from the mortgage or conveyance records.

There are not enough facts given in this example to know when the collateral mortgage package begins to affect third parties, for one does not know when a security interest was given in the collateral mortgage note. A collateral mortgage package begins to affect third parties only from the earliest concurrence of a perfected UCC9 security interest in the collateral mortgage note and registry of the collateral mortgage in the public records (see Section 13.5(b), above). One can ascertain, however, that the effects of the collateral mortgage will cease as to third parties on February 1, 2021, for the reasons stated above.

20.3. A Mortgage May Be Cancelled Either before or after the Effects of Recordation Have Ceased

Mortgages may be cancelled by the holder of the mortgage before the effects of recordation cease. Any person or entity may cancel a mortgage after the effects of recordation cease.

20.3(a). Cancelling a Mortgage before the Effects of Recordation Have Ceased

Mortgages may be cancelled before the effects of recordation cease (C.C. art. 3366). Special forms for this may be required by the Clerk of Court (C.C. of art. 3366(A) and R.S. 9:5166). The effects of the mortgage cease upon the recordation of the cancellation (C.C. art. 3366(B)).

The typical way a cancellation is accomplished is that the creditor who holds the note paraphed for identification with the mortgage goes to the clerk's office with the proper cancellation form. The creditor attaches the note, marked "paid," to the form (R.S. 9:5170); the clerk files the originals and records a copy of them in the mortgage records (see Section 19.6, above).

If there had been a paraphed note but it has been lost or destroyed (see Section 12.4(C), above), cancellation may be accomplished by recording an appropriate affidavit from the notary or title insurer (R.S. 9:5167–5158).

If there is no note paraphed for identification with the act of mortgage, the mortgage may be cancelled by an affidavit "*signed by the obligee of record of the mortgage or privilege that acknowledges the satisfaction or extinction of the secured obligation*" (R.S. 9:5169).

There are special rules, contained in R.S. 9:5557, concerning the obligation of creditors to grant a release of mortgages recorded prior to January 1, 2012. For these mortgages, the debtor may request in writing that the creditor file an act of cancellation when the debt that the mortgage secures has been satisfied (R.S. 9:5557(B)). A creditor has sixty days to act on that request and cancel the mortgage; the failure of the creditor to timely cancel the mortgage allows the debtor to file suit to get the mortgage erased and to hold the recalcitrant creditor liable for "*costs, reasonable attorneys fees, and damages....*" (R.S. 9:5557(B)).

While R.S. 9:5557 applies to all mortgages recorded prior to January 1, 2012, there is no such blanket rule applying to mortgages recorded after January 1, 2012. Rather, R.S. 9:5165 provides a different rule for residential mortgages as well as mortgages for the purchase or financing of "*one-to-four family residen-*

tial immovable property," and this rule applies only to such mortgages recorded after January 1, 2012. For these mortgages, the debtor may request, in writing, that the lender or mortgage servicer cancel the mortgage when the mortgage has been extinguished (see C.C. art. 3319 and Section 20.9, below). The mortgagor must submit any required fee with the written request, but those fees may not exceed $100 (R.S. 9:5165(B)(5) and (6)). The lender has forty-five days to act (R.S. 9:5165(C)). There are special rules for situations in which a settlement agent is involved (R.S. 9:5165(B)(6) and (C)). A failure by a lender or settlement agent to act timely may render them liable for damages and attorney's fees (R.S. 9:5165(C)(2) and 5165(E)).

Third parties, however, may not rely on an act of cancellation as definitively erasing a mortgage, even though R.S. 9:5174 provides for the liability of those who incorrectly or fraudulently request a cancellation. The reason third parties may not rely on the act of cancellation is that Louisiana jurisprudence has held that a fraudulently cancelled mortgage remains effective as to third parties. Because no person canceling a mortgage ever indicates that the request for cancellation is fraudulent, those who rely upon cancellations do so as a business risk; if the cancellation proves to be fraudulent, third parties are as affected by the mortgage as if it never had been cancelled. The only thing third parties can rely upon as a legal matter (as opposed to a business proposition or business risk assessment) is the failure of the holder of the mortgage to timely reinscribe it.

20.3(b). Cancelling a Mortgage after the Effects of Recordation Have Ceased

C.C. art. 3367 governs cancellation of mortgages after the effects of recordation have ceased. It provides that if "*the effect of recordation of a mortgage or privilege has ceased for lack of reinscription, the recorder upon receipt of a written signed application shall cancel its recordation.*"

20.4. How Long Third Parties Are Affected by a Recorded Judicial Mortgage

A judicial mortgage secures a judgment. Under C.C. art. 3359, the effect of recordation of a judgment creating a judicial mortgage ceases "*ten years after the date of the judgment.*"

A Louisiana judgment itself will prescribe, unless it is revived by court action (see Section 20.8(c), below; also see special rules on judicial mortgages from out-of-state courts (Section 17.3(b), above).

20.5. How Long Third Parties Are Affected by a Recorded Legal Mortgage

C.C. art. 3360 sets forth the rules on how long a legal mortgage affects third parties. For legal mortgages affecting a tutor, curator, or interdict, the effect of the legal mortgage *"ceases four years after the tutorship or curatorship termi-nates, or, if the tutor or curator resigns or is removed, four years after the judg-ment that authorizes the resignation or removal."*

There are separate rules in C.C. art. 3360(B) for legal mortgages securing the obligations of a curator of an absent person or a succession representative. These legal mortgages cease to affect third parties *"four years after homologation of his final account, or, if the curator or representative resigns or is removed, four years after the judgment that authorizes that resignation or removal. In any event, the effect of recordation ceases ten years after the date of the act of mortgage."*

20.6. Special Rules When a Mortgage Secures a Federal Obligation

When a mortgage secures an obligation to a federal agency, such as the Farmers Home Administration, federal courts have held that 28 U.S.C. §2415 supersedes state law. The federal courts have held that even if the prescription has run on the obligation the mortgage secures, and even if the effects of reg-istry have ceased as to third parties under the Civil Code, nonetheless, under federal law, these mortgages remain in existence forever and the federal agen-cies (and those who purchase the mortgages from the federal agencies) can foreclose on them *in rem* (see Section 12.11, above, about *in rem* obligations).

At least one Louisiana intermediate appellate court has refused to follow the federal jurisprudence in this regard. This remains a developing area of the law.

20.7. The Effect on Third Parties of Amending the Principal Obligation Secured by the Mortgage

While normally the length of time that a mortgage affects third parties is determined by comparing the date of the document to the due date of the ob-ligation secured by the mortgage (see Section 20.2(a), above), the parties may extend the effects of recordation by amending the obligation secured by the mortgage.

Under C.C. art. 3361, if, *"before the effect of recordation ceases an instrument is recorded that amends a recorded mortgage, pledge, or privilege to describe or modify the maturity of a particular obligation that it secures, then the time of cessation of the effect of the recordation is determined by reference to the maturity of the obligation last becoming due described in the mortgage, pledge, or privilege as amended."*

In other words, if the parties record a document in the mortgage records evidencing an amendment that extends the maturity date of the mortgage note, the effects of recordation may be extended.

Determining the effects of the extension requires two calculations. First, one looks at the original date of the mortgage, pledge, or privilege and the original maturity date of the obligation the mortgage, pledge, or privilege secures. Second, one looks at the amended maturity date of the obligation the mortgage, pledge, or privilege secures.

If the new, amended maturity date is less than nine years from the date of the original document (before it was amended), the effect of recordation ceases ten years from the date of the original execution date of the obligation secured by the mortgage, pledge, or privilege (C.C. art. 3357). If, however, the extended maturity date is nine years or more from the date of the original execution date of the obligation secured by the mortgage, pledge, or privilege, the effects of recordation will cease six years from the extended maturity date (C.C. arts. 3358, 3361).

20.7(a). Example #1

The facts are similar to those in Section 20.2(a)1, Example #1.

Debtor #3 borrows $10,000 from Creditor #3 represented by a negotiable promissory note and grants a mortgage on Debtor #3's property to secure the $10,000 note. The note, which is due in monthly installments over five years, is signed and dated January 15, 2011. The mortgage is signed and dated the same day and the note is paraphed *ne varietur* for identification with the Act of Mortgage (see Section 12.4(c), above, on paraphing notes *ne varietur*).

Creditor #3, however, does not file the mortgage for recordation with the Clerk of Court (see Chapter 19, above) until May 1, 2011.

On July 1, 2015, Creditor #3 and Debtor #3 enter into a document, which they record in the parish mortgage records, extending the maturity of the note from the original maturity date of January 15, 2016 (five years from the date the note was signed) to January 15, 2030 (19 years from the date the note was signed).

Under C.C. art. 3361, one must compare the new maturity date (January 15, 2030) to the original execution date of the note (January 15, 2011). Since the new maturity date is more than nine years from the original execution date, C.C. art. 3358 controls the calculation, and now the mortgage will affect third parties until January 15, 2036 (six years from the new maturity date).

20.7(b). Example #2

The facts are similar to those in Section 20.7(a), Example #1, above, but instead of the July 1, 2015 document extending the maturity date until January 15, 2030, it only extends the maturity date from the original maturity date of January 15, 2016 (five years from the execution of the note) to January 15, 2019 (eight years from the execution of the note).

As in the previous example, under C.C. art. 3361, one must compare the new maturity date (January 15, 2019) to the original execution date of the note (January 15, 2011). Since the new maturity date, however, is still less than nine years from the original execution date, C.C. art. 3357 controls the calculation, and the effect of the mortgage as to third parties will expire January 15, 2021.

20.8. Reinscription, in General

Reinscription is the method by which one extends the last date which a recorded mortgage or privilege may affect third parties. Reinscription generally can be done by the creditor unilaterally, without the debtor's consent, and even without the debtor's knowledge.

If accomplished timely and in the proper form, reinscription not only extends the last date on which the mortgage or privilege will affect third parties, it also preserves the original date when the mortgage or privilege first began to affect third parties. If reinscription is accomplished in the proper form but is not timely filed, special rules apply; in general, an untimely reinscription results in a new ranking date. In other words, the original date that the mortgage or privilege first began to affect third parties is lost and the mortgage or privilege will affect third parties only from the date of reinscription.

Reinscription only preserves the effect of the mortgage or privilege; it does not validate the obligation that the mortgage or privilege secures. Third parties cannot ascertain from the mortgage records whether the obligation has been paid off or has prescribed; therefore, third parties examining the public records must assume that the entire debt remains outstanding (see the discussion at Sections 24.2, below) and that the obligation has not prescribed. In litigation, however, the creditor must prove the validity of the principal obligation, for if the principal obligation is extinguished or unenforceable, the accessory obligation of the mortgage or privilege is unenforceable as well (see Sections 20.9 and 24.3, below).

20.8(a). The Civil Code's Reinscription Formalities Must Be Followed

The Civil Code provides certain formalities for acts of reinscription. The Civil Code's form requirements are the "exclusive" method of creating an effective act of reinscription (C.C. art. 3363). A failure to use the proper form will render the purported reinscription ineffective.

The Civil Code was amended to provide mandatory formalities; these amendments legislatively overrule earlier jurisprudence that had allowed certain documents to function as acts of reinscription. Therefore, under C.C. art. 3363, neither "*an amendment of an instrument creating a mortgage or pledge, or evidencing a privilege nor an acknowledgment of the existence of a mortgage, pledge, or privilege by the mortgagor, pledgor, or obligor constitutes a reinscription of the instrument.*"

20.8(b). Reinscription of Conventional Mortgages

C.C. art. 3362 provides the requirements for reinscribing mortgages, pledges of a landlord's rental stream, and privileges affecting immovable property. C.C. art. 3362 allows the creditor to act unilaterally; no notice need be given to the debtor concerning the reinscription. There is no need for a debtor to sign any document concerning reinscription.

Under C.C. art. 3362, a creditor must record in the mortgage records a "*notice of reinscription.*" The notice must be "*signed*" by the creditor. There is no requirement that the notice of reinscription be signed by the debtor or be done in the presence of witnesses. There is also no requirement that the notice of reinscription must be by an authentic act.

C.C. art. 3362 requires that the notice of reinscription contain:

- the "*name of the mortgagor or pledgor, or the name of the obligor of the debt secured by the privilege as it appears in the recorded instrument*";
- the "*registry number or other appropriate recordation information of the instrument or of a prior notice of reinscription*"; and
- a declaration that "*the instrument is reinscribed.*"

20.8(c). Reinscription of Judicial Mortgages

C.C. art. 3362 must be used for reinscription of judicial mortgages, but the act of reinscription does not validate the judicial mortgage (see Chapter 17, above, on judicial mortgages). A timely filed notice of reinscription extends the effect of the recordation of the judicial mortgage for ten years from the date of the recordation of the notice (C.C. art. 3364), but the judgment creditor must be sure that the judgment itself does not prescribe.

Because a Louisiana judgment prescribes in ten years from the date of its rendition (C.C. art. 3501), and because of the effect of a judicial mortgage *"ceases ten years after the date of the judgment"* (C.C. art. 3359), a judgment creditor who wishes to keep a recorded judicial mortgage effective for more than ten years must not only file the act of reinscription in the mortgage records, but also revive the judgment pursuant to C.C.P. art. 2031. While it is not necessary to record the judgment of revival in the mortgage records, many cautious judgment creditors do this, in addition to filing the act of reinscription, to put third parties on notice that the judgment remains valid.

Under C.C. art. 3501, a judgment of a Louisiana state court prescribes *"ten years from its signing if no appeal has been taken, or, if an appeal has been taken, it is prescribed by the lapse of ten years from the time the judgment becomes final."* Because a suit to revive a judgment must be brought within this ten year period, and because the effect of a judicial mortgage ceases *"ten years after the date of the judgment"* (C.C. art. 3359), it is important that a timely suit to revive the judgment be brought early enough so that the revival judgment can be obtained in the ten year period.

What if a creditor did not file suit to revive a judgment until a week before the ten year prescriptive period was about to run? In such a case, it is unlikely that the revival judgment can be obtained within the ten year period and recorded. In such a situation, the judgment creditor will nonetheless need to record the act of reinscription under C.C. art 3362 before ten years from the date of the original judgment lapses while also pursuing the revival action. Louisiana statutes previously contained a provision dealing with such circumstances, allowing a creditor who filed a timely suit for revival to record a notice of *lis pendens* in the mortgage records. This notice of *lis pendens* preserved the effect of the judicial mortgage and its original ranking date as to third parties as long as the revival judgment was obtained within a statutorily-prescribed period of time after the filing of the revival suit. This statute, however, has been repealed.

While there is no case on point under the current law, cautious creditors, when they file their revival suit near the time that the judgment may lapse, typically file not only the notice of reinscription of the judicial mortgage under C.C. art. 3362, but also a notice of *lis pendens* in every parish where the original judgment was recorded.

This practitioner's approach is bolstered by C.C. art. 3368, which permits cancellation of a judicial mortgage if a suit for revival has not been filed. C.C. art. 3368 provides that *"[n]otwithstanding the reinscription of a judicial mortgage,"* the judicial mortgage may be cancelled *"upon any person's written request to which is attached a certificate from the clerk of the court rendering the judgment that no suit or motion was filed for its revival within the time required by Article 3501 or of a certified copy of a final and definitive judgment of the court rejecting the demands of the plaintiff in a suit or motion to revive the judgment."* With the *lis pendens* of record, it may be difficult for *"any person"* seeking cancellation of the judicial mortgage to show that no timely suit for revival of the judgment has been filed.

20.8(d). Reinscription of Legal Mortgages

The Civil Code does not provide any special method to reinscribe legal mortgages. It appears that the mechanism for reinscription is via the notice of reinscription under C.C. arts. 3362 and 3363.

The notice of reinscription should continue the effects of recordation for *"ten years from the date the notice is recorded"* (C.C. art. 3364). As in the case of all mortgages, however, the mortgagee must make arrangements to assure that the obligation which the legal mortgage secures does not prescribe, for if that obligation ceases to be enforceable, the accessory obligation of mortgage also will become unenforceable (C.C. art. 3319(3)).

20.8(e). When a Reinscription Is Not Timely Filed

C.C. art. 3365 deals with the effect of an untimely reinscription. In general, an untimely reinscription results in the following: (a) third parties are not affected by the mortgage, pledge, or privilege after the effects of the original inscription have ceased but may become affected again by the mortgage, pledge, or privilege once the untimely "reinscription" is made; (b) the original date when the mortgage, pledge, or privilege began affecting third parties is lost (there will be no "retroactive rank" once the new, untimely reinscription is filed); (c) a new effective date begins upon the date of the untimely reinscription; and (d) the untimely reinscription extends this new effective date for ten years.

C.C. art. 3365(A) provides that a notice of reinscription *"that is recorded after the effect of recordation of the instrument sought to be reinscribed has ceased,*

again produces the effects of recordation, but only from the time the notice of rein-
scription is recorded. The effect of recordation pursuant to this Paragraph shall
continue for ten years from the date on which the notice of reinscription is recorded,
and the instrument may be reinscribed thereafter from time to time as provided
by Article 3362."

20.8(f). Examples Concerning Reinscription of Mortgages

The following examples deal with what happens if a mortgage is timely reinscribed or is untimely reinscribed.

20.8(f)(1). Example #1

On March 1, 2000, Debtor #4 gave a conventional mortgage to Creditor #4
to secure a March 1, 2000, note payable in monthly installments over the course
of seven years, with the last payment being due March 1, 2007. Creditor #4
recorded the mortgage on April 1, 2000, in the parish mortgage records. In
early 2008, when Debtor #4 had not timely paid the note in full, although
Debtor #4 had been making interest-only payments, Creditor #4 filed an appropriate act of reinscription of the March 1, 2000, mortgage. The filing and
recordation of the reinscription occurred on February 27, 2008.

In the meantime, on December 1, 2006, Debtor #4 had given a mortgage
on the same property to Lender, who had promptly recorded the mortgage.
That mortgage secured a note payable in monthly installments over the course
of thirty years.

In this case, Creditor #4's mortgage was timely reinscribed, because the note
secured by the mortgage was due in less than nine years from the date of the
document and therefore Creditor #4's mortgage would start to affect third parties on the date it was recorded (April 1, 2000) (see Sections 19.7 and 20.2(a)1,
above) and would continue to affect third parties for ten years from the date
of that document—until March 1, 2010 (C.C. art. 3357).

The timely reinscription on February 27, 2008, by Creditor #4 preserved
the original effective date of the mortgage as to third parties (April 1, 2000)
and extended that effective date for ten years from the recording of the act of
reinscription. Therefore, the mortgage will affect third parties until February
27, 2018—ten years from the filing of the timely notice of reinscription (C.C.
art. 3364).

Because Creditor #4's timely reinscription preserved the original April 1,
2000, ranking date, Creditor #4's mortgage outranks Lender's mortgage.

Additionally, if Creditor #4 records another act of reinscription at any point before the extended effect of recordation of Creditor #4's mortgage ceases on February 20, 2018, that second act of reinscription will extend the effective date another ten years from the act of reinscription (C.C. art. 3364). There is no prohibition against a creditor filing multiple timely acts of reinscription to keep the mortgage effective as to third parties and to preserve the original ranking date (in this case, April 1, 2000).

20.8(f)(2). Example #2

The facts are the same as in Section 20.8(f)1, Example #1, except that instead of recording the act of reinscription on February 27, 2008, Creditor #4 recorded the act of reinscription on March 15, 2010.

In this instance, the act of reinscription is untimely, because although Creditor #4 recorded the act of reinscription within ten years of the original inscription (April 1, 2000), the effect of the original inscription ceased ten years from the date of the document (which was March 1, 2000), not ten years from the date of the original recordation (see Sections 19.7 and 20.2(a)1, above).

Because the reinscription was untimely, Creditor #4 obtained a new ranking date of March 15, 2010, the date of the untimely reinscription. Creditor #4's mortgage will affect third parties from March 15, 2010, until March 15, 2020, because even an untimely act of reinscription lasts for ten years from the filing of the notice of reinscription (C.C. art. 3365(A)), but it does not preserve the original ranking date of the mortgage.

Because Creditor #4's mortgage now ranks from March 15, 2010, it is outranked by Lender's mortgage.

20.8(f)(3). Example #3

The facts are the same as in Section 20.8(f)2, Example 2, except that on March 4, 2010, Interested Party files a request for cancellation of Creditor #4's mortgage under C.C. art. 3367 (see Section 20.8(e), above). One should observe that March 4, 2010 is after the lapse of the effective date of Creditor #4's mortgage (which ceased affecting third parties on March 1, 2010) and before Creditor #4's attempt an untimely reinscription on March 15, 2010.

Under C.C. art. 3367, the Interested Party's act of cancellation must be honored. Although there are no cases on point under this article, some may argue that once Interested Party acts, Creditor #4's attempted reinscription on March 15, 2010 may not be valid. C.C. art. 3365 seems to resolve this claim, because it states that reinscription "*does not require that the mortgage or pledge or evi-*

dence of the privilege be again recorded, even if the original recordation has been cancelled."

20.9. Extinction of a Mortgage

C.C. art. 3319 states that a mortgage is extinguished in one of seven ways:

- "*(1) By the extinction or destruction of the thing mortgaged.*
- "*(2) By confusion as a result of the obligee's acquiring ownership of the thing mortgaged.*
- "*(3) By prescription of all the obligations that the mortgage secures.*
- "*(4) By discharge through execution or other judicial proceeding in accordance with the law.*
- "*(5) By consent of the mortgagee.*
- "*(6) By termination of the mortgage in the manner provided by Paragraph D of Article 3298.*
- "*(7) When all the obligations, present and future, for which the mortgage is established have been incurred and extinguished.*"

20.9(a). Extinction of a Mortgage by Destruction of the Thing Mortgaged

It is seldom that immovable property subject to a mortgage is destroyed, but mortgages are not limited to immovable property. Mortgages under C.C. art. 3286 may also exist on usufructs (see Section 14.2, above), servitudes, a lessee's rights in a lease (see Section 14.3, above), and property "*made susceptible of conventional mortgage by special law.*"

If a usufruct, lease, or servitude terminates, the thing mortgaged has been extinguished (C.C. art. 3319(1)), and the mortgage ceases to be enforceable.

20.9(b). Extinction of a Mortgage by Confusion

Except for situations involving third party possessors (see Section 21.6, below), if a creditor who holds a mortgage becomes the owner of the property that is mortgaged, then the mortgage is extinguished by confusion (C.C. art. 3319(2)).

Parties to a mortgage may not agree, in advance of a default, that the lender will become the owner of the property upon the default. As the Louisiana Supreme Court has stated, since "the edict of Constantine" such clauses "are contra bonos mores ... and are unconscionable."

On the other hand, nothing prevents parties to a mortgage, after a default has occurred, to agree to transfer the property from the debtor to the creditor in exchange for a complete or partial extinguishment of the obligation the mortgage secures (C.C. arts. 2655–2659). The problem with a giving in payment, however, is that while it extinguishes the mortgage through confusion, it does not extinguish inferior mortgages and privileges.

For example, if Creditor held a valid mortgage on Debtor's property that was dated, recorded, and effective against third parties on May 1, 2015, and Bank held a second mortgage on Debtor's property dated, recorded, and effective against third parties on June 1, 2015, it is clear that if Debtor defaults on the obligation Creditor's mortgage secures, Creditor may foreclose on the property and, in the process, extinguish Bank's second mortgage (C.C.P. art. 2376 and Chapter 39, below), transforming Bank into an unsecured creditor.

On the other hand, if instead of foreclosing, Creditor agreed that Debtor could transfer the property to Creditor in satisfaction of the obligation the mortgage secures, Creditor has created a serious problem for itself. This is because the transfer of the property from Debtor to Creditor has extinguished not only the obligation that the mortgage secures but also has extinguished the mortgage by confusion (C.C. art. 3319(2)). Yet, the transfer has had no impact on Bank's mortgage. The result is that, after the transfer, Creditor owns the property subject to Bank's mortgage, which is now a first mortgage on the property.

This is why cautious creditors contemplating taking mortgaged property in satisfaction of an obligation want to perform a title examination (see Chapter 23, below) to make sure that there are no superior or inferior mortgages, liens, or encumbrances on the property.

20.9(c). Extinction of a Mortgage by Prescription of the Obligation the Mortgage Secures

Because a mortgage is an accessory obligation (C.C. art. 3282), a mortgagee *"may enforce the mortgage only to the extent that he may enforce any obligation it secures."*

While third parties cannot ascertain from the public records whether the obligation the mortgage secures has prescribed, they must make the assumption that prescription has not run and that the accessory obligation of mortgage remains enforceable (see Section 24.2, below).

On the other hand, as between the parties, the creditor may only enforce the mortgage if the principal obligation it secures has not prescribed, and the creditor who brings a foreclosure action must prove the validity of the principal obligation.

Therefore, a creditor secured by a mortgage cannot rest on the assumption that just because third parties may be potentially affected by the mortgage, the mortgage remains enforceable between the parties. This point can be illustrated by referring to the situation described in Example #1, Section 20.8(f)(1), above. In that example, on March 1, 2000, Debtor #4 gave a conventional mortgage to Creditor #4 to secure a March 1, 2000 note payable in monthly installments over the course of seven years, with the last payment being due March 1, 2007. Creditor #4 recorded the mortgage on April 1, 2000 in the parish mortgage records. In early 2008, when Debtor #4 had not timely paid the note in full, although Debtor #4 had been making interest-only payments, Creditor #4 filed and recorded an appropriate act of reinscription of the March 1, 2000 mortgage on February 27, 2008.

If Debtor stopped making interest payments on February 28, 2007, and did nothing further to acknowledge the obligation the mortgage secures, the March 1, 2000 note will have prescribed on February 28, 2012, five years from the date Debtor ceased making interest payments (C.C. art. 3498). While third parties examining the mortgage records must assume that the mortgage remains effective against them until February 27, 2018, ten years after the date of the timely reinscription (C.C. art. 3364), the prescription of the mortgage note renders the mortgage ineffective as between the parties to it. If Creditor brought suit any time after February 28, 2012 (five years from the last payment on the note that the mortgage secures) to enforce the mortgage, both Debtor and third parties could challenge its validity (C.C. art. 3341). The fact that the inscription of the mortgage had not lapsed would be no defense if the obligation the mortgage secured had prescribed.

20.9(d). Extinction of a Mortgage by Judicial Proceedings and Consent of the Mortgagee

C.C. art. 3319 states that a mortgage may be extinguished, among other ways, "(4) *By discharge through execution or other judicial proceeding in accordance with the law*" and "(5) *By consent of the mortgagee.*"

A judgment in either an ordinary proceeding that recognizes the mortgage or in an executory proceeding (see Chapter 38) results in a judicial sale. At the judicial sale, the mortgage of the foreclosing creditor is extinguished and the creditor receives a privilege on the proceeds of the sale.

The mortgagee/creditor may always consent to the extinguishment of the mortgage (see Section 20.3(a), above).

20.9(e). Extinction of a Mortgage That Secures Future Advances

C.C. art. 3319 deals with mortgages that may secure future advances. These mortgages are extinguished "*By termination of the mortgage in the manner provided by Paragraph D of Article 3298*" or "*(7) When all the obligations, present and future, for which the mortgage is established have been incurred and extinguished.*"

C.C. art. 3298(D) permits the borrower to terminate the mortgage "*when an obligation does not exist and neither mortgagor nor the mortgagee is bound to the other or to a third person to permit an obligation secured by that mortgage to be incurred.*"

A properly documented future advance mortgage to secure a fluctuating-line of credit does not describe but a single note (see Section 13.3(b)(4), above). If this line of credit has been paid off, C.C. art. 3298(D) provides a mechanism for the debtor to compel the creditor to terminate the mortgage. Under this provision, the debtor must give "*reasonable notice*" to the creditor of the debtor's desire to terminate the agreement and the parties "*may contract with reference to what constitutes reasonable notice.*"

Chapter 21

The Rights of
Third Party Possessors

21.1. Third Party Possessors: An Overview

"Third party possessors" are those who own property encumbered by a mortgage but are *"not personally bound for the obligation the mortgage secures"* (C.C. art. 3315). This book refers to them as "third party possessors" because that is the phrase most lawyers use, reflecting the fact that these persons are both third parties to the mortgage and are possessors of the property affected by the mortgage.

The importance of a third party possessor arises if there is a foreclosure sale of the property. In such an instance, the third party possessor's rights may be extinguished by the sale (C.C.P. art. 2376), but the Civil Code allows the third party possessor the possibility of realizing some value from the improvements that the third party possessor has placed upon the property.

21.2. The Definition of a Third Party Possessor

C.C. art. 3315 defines a *"third possessor"* as *"one who acquires mortgaged property and who is not personally bound for the obligation the mortgage secures."* Therefore, a current owner is not a third party possessor if (a) the owner is a mortgagor, whether the mortgage was granted to secure the owner's personal obligation or was granted *in rem* (either to secure the debt of the owner or of another, see Comments to C.C. art. 3315 and Section 12.11, above) or (b) the owner has assumed a prior mortgage on the property (C.C.P. art. 2702, and Section 19.5, above).

The following types of acts give rise to third party possessor status for the purchaser of property: a sale "subject to" a mortgage (see Comments to C.C. art. 3315 and Section 21.5(b), below), a cash sale (see Section 21.5(c), below), or a quit-claim deed (see Section 21.5(e) below). On the other hand, a "sale with assumption of mortgage" means that the buyer has become personally liable on the obligation the mortgage secures; therefore, such a buyer is not a third party possessor (see Section 19.5, above, and Section 21.5(d), below).

The reason that cash sales give rise to third party possessor status for the buyer is that the seller, in the cash sale, has failed to disclose the existence of preexisting mortgages and encumbrances; without an express assumption of the mortgage by the buyer, the buyer is not obligated to recognize the mortgage, acknowledge its validity or existence, or be bound by it in any fashion. The preexisting mortgage continues after the transfer of the property to the buyer (C.C. arts. 3278 and 3279), but the buyer has no personal liability to the mortgage holder (C.C. art. 3315). The seller in a cash sale who fails to disclose an existing encumbrance on the property has breached the seller's warranties (see Section 21.5, below).

The reason that a sale "subject to" a mortgage gives rise to third party possessor status for the buyer is that the seller, in such a sale, has disclosed that an existing mortgage encumbers the property, but the "subject to" language means that the buyer, while recognizing that the mortgage exists, is not undertaking any personal liability to pay the mortgagee (see Section 21.5(B), below). The buyer is merely acknowledging that if the preexisting mortgage is not paid, the property may be seized and sold by the holder of the mortgage.

The reason that a quit-claim deed gives rise to third party possessor status for the buyer is that the seller, in such a sale, has expressly indicated that the seller is not warranting anything about the property (see Section 21.5(e), below). The seller in a quit-claim deed is not even warranting that the seller has title to the property. Whether or not the buyer has performed a title examination (see Chapter 23, below) prior to buying property under a quit-claim deed, the buyer under a quit-claim deed has not undertaken any personal obligation to pay any preexisting mortgage or encumbrance.

21.3. Liability of a Third Party Possessor

While a third party possessor's property may be encumbered by a prior mortgage, the third party possessor is not personally liable on the obligation the mortgage secures, because, by definition, third party possessor status does not apply to a buyer who has assumed a mortgage (see Section 21.2, above). Even though the third party possessor is not personally liable for the mortgage, the holder of the mortgage may still seize and sell the property and obtain a privilege on the proceeds of the sale, because the mortgage, as an indivisible real right, remains on the property even after the original mortgagor sells the property (see Section 11.4, above).

While a third party possessor is not personally liable to pay preexisting mortgages, C.C. art. 3316 creates liability for third party possessors who "trash" the property to the detriment of secured creditors. It provides that the *"deteriorations, which proceed from the deed or neglect of the third possessor to the prejudice of the creditors who have a privilege or a mortgage, give rise against the former to an action of indemnification."* Note that this liability is merely for the "deteriorations" to the property from the time the third party possessor came into possession; it does not make the third party possessor liable to the mortgage holder for the obligations the mortgage secures.

21.4. The Four Main Rights of a Third Party Possessor

The statutory rights of a third party possessor are found in two locations: C.C. art. 3317 and C.C.P. art. 2703. The third party possessor has four main rights: the right to bring an action in warranty against the seller (Section 21.5(a), below); the right of payment (Section 21.6, below); the right to arrest the seizure and sale (Section 21.7, below); and the right to claim enhanced value (Section 21.8, below).

21.5. A Third Party Possessor's Warranty Rights

One who sells property to a third party possessor usually explicitly or implicitly warrants the title to the property and the right of possession (see Section 21.5(a), below), except in the case of quit-claim deeds (see Section 21.5(e), below). Thus, warranties exist in every act of cash sale (see Section 21.5(c), below) and even in acts of sale that are "subject to" a mortgage (see Section 21.5(b), below). However, there is no warranty when a sale is by a quit-claim deed (see Section 21.5(e), below).

21.5(a). The Seller's Warranty of Title and Warranty against Eviction

Every sale of immovable property contains both a warranty against eviction and a warranty of title (C.C. arts. 2500–2517).

These warranties are "implied in every sale" (C.C. art. 2503), although the parties may increase the warranty, decrease it, or even eliminate it (C.C. art. 2503).

These warranties against eviction and of title include a warranty that "*covers encumbrances on the thing that were not declared at the time of the sale, with the exception of apparent servitudes and natural and legal nonapparent servitudes, which need not be declared.*" (C.C. art. 2500). If the seller has not disclosed items that impact title or that could cause an eviction, the seller is liable to the purchaser. A detailed discussion of the Civil Code warranty rules is beyond the scope of this Précis; however, the following sections detail how the warranty articles interact with acts of sales subject to a mortgage, acts of cash sale, acts of sales with assumption of mortgages, and quit-claim deeds.

21.5(b). Sales "Subject to a Mortgage" and the Seller's Warranty

A seller who sells by an act of "sale subject to mortgage" is indicating that the seller has revealed the existence of the prior mortgage; therefore, the buyer cannot claim a breach of warranty of title concerning the mortgage or a warranty against eviction if the mortgage holder forecloses.

If the seller has retained real security (such as a vendor's privilege or mortgage) to assure payment of the purchase price, the buyer may be a third party possessor as to the preexisting mortgage but not a third party possessor as to the seller. Section 21.11(e), below, gives an example of a purchaser of property who is a third party possessor as to some creditors holding mortgages but not as to others.

21.5(c). Cash Sales and the Seller's Warranty

A seller who sells by an act of "cash sale" that does not reveal any prior encumbrances is warranting that the title is free and clear of encumbrances. A "cash sale" document states, on its face, that the seller has received the entire purchase price at closing. Nothing more is owed to the seller, and the seller does not retain any rights in the property, whether by security interest or otherwise.

If there exists a prior encumbrance of record, the buyer who purchases via a "cash sale" may sue the seller for a breach of warranty of title, even if the mortgage holder does not foreclose. The buyer may also sue for breach of warranty against eviction even if the mortgage holder does bring foreclosure proceedings.

21.5(d). Sales with Assumption and the Seller's Warranty

A seller who sells by an "act of assumption" has revealed the existence of the prior mortgage. By "assuming" the mortgage, the buyer has become personally bound on the obligation the mortgage secures; the buyer is now liable *in solido* with the original obligor (see Section 19.5, above). Therefore, the rules of recordation of the mortgage are inapplicable to the buyer (see Section 19.5, above), and the buyer may not bring an action for breach of the warranty of title or breach of the warranty against eviction concerning that mortgage.

21.5(e). Quit-Claim Deeds and the Seller's Warranty

A seller who sells by a "quit-claim" deed makes no warranty whatsoever and is waiving all implicit warranties. C.C. art. 2502 describes what lawyers call a quit-claim deed and states that the seller transfers rights without warranting them and the seller "*does not owe restitution of the price to the [buyer] in case of eviction, nor may that transfer be rescinded for lesion.*"

The official comments to C.C. art. 2502 describes the implications of a quit-claim deed: "At common law, the distinguishing factor of a quitclaim deed is that it is an instrument that purports to convey nothing more than the interest or estate of the grantor, if any he has, at the time of the conveyance, rather than the property itself. Conveyance by quitclaim does not include any implication that the vendor has good title to the property, or even that he has any title at all. Thus, the purchaser by quitclaim deed is put on immediate notice that he is not acquiring land but merely the interest of his vendor in the land … What is called quitclaim at common law is an assignment of rights without warranty in the civil law."

21.6. The Third Party Possessor's Right Of Payment

If a foreclosure is threatened or instituted, the third party possessor has the legal right to pay "*the balance due on the indebtedness, in principal, interest, at-*

torney's fees, and costs" (C.C.P. art. 2703(1)). In other words, the third party possessor may pay off the obligation that the mortgage secures and be subrogated to the rights of the mortgagee.

As background to this concept, remember that when one buys property "subject to" a mortgage, the seller has revealed the existence of the prior mortgage and has not breached the warranty of title (see Section 21.5(a), above). The purchase price listed in the "sale subject to the mortgage" takes into account the balance on the existing mortgage, although the purchaser has no personal liability for that sum. For example, if property is listed for sale for $100,000 and is encumbered by a $25,000 preexisting mortgage placed on the property by the seller, the buyer who bought the property for $100,000 "subject to" the mortgage usually would pay the seller in cash only $75,000, because the mortgage would remain in place after the sale.

Therefore, if the buyer later pays off the mortgage holder, as allowed by C.C.P. art. 2703(1), the buyer is entitled to legal subrogation under C.C. art. 1829(2), which grants legal subrogation to a buyer *"of movable or immovable property who uses the purchase money to pay creditors holding any privilege, pledge, mortgage, or security interest on the property."* If a buyer does this, the buyer has recourse against the seller (see C.C. art. 3317 and Comment (c) to that article).

Alternatively, instead of paying off the obligation secured by the mortgage and extinguishing the mortgage, the third party possessor could purchase the obligation secured by the preexisting mortgage. Now, the buyer would be both owner of the property and the holder of the preexisting mortgage, but C.C. art. 3317 contemplates this situation and provides that, if this occurs, the mortgage is not extinguished by confusion. C.C. art. 3317 states that a *"third possessor who performs the obligation secured by the mortgage is subrogated to the rights of the obligee. In such a case, the mortgage is not extinguished by confusion as to other mortgages, privileges, or charges burdening the mortgaged property when the third possessor acquired the mortgaged property and for which he is not personally bound."*

21.7. The Third Party Possessor's Right to Arrest the Seizure and Sale

A third party possessor is not a party to the mortgage. Therefore, the third party possessor may claim that the mortgage does not affect him because the mortgage is invalid, extinguished, or not properly recorded or reinscribed.

Under C.C.P. art. 2703(2), the third party possessor may *"[a]rrest the seizure and sale on any of the grounds mentioned in [C.C.P. art.] 2751, or on the ground that the mortgage or privilege was not recorded, or that the inscription of the recordation thereof had preempted."*

Note that an owner of property who is a mortgagor (and owners who are not third parties to the mortgage) cannot claim that mortgage was not properly recorded or reinscribed. The reason is that recordation is irrelevant to the validity of a mortgage between the parties to it (see Section 19.2, above). Recordation (and thus arguments about recording and reinscription) are relevant only when third parties are involved.

21.8. The Third Party Possessor's Right to Claim Enhanced Value

Even if the third party possessor does not have enough money to pay off the foreclosing creditor (see Section 21.6, above), and even if the third party possessor cannot contest the foreclosure suit because the mortgage is valid as to third parties (see Section 21.7, above), the third party possessor may claim enhanced value by intervening into the foreclosure proceedings.

C.C.P. art. 2703(3) states that the third party possessor may intervene *"in the executory proceeding to assert any claim which he has to the enhanced value of the property due to improvements placed on the property by him, or by any prior third possessor through whom he claims ownership of the property."*

If the holder of a prior mortgage brings suit by ordinary proceedings, seeking a personal judgment on the principal obligation secured by the mortgage and recognition of the mortgage, the third party possessor also may intervene into that proceeding (*cf.* C.C.P. art. 1092).

21.9. The Limits of a Third Party Possessor's Claims to Enhanced Value

The third party possessor's rights to claim enhanced value is limited to the lesser of (a) the cost of the improvements made by the third party possessor, or (b) the amount that the property value has been enhanced by these improvements.

C.C. art. 3318 provides that a third party possessor *"may recover the cost of any improvements he has made to the property to the extent the improvements have enhanced the value of the property, out of the proceeds realized from en-*

forcement of the mortgage, after the mortgagee has received the unenhanced value of the property."

The improvements on which a third party possessor may base a claim are not a narrow category. They can include items such as erecting a building on the property, adding onto an existing structure, repairing or replacing a roof, or even renovating a kitchen or bathroom. The issue is not whether the improvements are big or small, but rather whether the third party possessor has made any improvements that have enhanced the property's value.

21.10. The Procedure by Which a Third Party Possessor Claims Enhanced Value

To understand how a third party possessor claims enhanced value, one must consider how a foreclosure by executory process operates. For a discussion of executory process, see Sections 38.1(b) and 38.1(c), below. For examples, see Sections 21.11(a) through 21.11(e), below.

The appraisal by the foreclosing creditor is based on the current value of the property. The third party possessor is concerned, however, not only with the current value of the property, but also with the difference between (a) the current value of the property with enhancements or improvements and (b) the value of the property had the improvements not been made. The reason for this concern is that only by proving these items may the third party possessor claim rights under C.C. art. 3318, which gives the third party possessor the right to claim the lesser of the costs of improvements or the value of the enhancement to the property resulting from the improvements (see Section 21.9, above).

Therefore, the third party possessor will need to show what the appraised value of the property is (at the time of foreclosure) without the enhancements. In other words, an appraiser hired by the third party possessor will need to consider what the property would have been worth at the time of foreclosure if the enhancements had not been made.

Since the creditor's appraiser is concerned only with the current value of the property as it currently exists, the only way for the third party possessor's rights to be protected and for the third party's appraisal to be properly asserted is for the third party possessor (a) to intervene in the proceedings under C.C.P. art. 1092 (and under C.C.P art. 2703 for executory proceedings) prior to the judicial sale and (b) to seek a court order allowing the third party possessor to have a separate appraisal to show the difference between the existing value of the property as it currently exists and what the value of the property would be if the improvements had not been made.

C.C.P. art. 1092 provides in part that, when "*the intervener claims such a mortgage or privilege only on part of the property seized, and the intervention is filed prior to the judicial sale, the court may order the separate sale of the property on which the intervener claims a mortgage or privilege; or if a separate sale thereof is not feasible or necessary, or the intervener has no right thereto, the court may order the separate appraisement of the entire property seized and of the part thereof on which the intervener claims a mortgage or privilege.*"

Louisiana jurisprudence has recognized the right of a third party possessor to obtain a separate appraisal. The third party possessor's claim to enhanced value is akin to that of a privilege (since it may outrank a portion of a prior mortgage, as the examples in 21.11, below, demonstrate). This is because the enhanced value affects only a portion of the property (the portion of the property that has been "enhanced").

The third party possessor, to fully protect its rights, will not only need a separate appraisal but also will need to be able to prove the costs of the improvements that have been made to the property (see Sections 21.9, above, and 21.11, below).

21.11. How the Proceeds of a Sheriff's Sale Are Distributed When a Third Party Possessor Properly Claims Enhanced Value

There is a four-step process in distributing the proceeds of a sheriff's sale when a third party possessor has timely intervened, obtained a separate appraisal to prove the enhanced value, and proven the cost of the improvements. Set forth below is the four-step process required by C.C. art. 3318 and the jurisprudence. This description, however, omits discussion of payment of the sheriff's costs commission for conducting the sale (R.S. 33:1428(A)(7)(a)).

First, the proceeds of the sale are distributed to the foreclosing creditor up to value of the property, not including the enhancements and improvements made by the third party possessor. This step is sometimes referred to as the "unenhanced value."

Second, any sales proceeds that remain are distributed to the third party possessor to the lesser of the cost of the improvements or the enhanced value the improvements created.

Third, any sales proceeds that remain are distributed to the foreclosing creditor until the foreclosing creditor's debt is paid in full.

Fourth, any sales proceeds that remain are distributed to inferior secured creditors on the property and then to the third party possessor.

The following examples illustrate how this works. Each of these examples assumes the same basic set of facts.

The facts are:

- Debtor granted a $100,000 mortgage on vacant tract of land to Creditor to secure a $100,000 loan made by Creditor to Debtor. This is the only encumbrance on the property.
- Debtor sells the property to TPP, a third party possessor, by an "act of sale subject to mortgage" that reveals the existence of the mortgage held by Creditor (see Section 21.5(b), above).
- Three years after buying the tract, TPP erects a home on the property.
- One year after TPP's building the home, Creditor institutes executory proceedings to foreclose on the property because of a default by Debtor in the payment of the obligation secured by the mortgage.
- In the executory proceedings Creditor proves that the debt secured by the mortgage is $100,000 (in principal and interest).
- In the foreclosure proceedings, the Creditor submits an appraisal showing that, at the time of foreclosure, the property is worth $100,000.
- The sheriff's sale brings in $100,000 (net of the sheriff's commission and the costs of the proceedings).

21.11(a). Example #1

TPP, who built the home, does nothing. TPP does not intervene in the sale.

In this instance, TPP has not properly or timely claimed the rights to enhanced value. Therefore, Creditor gets the entire $100,000 of the sales proceeds.

21.11(b). Example #2

TPP, who built the house, intervenes and proves that the house cost $80,000 to build. TPP also submits an appraisal showing that the value of the tract of land without the house is $45,000.

Thus, in this example, TPP's appraisal of $45,000 reflects the value the land without improvements *as of the time of foreclosure* (not at the time the TPP acquired it and not at the time of the construction of the improvements); this is because TPP must prove "enhancement" at the time of foreclosure. Therefore, TPP's appraiser must appraise the land at the time of foreclosure as if these improvements had not been made. There is no need for TPP's appraiser to appraise the land with the improvements; the creditor's appraiser has already done this.

Under this example, the enhanced value resulting from the construction of the house is $55,000 ($100,000 current value with enhancements minus $45,000 of value without enhancements). Because the enhanced value ($55,000) is less than the costs of the improvements ($80,000), TPP may claim only the lesser of those two figures, or $55,000.

In this situation, the $100,000 sheriff's sales proceeds would be distributed as follows. This chart also tracks how the distribution of the sales proceeds affects Creditor's claim against Debtor for the $100,000 loan secured by the mortgage on which Creditor is foreclosing:

TO	FOR	AMOUNT	Subtotal of Distribution of Sheriff's Sale Proceeds	Balance of $100,000 Debt Owing from Debtor to Creditor
Foreclosing Creditor	Value of property without enhancements	$45,000	$45,000	$55,000
TPP	Lesser of costs or enhancement	$55,000	$100,000	$55,000
Foreclosing Creditor	Balance (if any) to apply to Debtors' obligation to Creditor	$0		$55,000
TPP	Balance (if any) to TPP (because there are no inferior secured creditors)	$0		$55,000

Note that in this instance, although the property is worth $100,000, Creditor gets only $45,000 from the sales proceeds.

Creditor will have an unsecured claim against the Debtor for $55,000 (the difference between what Creditor received at the sheriff's sale and what Debtor owes Creditor).

Creditor has no claim against TPP for the $55,000. As a third party possessor, TPP has no personal liability to Creditor.

It should be observed that there is at least one Louisiana intermediate appellate court case indicating that the enhancement is the difference between the current value of the property and the value of the property at the time the TPP purchased it. No Louisiana Supreme Court decision has validated this approach, and it is submitted that this appellate case may have employed the wrong analysis.

The appraisal that the foreclosing creditor submits must indicate the value of the property at the time of foreclosure. There is no legal reason why the "enhancement" value should be measured at a different point in time. For example, if TPP bought the property and built a house before a hurricane, then a hurricane hit and seriously damaged the house, and then the foreclosure occurred before the TPP could do repairs, it could not be proper to measure "enhancement" based on the pre-hurricane value; the only appropriate test of enhancement should be the difference between the value of the property at the time of foreclosure with enhancements (as shown by Creditor's foreclosure sale appraisal), and the value of the property at the time of foreclosure as if the enhancements (in their condition at the time of foreclosure) did not exist (see Section 21.11(d), Example #4, below). This "value without enhancement" procedure is something appraisers commonly perform.

Therefore, in this Example #2 and the following examples, this Précis has not followed the indication of the intermediate appellate court and will proceed with the belief that the proper analysis reflects that "enhancement" is properly measured by the difference between the total value of the property at the time of foreclosure sale and the value of the property at the time of foreclosure sale as if the enhancements (in their current condition) had not been made.

21.11(c). Example #3

TPP, who built the house, intervenes and proves that the house cost $20,000 to build. TPP also submits an appraisal showing that the value of the tract of land without the house is $45,000.

Therefore, the enhanced value caused by the construction of the house is $55,000 ($100,000 current value with enhancements minus $45,000 of value without enhancements). Because the enhanced value ($55,000) is more than the costs of the improvements ($20,000), TPP may claim only the lesser of those two figures, or $20,000.

In this situation, the $100,000 sheriff's sales proceeds would be distributed as follows:

TO	FOR	AMOUNT	Subtotal of Distribution of Sheriff's Sale Proceeds	Balance of $100,000 Debt Owing from Debtor to Creditor
Foreclosing Creditor	Value of property without enhancements	$45,000	$45,000	$55,000
TPP	Lesser of costs or enhancement	$20,000	$65,000	$55,000
Foreclosing Creditor	Balance (if any) to apply to Debtors' obligation to Creditor	$35,000	$100,000	$20,000
TPP	Balance (if any) to TPP (because there are no inferior secured creditors)	$0		$20,000

Note that now Creditor gets only $80,000 from the sales proceeds and has an unsecured claim against Debtor for $20,000.

21.11(d). Example #4

TPP, who built the house, intervenes and proves that the house cost $120,000 to build. TPP also submits an appraisal showing that the value of the tract of land without the house is $10,000. This situation of the cost to build a house being greater than the property is worth today is not necessarily unusual; consider housing values in areas damaged by hurricanes or flooding where the foreclosure occurs before the damage has been fully repaired.

In this example, the enhanced value caused by the construction of the house is $90,000 ($100,000 current value with enhancements minus $10,000 of value without enhancements). Because the enhanced value ($90,000) is less than the costs of the improvements ($120,000), TPP may claim only the lesser of those two figures, or $90,000.

In this situation, the $100,000 sheriff's sales proceeds would be distributed as follows:

TO	FOR	AMOUNT	Subtotal of Distribution of Sheriff's Sale Proceeds	Balance of $100,000 Debt Owing from Debtor to Creditor
Foreclosing Creditor	Value of property without enhancements	$10,000	$10,000	$90,000
TPP	Lesser of costs or enhancement	$90,000	$100,000	$90,000
Foreclosing Creditor	Balance (if any) to apply to Debtors' obligation to Creditor	$0	$0	$90,000
TPP	Balance (if any) to TPP (because there are no inferior secured creditors)	$0	$0	$90,000

Now, the bulk of the sales proceeds have gone to TPP, while Creditor is left with a $90,000 unsecured claim against Debtor.

21.11(e). Example #5

In this example, the facts are slightly different from the ones above. Instead of the Creditor's appraisal at sheriff's sale being $100,000, the property appraises for $150,000 and sells for that amount (net of sheriff's commissions and court costs).

Additionally, to build the house, TPP had borrowed $90,000 from Lender, and Lender secured that loan by a $90,000 second mortgage on the property (Creditor holds the first mortgage).

The home cost the entire $90,000 to build, and TPP's separate appraisal shows that the value of the tract without the house is $63,000. Therefore, the house enhanced the property value (at the time of foreclosure) by $87,000 ($150,000 value of land with the house minus $63,000 value of land without the house).

Under these facts, Lender can intervene and claim TPP's third party possessor rights. This is because while TPP is a third party possessor as to Creditor, TPP is personally liable to Lender and is not a third party on Lender's mortgage. Lender's mortgage encumbers all of TPP's rights in the property, including the right to claim enhanced value. Therefore, under the jurisprudence, Lender can intervene and asserts TPP's third party possessor rights. The distribution would be as follows:

TO	FOR	AMOUNT	Subtotal of Distribution of Sheriff's Sale Proceeds	Balance of $100,000 Debt Owing from Debtor to Creditor	Balance of $90,000 Debt Owing from TPP to Lender
Foreclosing Creditor	Value of property without enhancements	$63,000	$63,000	$37,000	$90,000
Lender (claiming TPP's third party possessor status)	Lesser of costs or enhancement	$87,000	$150,000	$37,000	$3,000
Foreclosing Creditor	Balance (if any) to apply to Debtors' obligation to Creditor	$0	$0	$37,000	$3,000
Lender (claiming TPP's third party possessor status)	Balance (if any) to inferior creditor Lender, and then to TPP	$0	$0	$37,000	$3,000

Note that although Creditor was owed $100,000, and although the property sold for $150,000, Creditor (who held the first mortgage) gets only $63,000 of the sales proceeds and has an unsecured claim against Debtor for $37,000. On the other hand, because of the third party possessor rules, Lender, who held a second mortgage, gets more from the sale ($87,000) than does the first mortgage holder.

Also note that as a result of this transaction, Debtor is left owing $37,000 to Creditor on an unsecured claim, while TPP owes Lender only $3,000 as an unsecured claim.

This example demonstrates the powerful nature of the third party possessor's rights and the importance of inferior creditors considering intervening into the proceedings if they can prove that the third party possessor is personally liable to them.

Chapter 22

The Resolutory Condition, Rights of First Refusal, and Rights of Redemption

22.1. An Overview of the Resolutory Condition, Rights of First Refusal, and Rights of Redemption

Mortgages may secure creditors regardless of whether the creditor's right arises as a seller or as a third party lender. Sellers who retain mortgages to secure a portion of the purchase price, however, get additional rights that mere lenders (who are not sellers) do not have.

Sellers, in addition to being able to contract for mortgages to secure the purchase price of property sold on credit, can obtain four other important rights. Two arise as a function of a credit sale: the resolutory condition and the vendor's privilege (see Chapter 33, below). The remaining two (the right of first refusal and the right of redemption) are contractual rights that the seller must expressly seek and set forth in the act of sale.

A resolutory condition essentially unwinds a sale and puts the buyer and seller back into the position they were prior to the sale. Resolutory conditions arise by operation of law as an aspect of certain sales (see Section 22.2, below).

A vendor's privilege arises by operation of law in a credit sale if the sales document is recorded in the parish mortgage records (see Chapter 33 below).

A right of first refusal, in contrast to a resolutory condition, does not arise by operation of law but rather is a result of an express clause contained in the act of sale or a related document. A right of first refusal runs in favor of the seller; when the seller exercises its right of first refusal, the seller is insisting on specific performance of the contract or sale. If the buyer desires to sell the property to a third party, a right of first refusal essentially requires the buyer to grant the seller the right to purchase the property on the same terms and conditions upon which the buyer and third party had agreed (see Section 22.3(a), below).

A right of redemption, like the right of first refusal, does not arise by operation of law but rather is the result of an express clause in the act of sale or a related document. Unlike the right of first refusal, the right of redemption is not dependent on the act of the buyer in finding a third party purchaser. Rather, a right of redemption allows the seller to unilaterally regain ownership of the property by paying a predetermined price to the buyer (see Section 22.4, below).

The result of the successful exercise of the resolutory condition, the right of first refusal, and the right of redemption are, in one sense, the same; the seller regains ownership of the property that had been sold to the buyer and the seller may judicially extinguish all inferior transfers, mortgages, liens, and encumbrances by the buyer. The impact on third parties of the successful exercise of the resolutory condition, the right of first refusal, and the right of redemption are also similar: these rights "run" with the property, impact future owners of the property, and can result in extinguishing of all transfers, sales, privileges, mortgages, liens, and encumbrances placed on the property by the buyer or any future owner.

The resolutory condition, the right of first refusal, and the right of redemption differ, however, in how they are exercised, what they mean for the parties and third parties, and in the applicable maximum length for which they may be contracted or utilized.

22.2. The Resolutory Condition

Resolutory conditions arise by operation of law in every act of sale of immovable or movable property where, after the sale has been completed, the buyer must pay the seller or render some additional performance to the seller.

22.2(a). Definition of a Resolutory Condition

A resolutory condition arises in every act of sale where the "*buyer fails to pay the price*" (C.C. art. 2561). Resolutory conditions do not arise if no sale is involved, for resolutory conditions are granted only to sellers of property.

When a resolutory condition exists, the seller "*may sue for dissolution of the sale*" (C.C. art. 2561). Thus, a resolutory condition does not seek specific performance to compel the buyer to pay the purchase price; rather, a resolutory condition "unwinds" a sale and puts the parties back into the position that they occupied immediately before the sale, with the seller regaining ownership of the property.

Every credit sale gives rise to a resolutory condition, and every credit sale of immovable property is always secured by both a resolutory condition (which arises by operation of law from the fact of a credit sale) and a vendor's privilege (which arises by operation of law, if the credit sale is filed for recordation in the mortgage records, see Chapter 33, below), unless the parties expressly waive these rights in writing.

While a seller may also retain a mortgage (a consensual security device) to secure the credit portion of the purchase price, the Louisiana State Law Institute comments to C.C. art. 2561 note that a seller's right to exercise the resolutory condition "*is not dependent upon the existence of a security device such as a mortgage or privilege.*"

The resolutory condition is not limited to the failure to pay the purchase price. Resolutory conditions also may arise when part of the consideration for the sale is a future act of the buyer that the buyer fails to perform.

For example, assume that Seller sells Lot A to Buyer. Lot A fronts on a Road A. Seller retains ownership of adjacent Lot B that fronts on Road B. Buyer agrees in the act of sale that if Buyer ever develops Lot A into a subdivision, Buyer will grant Seller and any future owner of Lot B a servitude across Lot A to access Road A.

In this example, Buyer has created a resolutory condition. If Buyer develops the subdivision and does not give road access to Seller or his successors and assigns, they may exercise the resolutory condition to unwind the sale. As this example shows, a resolutory condition can exist even if what remains to be done by a buyer is an obligation to perform rather than an obligation to pay.

22.2(b). The Effect of a Resolutory Condition on Third Parties

In a sale of immovable property, a resolutory condition exists without special terminology or "magical words" as long as it is apparent on the face of the document in the public records that a portion of the purchase price has not been paid or that something remains to be done by the buyer for the seller. If the document in the public records does not reveal this, there is no resolutory condition even if the seller can demonstrate, in court, that the purchase price was not paid.

Because of the public records doctrine, third parties can ascertain whether a resolutory condition exists by examining the act of sale. A resolutory condition exists even if the credit sale is never filed for recordation in the mortgage records. Filing of the credit sale in the conveyance records is sufficient for the resolutory condition affect third parties (see Law Institute comment (h) to C.C. art. 2561).

By contrast, a resolutory condition in a sale of movables is not dependent on the language of the document; if the seller can demonstrate that the purchase price was not paid and the buyer remains in possession of the movable, the seller can exercise the resolutory condition.

22.2(c). Extensions of Time and Resolutory Conditions

The ability of a court to grant an extension of time to a buyer when a seller wishes to exercise the resolutory condition depends on whether the sale is of a movable or an immovable.

Under C.C. art. 2562, if the sale is of an immovable *"and there is no danger that the seller may lose the price and the thing, the court, according to the circumstances, may grant the buyer an extension of time, not in excess of sixty days, to make payment, and shall pronounce the sale dissolved if the buyer fails to pay within that time. When there is such a danger, the court may not grant the buyer an extension of time for payment."*

Yet, under C.C. art. 2563, there are instances by which a buyer may avoid automatic dissolution. Art. 2563 states that this occurs, despite "automatic" dissolution language in the contract, *"for as long as the seller has not given the buyer notice that he avails himself of that clause or has not filed suit for dissolution,"* the resolutory condition is not triggered.

By contrast, under C.C. art. 2564, if the sale is of a movable *"and the seller chooses to seek judicial dissolution of the sale because of the failure of the buyer to perform, the court may not grant to the buyer any extension of time to perform."*

22.2(d). The Prescriptive Period on the Resolutory Condition

There is a difference in the prescriptive period applicable to contracts creating resolutory conditions that arose before January 1, 1995, and those that arose after that date. For sales that occur after January 1, 1995, the seller's right to exercise the resolutory condition prescribes at the same time as the note that the buyer gave for the unpaid portion of the purchase price (C.C. art. 2561).

Prescription on a negotiable instrument is five years from the date it is due (C.C. art. 3498).

For sales that occurred before January 1, 1995, however, the Louisiana Supreme Court has ruled that the right to exercise the resolutory condition expires ten years after the last payment date of the note the buyer gave for the unpaid portion of the purchase price. In other words, for pre-January 1, 1995, sales, it is possible that the resolutory condition can be exercised by a seller even if the note for the purchase price may have prescribed and the accessory obligation of mortgage rendered unenforceable because the principal obligation which it secures has prescribed.

The following two examples illustrate issues that arise involving resolutory conditions for sales occurring before and after January 1, 1995.

22.2(d)(1). Resolutory Condition, Example 1

On March 1, 1990, Seller sold to Buyer immovable property by an "Act of Sale With Mortgage." This document consists of a credit sale in which Seller has retained a mortgage to secure the payment of the financed portion of the purchase price.

Buyer gave Seller a note payable in monthly installments over the course of thirty years, with the last payment due March 1, 2020. The note was described in the act of sale and the note was secured by a mortgage on the property; the mortgage was contained in the "act of sale" document; there were not two separate documents.

Seller promptly recorded the Act in both the mortgage and conveyance records of the parish where the property is located.

Even though the final payment is not due until 2020, because this transaction occurred before January 1, 1995, the jurisprudential rules that controlled the transaction pre-amendment to C.C. art. 2561 apply. If Buyer does not timely make all payments and does not acknowledge the obligation (thereby interrupting prescription), the note will prescribe on March 1, 2025 (the note is due March 1, 2020; prescription on a note is five years, C.C. art. 3498). Even if the note had been acknowledged to interrupt prescription, however, absent a lawsuit foreclosing on the mortgage or challenging it, the mortgage will cease to affect third parties on March 1, 2026, because third parties cannot ascertain from the public records whether prescription has been interrupted on the note (see Section 20.2(a), above, and Section 24.2, below).

Yet, although the mortgage will cease to affect third parties in 2026, under Louisiana Supreme Court jurisprudence, the resolutory condition will continue to affect third parties until March 1, 2030 (ten years from the date the last payment on the note became due). It is worth observing that the ten year period runs from the date the last payment was due on the note; it does not run ten years from the date of the prescriptive period on the note.

This result occurs even though the note may have prescribed; remember that third parties cannot ascertain from the public records whether prescription has run on the note.

Further, Seller could exercise the resolutory condition even if Seller had then sued Buyer on the mortgage after the mortgage note had prescribed but before the mortgage inscription lapsed. Seller would lose, because the mortgage, being an accessory obligation, would have been extinguished by operation of law (C.C. arts. 3282 and 3319).

Moreover, Seller could exercise the resolutory condition even if the inscription of the mortgage had lapsed for failure to timely reinscribe it (see Sections 20.2 and 20.8, above). The rationale behind this jurisprudence, which was overruled by the Civil Code amendments that became effective in 1995, was that a resolutory condition was not an action for specific performance on the note and the mortgage that secured it; rather, it was a separate action to dissolve the sale that was independent of the enforceability of the note. As observed above, however, for all transactions after January 1, 1995, this former jurisprudential rule has been legislatively superseded, but those examining title must be aware of it when looking at transactions that occurred prior to January 1, 1995.

22.2(d)(2). Resolutory Condition, Example 2

On June 1, 2000, Seller sold to Buyer immovable property by an "Act of Sale With Mortgage." Buyer gave to Seller a note payable in monthly installments over the course of twenty years, with the last payment due June 1, 2020. The note is described in the act of sale and the note was secured by a mortgage on the property; the mortgage was contained in the "act of sale" document; there were not two separate documents.

Seller promptly recorded the Act in both the mortgage and conveyance records of the parish where the property is located.

Because this transaction occurred after January 1, 1995, the statutory rules under current C.C. art. 2561 apply. If Buyer does not timely make all payments and does not acknowledge the obligation (thereby interrupting prescription), the note will prescribe June 1, 2025, because the note is due June 1, 2020. Prescription on a note is five years (C.C. art. 3498). Once the note has prescribed, the resolutory condition becomes unenforceable by virtue of C.C. art. 2561.

22.2(e). Effect of Exercising a Resolutory Condition

If a seller exercises the resolutory condition by judicial action, all inferior liens, encumbrances, and transfers by the buyer will be erased from the public records. Because third parties can ascertain the existence of a resolutory condition from the public records, third parties are put on notice that their rights in the property may be extinguished if the seller timely exercises the resolutory condition.

A seller who exercises the resolutory condition must restore the buyer to the same condition the buyer had prior to the act of sale; therefore, the seller must refund all monies received from the buyer. A seller who exercises the resolutory condition can deprive the buyer of increases in the value of the property (see Section 22.2(e)(1), Example 3, below).

22.2(e)(1). Resolutory Condition, Example 3

The facts here are the same as in Section 22.2(d)(1), Example 1, above. On March 1, 1990, Seller sold to Buyer immovable property by an "Act of Sale With Mortgage." Buyer gave Seller a note payable in monthly installments over the course of thirty years. The note was described in the act of sale and the note was secured by a mortgage on the property; the mortgage was contained in the sale document. The Seller promptly recorded the act in both the mortgage and conveyance records of the parish where the property is located. The price in the act of sale is $100,000. Further assume that Buyer makes no improvements to the property and that it remains vacant land.

If, on December 1, 2019, Buyer defaults and Seller sues for dissolution under the resolutory condition, Seller must refund to Buyer all the payments Buyer made to Seller. As a result of the dissolution suit, Seller will regain ownership of the property. If the property is worth $350,000 at this point, Buyer has no right to any increase in the value. This is in contrast to what would be the case if, instead of dissolving the sale, Seller had sought specific performance and foreclosed on its mortgage. In that case, Buyer would be entitled to the value of the equity in the property that exceeded the pay-off of the mortgage (assuming that there were no inferior mortgages or encumbrances).

22.3. The Right of First Refusal

A right of first refusal is a contractual clause inserted into a contract of sale granting the seller certain rights. In essence, the buyer agrees it cannot sell the item or property to a third party without first offering to sell the property back to the original seller on the same terms and conditions offered by the third party buyer.

22.3(a). Definition of a Right of First Refusal

A right of first refusal is a contract by which an owner agrees *"that he will not sell a certain thing without first offering it"* to the person in whose favor the right of first refusal runs (C.C. art. 2625).

The existence of a right of first refusal in a document does not prevent a sale to a third party. Rather, the third party buys the property subject to the right of first refusal. Thus, a purchaser who buys property where a valid right of first refusal exists must be aware that the holder of the right could step in later, claim that proper notice was not given to the holder, exercise the right of first refusal, and dissolve the sale by which the current owner bought the property.

A right of first refusal may run in favor of one who sold the property to the current owner and may be contained in the act of sale. A right of first refusal may also be contractually obtained by one who never had any ownership rights in the property. To affect third parties concerning immovable property, a right of first refusal must be recorded in the conveyance records of the parish where the property is located (see Section 22.3(b), below).

The price for the right of first refusal *"must be on the same terms"* (C.C. art. 2626) that the current owner (the original buyer) has offered the property for sale to another unless the original buyer and seller had agreed otherwise.

22.3(b). The Effect of a Right of First Refusal

A right of first refusal concerning immovable property is a real right; to affect third parties, it must be recorded in the conveyance records of the parish where the property is located (C.C. arts. 2629, 3338).

By contrast, a right of first refusal on movables does not require filing or recordation and affects third parties *"who, at the time of acquisition of a conflicting right, had actual knowledge of that transaction"* (C.C. art. 2629).

While the Civil Code does not expressly limit rights of first refusal to contracts of sale (where the seller retains a right of first refusal should the buyer ever decide to sell the property to a third party), unless the document is carefully drafted, a right of first refusal in favor of one who is not the seller may be treated as an option to purchase, which is subject to different rules (see C.C. art. 2620).

Because a right of first refusal contained in an act of sale of immovable property imposes an obligation on the buyer to perform an act to complete the sale, if a seller puts a right of first refusal in a contract with the buyer, this may give rise to both a vendor's privilege by operation of law (see Chapter 33, below) and a resolutory condition (see Section 22.2(a), above).

C.C. art. 2627 controls the time frame in which a person must exercise a right of first refusal once notified that the owner is ready to sell to a third party. The time period is ten days for movables and thirty days for immovables, unless the parties have contracted otherwise. If the holder of the right of first refusal is not notified, however, of the pending sale to a third party, the right of first refusal is still valid, subject only to a lapse because of the running of prescription (see Section 22.3(c), below).

22.3(c). The Prescriptive Period on the Right of First Refusal

There is a difference in the prescriptive period that is applicable to rights of first refusal that arose in contracts executed before January 1, 1995, than to those afterwards. Prior to January 1, 1995, rights of first refusal were imprescriptible. Therefore, a right of first refusal granted in 1994 or even 1934 may still be valid today.

Under C.C. art. 2628, as amended effective January 1, 1995, a right of first refusal may not last longer than ten years, although the parties may contract for a shorter time frame. This amendment affects all rights of first refusal entered into after the effective date of the amendment.

In light of C.C. art. 2628 as it currently exists, if the parties in any contract executed after January 1, 1995, attempt to contractually grant a right of first refusal lasting longer than ten years, the time frame will be reduced to ten years unless the right is *"granted in connection with a contract that gives rise to obligations of continuous or periodic performance,"* in which case the *"right of first refusal may be granted for as long a period as required for the performance of those obligations"* (C.C. art. 2628).

A word of caution is in order for those examining title. In construing C.C. art. 2628 and its effect on documents with rights of first refusal executed between 1995 and 2005, one should consult Louisiana Acts 2003, No. 1005 and Acts 2004, No. 24, because the latter act indicates that certain changes made effective July 2, 2003, were prospective only. A more detailed discussion is beyond the scope of this Précis.

22.4. The Right of Redemption

The right of redemption is a contractual right in contracts of sale; it gives the seller a right to regain ownership of the property that had been sold by paying a price to the buyer. Unlike a right of first refusal, the right of redemption is not dependent upon the buyer attempting to resell the property; the right of redemption may be unilaterally demanded by the seller at any time.

22.4(a). Definition of a Right of Redemption

C.C. art. 2567 defines a right of redemption as an agreement in a contract of sale through which the seller may regain ownership of property by paying an agreed-upon price to the buyer.

As the Law Institute comments to this article note, the price of the right of redemption *"may be higher or lower than the purchase price paid"* by the original buyer.

Because the right of redemption depends upon the unilateral act of the seller to exercise it and (unlike the right of first refusal) does not require a prior action by the buyer, a right of redemption does not give rise either to a vendor's privilege (see Chapter 33, below, on the vendor's privilege) or to a resolutory condition (see Section 22.2(a), above).

Louisiana law distinguishes between a right of redemption and an option to repurchase. To constitute a right of redemption, the seller must reserve that right in the act of sale. If the seller does not do so, any later agreement with the buyer to the same effect is treated as an option to repurchase.

22.4(b). The Effect of a Right of Redemption on the Buyer and Third Parties

If what is sold is an immovable and the right of redemption is contained in the act of sale that is filed for recordation in the conveyance records, the right of redemption is a real right that "follows the property" into the hands of third parties. Therefore, a seller may exercise the right of redemption against current owners of the property even if the original buyer has transferred ownership to a third party (C.C. art. 2572).

When the right of redemption is timely exercised, mortgages and encumbrances placed on the property by the buyer and any later purchaser are extinguished (C.C. art. 2588), subject to the public records doctrine. Since, in the sale of an immovable, the right of redemption normally would be contained in the recorded act of sale, third parties are put on notice that their liens, mortgages and encumbrances can be extinguished if the right of redemption is exercised.

Nonetheless, the buyer of property (and any third party purchaser) subject to a right of redemption is entitled to the fruits of the property (C.C. art. 2575). The buyer and any subsequent third party purchaser are also given certain rights in connection with improvements made on the property (C.C. art. 2577). The buyer may also exercise the right of discussion to prevent the redemption (C.C. art. 2574 and C.C.P. arts. 5151 *et seq.*). The buyer under a right of redemption, however, is liable for deterioration of the property (C.C. art. 2578).

If the seller exercises the right of redemption, the seller must reimburse "*the buyer for all expenses of the sale and for the cost of repairs necessary for the preservation of the thing*" (C.C. art. 2587).

Under C.C. art. 2569, a right of redemption may be treated as a security interest "*when the surrounding circumstances show the true intent of the parties was to make a contract of security.*" For immovable property, this rule must be read in conjunction with the public records doctrine (see Chapter 19, above). Sometimes a sale containing a right of redemption may be treated as a mortgage as between the parties while at the same time being treated as a sale subject to a right of redemption as to third parties. The following examples illustrate this.

22.4(b)(1) Example #1: A Sale That Is a Right of Redemption as to Third Parties but a Mortgage as to the Parties

In Year 1, Seller sells property to Buyer with a five year right of redemption. The sale with the right of redemption is recorded in the parish conveyance records. Buyer never leaves the property, and Seller never insists on taking possession of the property.

Because the Seller has permitted Buyer to remain on the property and there is no agreement between Buyer and Seller that Buyer is not occupying it as owner, the jurisprudence treats the transaction as a mortgage by Buyer in favor of Seller. This is not the case as to third parties, however. In this situation, there is no indication in the public records that this is not a sale with a right of redemption, and nothing in the public records indicates who is in possession of the property. Therefore, while as between Seller and Buyer it is a mortgage, third parties may treat this as a true sale with a right of redemption.

Thus, until the right of redemption expires at the end of Year 5, any person who wants to purchase the property from Buyer will take it subject to the right of redemption. If the sale from Buyer takes place in Year 4, Seller may exercise the right of redemption.

22.4(b)(2). Example #2: A Sale that Is a Right of Redemption Both as between the Parties and as to Third Parties

The facts are the same as in Example #1, Section 22.4(c)(1), above, except that one day after Buyer and Seller execute and record the act of sale with the right of redemption, Buyer executes a lease with Seller in which Buyer leases the property from Seller for five years. Buyer and Seller do not record the lease in the public records.

While the public records in both Example #1 and #2 do not contain an indication of who possesses the property, and while in both examples Buyer is in physical possession of the property, the result in Example #2 differs from Example #1. When Buyer executed the lease in favor of Seller, Buyer was acknowledging that he was no longer possessing the property as owner but was rather acknowledging Seller's ownership. This unrecorded lease makes the transaction a completed sale with a right of first refusal between the parties.

As to third parties, the results here are the same as in Example #1, above. Because there is no indication on the public records that this is not a sale with a right of redemption, and nothing on the public records indicates who is in possession of the property, third parties may treat this as a true sale with a right of redemption.

22.4(b)(3). Example #3: A Sale that Is a Purported Right of Redemption That Is Treated as a Mortgage Both as between the Parties and as to Third Parties

In Year 1, Seller sells property to Buyer. The act of sale states, in pertinent part: "This sale with a right of redemption is made to secure a debt that Seller owes Buyer."

Third parties looking at this document can ascertain that Seller is the debtor and Buyer is the creditor. Under Louisiana jurisprudence, both the parties to a document and third parties must treat such a transaction as a mortgage rather than as a sale (see Section 18.1, above). The purported "right of redemption" will be of no effect, both as between the parties and as to third parties, because in such a document, despite the language of sale, no title transfers from Seller to Buyer; it is merely a mortgage when the seller is a debtor of the buyer rather than a creditor of the buyer.

22.4(c). The Preemptive Period on the Right of Redemption

The rules concerning the timely exercise of the right of redemption are preemptive, not prescriptive, and these time frames run even as against minors (C.C. art. 2571).

C.C. art. 2568 sets the preemptive time periods. For immovable property, a seller must exercise the right of redemption before the shorter of (a) the contractual right of redemption or (b) ten years from the act of sale. For movable property, the maximum period for redemption is five years from the act of sale. The parties cannot contract for longer periods.

Chapter 23

Title Examination

23.1. An Overview of Title Examinations, Title Opinions, and Title Insurance

Title examinations, title opinions, and title insurance are three separate items, but students often confuse them.

A "title examination" is a review of documents obtained from the public records in an effort to collect all pertinent documents relating to a tract of immovable property.

A "title opinion" is a written opinion letter from a lawyer to a client evaluating who owns the property, what encumbrances may exist on the property, and determining whether the title contains a material defect. A "material defect" is a problem found in the title to immovable property that may require litigation to resolve or clear that defect.

Title insurance is an insurance policy issued by a company that agrees to pay up to the policy value if the title to immovable property has a material defect (see R.S. 22:511 *et seq.*).

A purchaser does not have valid, unencumbered title to property merely because the purchaser received a title opinion or a title policy. A lender does not have a valid first mortgage on property merely because the lender received a title opinion or title policy stating that the lender's mortgage is a first encumbrance. While title opinions and title insurance may give some degree of solace to purchasers and lenders who rely upon them, all title opinions and title insurance really do is provide the lender or purchaser with someone to sue in the event that the title contains a defect not noted in the title opinion or title insurance policy. This is not an insignificant right, however, for the fact that the issuer of the title opinion or title insurance can be sued makes them both more careful in their examination of title and more diligent in attempting to correct title defects that are discovered.

The process of conducting a title examination is described in Sections 23.2, 23.3, and 23.4, below.

Lawyers issue title opinions. Title insurance companies, through their agents (who are usually lawyers, see R.S. 12:804) issue title insurance policies based upon a lawyer's examination of the title. The recipients of title opinions and title insurance policies are lenders who seek to place a mortgage on immovable property, those intending to purchase immovable property, or both.

23.1(a). Title Opinions Are Seldom Used Today

Today, all but a tiny handful of closings (both commercial and residential) in Louisiana are done using title insurance rather than title opinions. A "closing" is the process of signing all the documents necessary to accomplish a sale of property, the financing of property, or both.

Until the mid-1970s, however, almost all closings in Louisiana took place using a title opinion issued by a lawyer. Giving a title opinion is part of the statutory definition of the practice of law (R.S. 37:212). If a lawyer's title opinion is erroneous, the lawyer may have committed malpractice and can be sued. If the lawyer is a member of a law firm, the law firm can be sued as well.

Prior to the mid-1970s, financial institutions in Louisiana, especially savings and loans that made residential loans, often used but one law firm and that firm did all the closings for the institution and issued every title opinion for that institution.

Therefore, prior to the mid-1970s, when title opinions were the primary way that lenders ascertained whether their mortgage was valid, lenders would allow only "approved" attorneys to issue title opinions to that institution. Getting on the "approved" list usually required either that the lawyer worked for a law firm known for its real estate expertise or that the lawyer had demonstrated to the institution the requisite real estate knowledge to issue the title opinion.

23.1(b). Title Insurance

The Louisiana Title Insurance Act (R.S. 22:511 *et seq.*) controls title insurance in the state. Louisiana law allows law firms to own title insurance agencies (R.S. 12:804) and to be title insurance agents.

A title insurance policy essentially provides that, if there is a problem with the title not noted on the face of the insurance policy, the insurer will either

(a) pay the policy limits to the insured party, or (b) attempt to clear the title defect. If the title insurance company is not able to clear the title defect, it pays up to the policy limits to the insured party.

There are three main reasons why title insurance is used for almost all residential and commercial property closings, not merely in Louisiana but also nationwide. First, lenders require their borrowers to pay for the lender's title insurance policy as part of the closing costs; therefore, the title policy costs the lender nothing. Second, if a title contains a defect, all the lender wants is to be paid the outstanding balance on its mortgage. It does not matter to the lender if the property has appreciated in value, because the lender is concerned about collecting the loan, and the title insurance proceeds will accomplish that task if there is a title defect. Third, the lenders' loan documents often allow them to have prior approval of which title insurance companies may issue title policies for their loans; thus, lenders have the ability to make sure that only national companies with large assets issue the title policies accepted by the lenders. While there is no assurance that a national title insurer will not have financial difficulties, it is easier for lenders to keep track of the reputation and solvency of a few national title insurance companies than having to ascertain the solvency and capabilities of every lawyer who wants to submit a title opinion for a closing.

23.2. Title Examinations Begin with an Abstract of Title

Both title opinions and title insurance policies require a title examination. A lawyer must review the documents found in the parish public records to ascertain who owns the property, whether there are any encumbrances on the property, and whether there are any material defects (see Section 23.1, above).

A title examination is the act of reading all of these documents and forming a legal opinion about all of the information found in the documents, as well as ascertaining what information is not present that might be pertinent in ascertaining the status of the title.

23.3. An Overview of Abstracts of Title

An abstract of title is a collection of all documents in the public records that may affect title to the property (see Section 23.3(h), below). Obtaining an abstract of title requires that someone locate and then obtain all the pertinent documents related to the property whose title is being examined.

While a detailed discussion of abstracts of title is beyond the scope of this Précis, this Section will describe, in general, the process of "running" an abstract.

The first step is to consult the indices to the parish's conveyance and mortgage records. The conveyance records contain a "Vendor" index and a "Vendee" index. The mortgage records contain a "Mortgagor" index and a "Mortgagee" index. Each index contains a reference to every document under the name of the vendor, vendee, mortgagor, or mortgagee. There is no index to these documents based on property description. Therefore, at the present time, one cannot look up "Lot 233, Oakmeadow Subdivision, East Baton Rouge Parish," to start the abstract process; one must know the name of the current owner or the current mortgage holder.

Of course, if a name is not found in the index (because the Clerk omitted it in error or otherwise), those reviewing the index cannot find the pertinent document. Even if the name is not found in the index, the document still affects third persons, because it is the process of registry, not the creation of indices, that affects third parties (see Chapter 19, above). Therefore, title opinions and title insurance policies expressly state that they were issued based on the indices examined as of the date of the examination. Title opinions and title insurance policies do not express any opinion or coverage for any matter not shown in the indices on the date of the examination.

The typical method of examining title includes: a review of vendee and vendor indices, then a review of the mortgagor indices, then a review of the map book, then a review of pertinent court proceedings, then a review of the UCC records, and finally a review of the Secretary of State's records.

Sections 23.3(a) through 23.3(h), below, give a generalized overview of how this process works. These sections all deal with the following example: Creditor has hired you to ascertain whether a loan it plans to make to Donna Debtor will be a first mortgage on Donna's property. Your work for Creditor will require a title examination. To perform the title examination, someone must review the public records and obtain copies of all the pertinent documents. The process usually follows this pattern:

23.3(a). How Far Back Should You Search?

The first question to address is how far back in the public records one should search.

To fully understand and evaluate the title, you should run the vendee index and the mortgagor index back to the patent—in other words, you should examine these indices back to the time that the property was transferred from the federal government or State of Louisiana to the first purchaser. If the title runs back before 1812 (when Louisiana became a state), you should examine the title back to the time it was transferred from the sovereign or governing entity to the first purchaser.

Some lawyers claim that you that need to run the title back only 55 years. This is a business decision, not a valid legal rationale for stopping at 55 years. The 55 year rule came from the theory that if one went back beyond 30 year's acquisitive prescription (C.C. art. 3486), plus the former age of majority (21 years), plus the former rule that minors had four years from the age of majority to bring certain actions, then one might assume that all problems with the title had been cured. This is an erroneous assumption. Stopping the abstract after 55 years does not mean that title is clear. For example, if there is a mortgage securing a note due in monthly installments, with the last installment due 60 years after the date of the note, that mortgage will affect third parties for six years after the majority date—in other words 66 years from the date of the document (see C.C. art. 3358 and Section 20.2(a), above). The fact that someone has acquired the property in the interim by 30-year's acquisitive prescription does not affect the validity of the mortgage, for the mortgage encumbers the property, not the ownership interest (see C.C. art. 3278 and Chapter 11, above). Likewise stopping the abstract after 55 years will not pick up a right of first refusal entered into long ago, for those rights can be imprescriptible if those rights were acquired prior to January 1, 1995 (see Section 22.3(c), above).

As a business matter, some lawyers and title insurers may decide to take the business risk that the chance of having a title defect in something older than 55 years is relatively small. The business risk is they can be sued if they are wrong. The fact that some people accept this as a risk of doing business does not mean that legally one can ascertain the status to title by stopping at the 55 year mark. The only safe and assured way of ascertaining the status of title is to run the title back to the patent.

23.3(b). Vendee Index

The place to start in creating an abstract of title is with the vendee index. You know that Donna Debtor is the ostensible owner of the property. Donna must have bought the property from someone.

You therefore start by examining Donna's name in the vendee index to ascertain from whom she purchased the property. You determine that Donna bought the property from Sally Seller. You make a note of the document number—both the conveyance record information and the "original bundle" information (see Chapter 19, above)—so that you can obtain a copy of that document from the Clerk of Court.

You then run Sally Seller's name through the vendee index to ascertain from whom she bought the property. You find that the indices reflect that she bought it from Candide Conveyor. As you did with the sale from Donna to Sally, you make a note of that document number so that you can obtain a copy.

For the reasons set forth in Section 23.3(a), above, you run all the names in the index back to the patent to ascertain who first purchased the property from the state or the sovereign. This may involve searching the records back to the early 1800s.

23.3(c). Vendor Index

Once you have run the vendee index, you take every name you have located and run each of those names over the same period of time in the vendor index. This is so that you can check to see whether the vendor and vendee indices match. If they do not, this can indicate a title defect.

For example, in your review of the vendee index (Section 23.3(b), above) you found that part of the chain of title involved Donna Debtor purchasing from Sally Seller who purchased from Candide Conveyor. What if, in your review of the vendor index, you found that the day before Candide Conveyor sold the property to Sally Seller, Candide signed an act of sale transferring this same property to Billy Buyer? If you found this, you would know that there is a question whether Candide had good and just title to transfer the property to Sally and thus whether Sally had good title to transfer it to Donna.

In addition, you want to ascertain whether anyone who is in the chain of title has granted a lease or servitude on the property; that information will be contained in the conveyance records. Some leases last 99 years. Some servitudes are given in perpetuity. Therefore, they may encumber the property, and you will need to obtain copies of these documents.

What if the vendor index contains a variation on the name in the vendee index? For example, what if the vendee index shows a purchase by Donna Debtor from Sally Seller, but the vendor index shows a sale from "*Susan Sallie* Seller" or from "*Salley Sellers*"? You'll want to get copies of these documents as well, because the point of reviewing the index is not to ascertain which of these transactions is controlling, valid, or involved the same person; rather, the purpose is to locate every document that *might* affect the title to the property. Therefore, you will obtain a copy of each sale because a legal opinion will be needed to determine whether that document affects title. Remember, the indices do not indicate the property description, only the names of vendors and vendee or mortgagor and mortgagee. If there is a brief property description in the indices, you cannot rely upon it, and all indices have a warning to this effect. The only way to ascertain whether the property in question is impacted by the documents listing "_Susan Sallie_ Seller" or "Sall_ey_ Sellers_" is to read those documents once you've assembled all the documents for the abstract.

Therefore, the only way to assure that the title is free from material defects is to examine in the vendor index every name you had picked up in the vendee index. For each of the transactions you locate in the vendor index, you make a note of the document number because you will need to obtain a copy of each of these documents.

23.3(d). Mortgagor Index

You next take every name you picked up in your examination of both the vendor and vendee indices and determine whether these names occur in the mortgagor index. This is because any one of these individuals or entities may have granted a mortgage or other encumbrance on the property.

As you did in your other indices examinations, for each of the transactions you locate in the mortgagor index, you make a note of the document number because you will need to obtain a copy of each of these documents.

23.3(e). UCC Index

The Louisiana Secretary of State's office maintains an index to all UCC filings (see Chapter 41, below). That index is searchable by the names of businesses and individuals; the search can be done online by those registered to conduct such searches.

If the property is a commercial tract (as opposed to a single-family residential home), those conducting title searches always search the UCC indices. This is because fixtures that are an integral part of commercial properties may be secured by a UCC9 fixture filing (see Section 41.1(g), below); the existence of such a filing may impact your client's evaluation of the transaction. For example, if the property whose title you are examining is a hotel and its central air conditioning units are subject to a fixture filing, your client, Creditor, may be reluctant to make the loan because, upon foreclosure, the UCC creditor could intervene and seize and sell the air conditioning units (see Section 41.1(g), below). A hotel in Louisiana without air conditioning units is worth far less than a hotel with functioning air conditioning.

Note that if one of the persons shown as owner of the property in the documents you have located is a corporation organized under the laws of another state, or is shown as an individual residing in another state, you may have to search the UCC records not just of Louisiana but also of the other pertinent states (see Section 41.1(d), below).

23.3(f). Obtaining and Performing an Initial Review of Documents Concerning Maps or Plats

Once you have ascertained from your searches of the vendor, vendee, mortgagor, and UCC indices which transactions might impact the property, you obtain copies of each of these documents.

You then examine each document to ascertain whether any of them refer to a map or plat, because, under Louisiana law, a map or plat controls over contrary information contained in a written description. Further, many times encumbrances are shown only on maps or plats, and there are indices to these as well.

For example, a plat of a subdivision may show building set-back lines, utility servitudes, servitudes of passage, or other information that will be pertinent to the lawyer examining the title.

If any of these documents refer to a map or plat, you must obtain a copy of that. Many Clerk of Courts' offices contain separate map or plat books.

23.3(g). Obtaining and Performing an Initial Review of Documents Concerning Other Information

Your review is not finished just because you have completed the steps listed above. Depending on the asset, the parties, and other information you have, you may need to review local property tax records, federal tax lien books kept by federal courts, federal court suit filings, and federal bankruptcy filings.

In addition, once you have assembled all the documents, you perform an initial review and look at the marital status of the parties shown on various documents. For example, if the sale document from Candide Conveyor to Sally Seller (which you located from your review of the vendor or vendee index) does not list Candide's marital status, but the sale from Candide to Billy Buyer (see Section 23.3(c), above) lists her as "Candide Conveyor, wife of Marvin Conveyor," then you have an indication that this property might be community property. You will have to perform an additional search in the court records and other pertinent records to ascertain whether Candide and Marvin had a separate property agreement, whether they had been divorced, or whether Marvin had died and his interest in the property (if any) is tied up in his estate.

23.3(h). Assembling All the Documents You Found and Creating the Abstract of Title

After you performed all of the tasks discussed in Sections 23.3(b) through 23.3(g), above, you will have assembled a stack of documents. This stack represents copies of every document you have ascertained might impact the title to the property.

This stack of documents is the "abstract of title," because you have abstracted from the public records those documents that appear to pertain to the property.

The next step is to examine the abstract.

23.4. The Title Examination Process

A title examination consists of reviewing each and every word in each and every document contained in the abstract of title (see Section 23.3(h), above) and forming a legal opinion about the status of the title.

A title examiner reviews the title to ascertain ownership and any impediments that might exist on the face of the public records to the current owner possessing full ownership of the property in question. This may involve, particularly for corporations, partnerships, and other business entities, whether the public records reflect the proper authorizations for those purporting to act on behalf of the entity.

A title examiner also reviews the documents to ascertain whether there are any encumbrances on the property. Those encumbrances might include but are not necessarily limited to: a mortgage, lease, servitude, usufruct, or privilege; a UCC9 fixture filing; building restrictions; deed restrictions; resolutory conditions (see Section 22.2, above); rights of first refusal (see Section 22.3, above); and rights of redemption (see Section 22.4, above).

The title examiner then reaches a legal conclusion on the status of the title and all potential encumbrances.

Some issues that are noted as potential issues in the title examination or that may impact the title may be acceptable to recipient of the title opinion or title insurance policy. For example, the buyer or lender may not be concerned if there is a servitude that does not impact the use of the property or that actually aids the property. Likewise, the buyer or lender may not be concerned with recorded building restrictions if the existing or contemplated building will not violate the restrictions. In these types of situations, the title opinion or title insurance policy will list these items as an exception to valid title, and the transaction will proceed to closing.

Some issues that are noted may be problems capable of being corrected prior to closing, such as the lack of a corporate authorization for a transaction. Sometimes the title examiner can correct this by approaching the corporation, obtaining the proper resolution for the transaction in question, and recording that documentation.

Some problems may be material issues that may prevent the closing from proceeding forward, such as ascertaining that the current owner's ownership interest is in doubt, or that a prior recorded mortgage exists when your client expected to have a first mortgage on the property but now cannot get that in light of the preexisting mortgage. The issue whether to proceed with the closing requires consultation with the client, explaining the issues, and determining: (a) whether the client is willing to proceed, understanding the risks; (b) whether the material issues can be resolved or "insured over" (whether title insurance will take on the risk and agree to pay if the problem is not resolved); (c) or whether the problem can be ultimately resolved by negotiating with those who have rights impacting the title or filing a lawsuit to clear the title to the property.

Chapter 24

Examples of Differences between Title Examination Issues and Litigation Issues Involving the Ranking of Mortgages and Privileges

24.1. An Overview of the Differences between Title Examination Issues and Litigation Issues

Both title examinations (see Chapter 23, above) and litigation involving title are concerned with ascertaining who has "good" title to property, whether the property is encumbered by one or more security devices that affect third parties, and if so, the rank of those security devices.

The primary differences between title examination issues and litigation is that a title examiner cannot ascertain all the "real" facts that might relate to the validity of the title or security interests. The title examiner is limited to making a determination based on what is (and is not) recorded in the public records. In contrast, litigation requires that the party claiming a security interest in property prove (as appropriate to the situation) the validity of title of the debtor or obligor, the principal obligation the security device secures, the outstanding balance on the principal obligation, and the rank of the creditor's security interest.

24.2. A Title Examiner Must "Assume the Worst" When Examining Title

A title examiner is primarily concerned with those things shown on the public record; under Louisiana law, when things that are required by law to be on the public record are not found there, third parties are not affected even if they otherwise are aware of these facts for reasons that are unrelated to the public records (see Section 19.3(a), above).

There are a number of critical issues that a title examiner cannot ascertain from the face of the public records. For example, a title examiner cannot know, by looking at the public records:

- what the balance is on a note secured by a mortgage (see, for example, Section 13.3(a), above);
- whether the note secured by the mortgage represents money loaned contemporaneously at the time of the note's creation or whether the note represents money that is to be advanced in the future (see Section 13.3(c), above);
- whether the note secured by the mortgage in fact has prescribed or been acknowledged;
- when a security interest was perfected in a collateral mortgage note, an important date because a collateral mortgage package takes its rank against third parties from the earliest concurrence of recordation of the mortgage and a perfected security interest in the collateral mortgage note (see Sections 13.5 and 13.5(b), above);
- whether a collateral mortgage secures a specific past debt, a specific set of future advances, or a fluctuating line of credit (see Section 13.10, above);
- or whether the note has been transferred from the original creditor to another creditor (see Sections 13.11–13.13, above).

Therefore, a title examiner must "assume the worst" in looking at the title. In other words, the title examiner must assume that every act that could help a creditor maintain the validity of its mortgage and its mortgage rank has been accomplished, unless there is something in the public records to the contrary. The title examiner, therefore, must assume that:

- the entire principal balance of the note is unpaid;
- interest has continued to accrue on the note according to the terms of the note;

- the debtor has acknowledged the note so that the note has not prescribed;
- the note for anything other than a collateral mortgage represents money loaned contemporaneously at the time of the note's creation so that whether it could be construed as an "ordinary" mortgage or a future advance mortgage, it will rank from the date of filing and timely recordation of the mortgage that the note secures (see Sections 13.2 and 13.3(b)2, above); and that
- a security interest in a collateral mortgage note was perfected prior to or at the same time as the filing of the collateral mortgage in the mortgage records, and the collateral mortgage note secures an amount at least equal to the amount of principal and interest accrued on the collateral mortgage note (see Sections 13.11–13.13, above).

24.3. A Creditor Bears the Burden of Proof in Litigation

In litigation, unlike title examinations, the creditor claiming a security interest bears the burden of proof. There is no "assumption" a court may make about the validity of the mortgage or the debt it secures.

The creditor must show, at a minimum, that:

- the principal obligation secured by the mortgage is valid, enforceable, and has not prescribed;
- the rank of the mortgage, which involves proving when the mortgage first began to affect third parties; and
- the inscription of the mortgage has not lapsed as to third parties (see Chapter 20, above).

Chapter 25

The Homestead Exemption

25.1. There Are Two Types of "Homestead Exemptions"

There are two different types of "homestead exemptions" in Louisiana; one relates to taxes and the other relates to foreclosures.

The homestead exemption from taxation (Louisiana Constitution, Art. VII, Section 20(A)) protects the first $75,000 in value of a home from property taxes. Therefore, a home that has a tax appraisal of $74,999 pays no property taxes. A home that has a tax appraisal of $80,000 pays taxes only on $5,000 of value ($80,000 − $75,000), not on the entire $80,000 value.

The homestead exemption from seizure and sale (R.S. 20:1) allows a home-owner to receive certain proceeds from a foreclosure sale before the foreclosing creditor. It allows the homeowner to realize at least some equity from a foreclosure sale; however, this right can be (and usually is) waived in a mortgage (see Section 25.2, below).

25.2. Waiving the Foreclosure Homestead Exemption

For purposes of the statutory homestead exemption applicable to foreclosure proceedings, a homestead is defined by R.S. 20:1(A)(1) as "*a residence occupied by the owner and the land on which the residence is located, including any building and appurtenances located thereon, and any contiguous tracts up to a total of five acres if the residence is within a municipality, or up to a total of two hundred acres of land if the residence is not located in a municipality."*

The homestead exemption (R.S. 20:1) allows the homeowner to receive the first $35,000 in value if a creditor sells the home. R.S. 20:1(A)(2) provides that this $35,000 exemption applies to any *"seizure and sale under any writ, mandate, or process whatsoever...."* This statute, however, allows a homeowner to waive the benefit of the exemption in a mortgage document (R.S. 20:1(D)).

There is a special homestead exemption for debts arising from *"catastrophic or terminal illness or injury"* (R.S. 20:1(A)(3). For these debts, *"the exemption shall apply to the full value of the homestead based upon its value one year before such seizure"* (R.S. 20:1(A)(2)).

Creditors typically have the homestead exemption expressly waived in mortgage documents, for the creditor wishes to obtain the maximum proceeds from the sale of the property if a foreclosure is required. Because the homestead exemption can be claimed by a spouse (R.S. 20:1(B)), creditors require the spouse to enter into the waiver of the homestead exemption.

Because the homestead exemption applies to certain insurance proceeds from disasters (R.S. 20: 1(A)(2)), creditors who wish to receive the full value on insurance policies (see R.S. 9:5386) may need to have the express homestead waiver in the act of mortgage.

In addition to the homestead exemption contained in R.S. 20.1, there is a separate statute protecting a debtor's homestead from being seized to satisfy a judgment for consumer credit card charges (R.S. 13:3851.1). The statute does not prevent recordation of the judgment creating a judicial mortgage; it instead prohibits seizure of the property unless the credit card debt was also secured by a conventional mortgage granted by the debtor.

25.3. Exceptions from the Statutory Foreclosure Homestead Exemption

La. R.S. 20:1(C) provides that, in addition to express waivers in mortgages, the homestead exemption does not apply when the following types of claims are involved: *"the purchase price of property or any part of such purchase price"* (see Chapter 33, below); *"labor, money, and material furnished for building, repairing, or improving the homestead"* (see R.S. 9:4801 et seq. and Chapter 37, below): *"liabilities incurred by any public officer, or fiduciary, or any attorney at law, for money collected or received on deposits"*; *"taxes or assessments"*; the lessor's privilege (see Section 31.2, below); and for amounts due *"a homestead or building and loan association for a loan made by it on the security of the prop-*

erty; provided, that if at the time of making such loan the borrower be married, and not separated from bed and board from the other spouse, the latter shall have consented thereto."

25.4. Bond for Deed Contracts and the Homestead Exemption

There has been no case testing whether the Civil Code's treatment of bond-for-deed purchasers as "owners" (for the purposes of the homestead exemption from taxation) complies with the constitutional definition of a homestead.

The Constitution states (Const. Art. VII (20)(A)(7)) that *"[N]o homestead exemption shall be granted on bond for deed property. However, any homestead exemption granted prior to June 20, 2003 on any property occupied upon the effective date of this Paragraph by a buyer under a bond for deed contract shall remain valid as long as the circumstances giving rise to the exemption at the time the exemption was granted remain applicable."*

Yet, R.S. 9:2948 makes a bond-for-deed purchaser who is occupying the property eligible for the homestead exemption. Whether this statute is sufficient to grant the exemption in light of the Constitutional provision remains to be seen.

Chapter 26

The Relationship between Lending and Insurance

26.1. Why Creditor-Drafted Documents Include Clauses about Insurance

When loans are secured by mortgages or security interests, creditors want to be sure that, if the property is damaged or destroyed, there is insurance to repair or replace the property or pay off the loan. The creditor does not purchase this insurance; instead, the loan documents typically require the debtor to purchase the insurance and provide proof of its existence to the creditor (see Section 26.2, below). A mortgage may also include a pledge of such insurance (see Section 15.2, above).

When loans are secured by a surety, many creditors want to be assured that if the surety dies, the surety had sufficient assets to satisfy the secured obligations. This means that creditors may wish to obtain an interest in a life insurance policy on the surety (see Section 26.4, below).

26.2. The Differences between "Simple" and "Standard" Loss Payee Clauses

Mortgages and security agreements usually contain a clause requiring not only that the debtor obtain and maintain property and casualty insurance to protect the collateral in the event of an accident, fire, or disaster, but also that the insurance contain a "loss payable" clause in favor of the creditor. A "loss payable" clause, in conjunction with language in the mortgage or security agreement or loan agreement, usually allows the creditor to collect the insurance and either apply it to the outstanding debt or allow the borrower to use the money to repair the property, restoring it to its original condition to protect the value of the collateral.

There are two types of loss payable clauses—(a) a simple clause, and (b) what is known as a "standard," "union," or "New York" clause. These three terms ("standard" clause, "union" clause, and "New York" clause) are different phrases for the same concept.

A simple loss payee clause states in essence that the creditor will be paid if the debtor can collect on the insurance. In other words, the creditor's rights derive from the rights of the debtor. If the debtor cannot collect (for example, because of fraud or arson), then the lender cannot collect.

A "standard," "union," or "New York" clause creates a separate contract of insurance between the insurer and the creditor. This separate contract protects the creditor not only from accidents and disasters but also from any loss resulting from the acts or neglect of the debtor.

Experienced creditors usually require either that the debtor's insurance contain either a "standard," "union," or "New York" clause in favor of the lender or that the debtor's insurance policy contain terms and conditions "satisfactory to" the creditor. The purpose of this "satisfactory to" provision is to allow the creditor to reject as insufficient any insurance a debtor furnishes that does not contain a "standard," "union," or "New York" clause.

26.3. How a Creditor Obtains a Security Interest in Casualty Insurance on Immovable Property

R.S. 9:5386 allows a mortgage to contain a pledge of "the mortgagor's rights under policies of insurance covering the immovable." This area is covered in more depth in Section 15.2, above.

The inclusion of such a "collateral assignment" in the mortgage, however, does not address the type of casualty insurance clauses that must be contained in the insurance policy. The creditor typically adds clauses to the "collateral assignment" language to mandate that the insurance policy contain a "standard," "union," or "New York" clause (see Section 26.2, above).

Certain lenders whose mortgages contain insurance assignments are subject to statutory requirements under R.S. 6:337, which controls how those insurance proceeds must be applied and allocated between repair costs and mortgage payments.

26.4. How a Creditor Obtains a Security Interest in Life Insurance Proceeds

The UCC provides the mechanism to obtain a security interest in life insurance. Under R.S. 10:9-203(b)(3)(A), 9-204(b)(4), 9-310(b)(8), 9-312, 9-314, and 9-329.1, the requirements are:

- The owner of the insurance policy executes a written security agreement in favor of the creditor (this is typically styled an "act of assignment"); and
- The insurer acknowledges that it has received notice of the security agreement.

In addition, if the owner retains the right to change the beneficiary, no consent of the beneficiary is required. If the beneficiary is irrevocable, however, the consent of the beneficiary is required.

It should be noted that filing a UCC financing statement is neither necessary nor required to perfect a security interest in life insurance (R.S. 10:9-310(b)(8)). This type of security interest is a private transaction among the owner of the policy, the creditor, and the insurer; yet, it affects third parties from the moment the UCC9 requirements are met.

Chapter 27

Default Clauses

27.1. An Overview of Default Clauses: Monetary v. Non-Monetary Defaults

Every note, mortgage, and security agreement contains default clauses. The purpose of these provisions is to allow the creditor to accelerate the entire debt if the debtor fails to perform even one of the obligations contained in the agreements the debtor has signed.

Default clauses fall into two main categories: monetary and non-monetary.

Monetary defaults occur when a debtor fails to timely make a required payment—for example, a debtor fails to make a timely payment of principal or interest.

A non-monetary default refers to those situations where the default is not caused by the failure to timely pay the creditor but rather by the actions or in-actions of the debtor or others (such as sureties). See Section 27.2, below, for examples of typical non-monetary default clauses. Many debtors and sureties mistakenly believe that if the principal and interest payments are timely made, they need not worry about the creditor accelerating the entire loan amount. If a non-monetary default occurs, the creditor may "call the loan," requiring immediate payment of the entire amount borrowed, even if a debtor has timely made all monetary payments of principal and interest.

Some default clauses are "ipso facto," while others depend upon the actions of the creditor. The phrase "ipso facto" in a mortgage means that when a provision of the document has been breached, the entire obligation, by reason of this fact (ipso facto), becomes immediately due and payable.

For some defaults, the loan documents, mortgage, or security agreement do not create an "ipso facto" default but rather permit the debtor to attempt to cure the default. Sometimes the "cure" occurs after notice from the creditor, such as a clause requiring the debtor to renew or replace insurance on the collateral within a time frame set by the creditor, or a provision giving a debtor the right to "reinstate" the loan if the debtor makes certain additional payments. Sometimes a cure is permitted for a certain period of time, such as a section of a mortgage or security agreement triggering an ipso facto default if the debtor allows a lien to be placed on the property, but providing that, if the debtor within thirty days of the lien's placement, files a good faith lawsuit to remove the lien, the default may not automatically accelerate the loan.

Whether a document contains an ipso facto default clause or not, almost all documents contain what is known as either a "preservation of rights" or "reservation of rights" provision. This provision states that the failure of the creditor to enforce its rights at any point in time in the past will not deprive the creditor of the ability to enforce that right or other rights in the future.

27.2. Typical Non-Monetary Default Clauses

The following are examples of typical non-monetary default clauses:

- Financial Statements. The debtor's or guarantor's failure to timely provide financial statements or financial information.
- Taxes. The debtor's failure to timely pay real estate taxes on real estate collateral.
- Insurance. The debtor's failure to insure the property or keep the insurance current.
- Liens and Encumbrances. The debtor's voluntarily placement of a second mortgage on real estate or the debtor's allowing a security interest, privilege (lien), or mortgage to impact the collateral.
- Environmental. The debtor's actions in allowing or failing to prevent the presence of toxic chemicals on the property or failing to comply with environmental laws.
- Bankruptcy. Although the Federal Bankruptcy Code prohibits a creditor from enforcing an ipso facto clause upon the bankruptcy of the debtor (11 U.S.C. §365(e)(1)), the Bankruptcy Code does not prohibit enforcement of an ipso facto clause against the debtor if the bankruptcy is of the surety.

Chapter 28

Civil Code Privileges: An Overview

28.1. What Is a "Privilege"

A privilege (which the common law calls a "lien") is defined by C.C. art. 3186 as "*a right, which the nature of the debt gives to a creditor and which entitles him to be preferred before other creditors, even those who have mortgages.*" This definition has remained unchanged for almost 150 years.

28.2. How Are Privileges Created?

A privilege can be created only by statute; parties cannot contractually agree to create a privilege. As the title to C.C. art. 3185 states, privileges are "*established only by law*" and are "*stricti juris*" (meaning that courts strictly and narrowly construe them).

Because privileges are created only by legislation, one must examine each privilege-creating statute to ascertain how the privilege arises. Some privileges, such as the vendor's privilege, arise from credit sales even if the act of sale says nothing about a privilege (C.C. arts. 3227, 3249(1), and see Section 31.1 and Chapter 33, below). Some privileges, such as the repairman's privilege, arise at the time repair work is done on a movable (C.C. arts. 3217(2), R.S. 9:4501, 4502; and see Section 31.3, below). Some privileges, such as the lessor's privilege, arise the moment a tenant leases an apartment, store, or commercial building (C.C. arts. 2707 *et seq.*, C.C. art. 3219, and see Section 31.2, below). Some privileges arise the moment someone performs an act, such as handling a funeral (C.C. art. 3192 *et seq.*, and see Section 29.2, below), providing food or medicines for a horse (R.S. 9:4661), or even picking moss (R.S. 9:4641).

Because privileges arise only by operation of law, one must examine the statutory language concerning each privilege to ascertain:

- when the privilege arises between the parties;
- whether the privilege affects immovable property, movables, or both;
- when the privilege starts to affect third parties and whether this requires recordation of a document in the public records;
- when the privilege ceases being effective between the parties;
- when the privilege ceases being effective as to third parties;
- whether the length of the privilege as to third parties can be extended by reinscription; and
- how the privilege ranks as to other privileges, mortgages, and security interests.

28.3. Special and General Privileges on Movables and Immovables: An Overview

Privileges can be classified according to whether they are general or special (C.C. art. 3190), and whether they affect only immovable property, only movable property, or both movable and immovable property.

A general privilege is not limited to a specific object or item. Rather, a general privilege affects all current and future assets of the debtor. Some general privileges affect only movable property, some affect only immovable property, and some affect both movables and immovables (see Chapters 29 and 30, below).

Special privileges, depending on the exact privilege in question, (a) may affect only a particular, specific item or (b) may affect an entire class of items of the type defined in a statute.

Examples of special privileges that affect only a specific item include: a repairmen's privilege, which exists only on the object being repaired (C.C. arts. 3217(2), R.S. 9:4501, 4502; and see Section 31.3, below); the vendor's privilege on the movable item sold on credit (C.C. art. 3227, and see Section 31.1, below); and the vendor's privilege on the immovable property sold on credit (C.C. art. 3249(1) and see Chapter 33, below).

Examples of special privileges that affect a certain defined class of items include the lessor's privilege on certain movable assets of the tenant (C.C. arts. 2707 *et seq.*, C.C. art. 3219, and see Section 31.2, below).

28.4. How Many Louisiana Privileges Exist?

There are over 1,500 privileges contained in Louisiana statutes. These privileges are found not just in the Civil Code or in R.S. 9 (the Civil Code ancillaries); rather, privileges are scattered throughout numerous titles of the Louisiana Revised Statutes. Examples include:

- the privilege banks have for storage costs on abandoned safety deposit boxes (R.S. 6:327);
- the privilege granted to municipalities and parishes in connection with correcting certain health or housing violations (R.S. 13:2575);
- the privilege of attorneys handling workers' compensation claims (23:1141); and
- the state's privilege on all property of the owner of an "uncontrollable, or wastefully burning well" when the state has taken control of the well to halt the problem (R.S. 30:32).

Each statute must be reviewed carefully to ascertain whether the privilege is general or special, whether the privilege applies to movables or immovables or both, and how the privilege is created and enforced.

28.5. Why Were Privileges Created?

Today, when the government seeks to either discourage some actions (outside of the criminal law context) or encourage others, the usual mechanism is through taxes, fees, tax credits, and tax exemptions. Imposing a tax or fee on something may tend to discourage people from purchasing an item or performing an activity (such as taxes on tobacco and liquor) while at the same time raising revenue for the state. In contrast, granting a tax credit or tax exemption tends to encourage people to undertake actions from which they might otherwise refrain or would not undertake as frequently; this is the concept behind the ability to deduct interest payments on home mortgages (it encourages home ownership), tax credits for first-time home buyers (which were offered in 2008–2010), tax credits for film productions made within the state, and tax credits for "angel investors"—those who help fund early stage, wealth-creating businesses.

At the time the Civil Code was originally enacted in the early 1800s and reworked in 1870, there was not the easy availability of credit from multiple sources that exists today, and taxes on transactions were minimal (the main form of taxation in those days was on the value of immovable property). The primary method by which behavior was encouraged in the 1800s was through the use of privileges. Under Louisiana law, all unsecured creditors have always ranked equally when they try to seize and sell a debtor's assets, but creditors secured by privileges or mortgages were able to get the sales proceeds before the unsecured creditors (C.C. art. 3134; also see Section 1.2, above).

Therefore, if the legislature wished to encourage treatment of those who were critically ill, it could do so by granting a privilege to those who supplied medical care and medicine (C.C. arts. 3199, *et seq.*, and see Section 29.4, below). If the legislature wanted to make sure that there was an ample supply of rental housing or an ample supply of farmland for rent, it could do so by creating a privilege in favor of lessors (C.C. arts. 2707 *et seq.*, C.C. art. 3219, and see Section 31.2, below). If the legislature wanted to make sure that buyers of movable and immovable property would not have to pay cash for all their purchases, it could create a vendor's privilege securing the debts owed to the seller for the purchase price (C.C. art. 3227 Section 31.1, below, and C.C. art. 3249(1) and Chapter 33, below).

Each of these original Civil Code privileges had a specific societal purpose in mind, and each was created to further an interest that the legislature believed important. These rights were deemed so important by the legislature that they were made privileges so that the parties would not have to specially contract for them; the privileges would arise merely by operation of law and thus encourage these kinds of activities.

Because privileges are created by statute, however, it soon became apparent that a creditor who wished to receive a statutory right elevating that creditor over other unsecured creditors could do so by encouraging the passage of special legislation instituting a privilege. There is nothing wrong with this, and often the interests of creditors who encouraged the creation of privileges and societal interests intertwined. It must be recognized, however, that the myriad of privileges that have been created since the 1800s do not reflect the kind of global vision of privileges that existed in the 1800s when privileges were confined almost exclusively to those in the Civil Code.

Chapter 29

The Civil Code's General Privileges

29.1. An Overview of the Civil Code's General Privileges

The Civil Code's listing of general privileges are found in C.C. arts. 3191 and 3252. These are:

- Funeral privileges (C.C. arts. 3191(1) and 3252(1)). This privilege affects both movables and immovables (see Section 29.2, below).
- Law charges and judicial expenses (C.C. arts. 3191(2) and 3252(2)). This privilege affects both movables and immovables (see Section 29.3, below).
- Last sickness expenses (C.C. arts. 3191(3) and 3252(3)). This privilege affects both movables and immovables (see Section 29.4, below).
- Servant's wages (C.C. arts. 3191(4) and 3252(4)). This privilege affects both movables and immovables (see Section 29.5, below).
- Suppliers of provisions (C.C. art. 3191(5)). This privilege affects only movables (see Section 29.6, below).
- Salaries of clerks and secretaries (C.C. arts. 3191(6) and 3252(5). This privilege affects both movables and immovables (see Section 29.7, below).
- Necessitous surviving spouse privilege (C.C. art. 3252). This privilege affects both movables and immovables (see Section 29.8, below).

The next sections will describe in further detail each of these privileges. Note, however, that the general privileges on movables occur by operation of law and affect all of the debtor's movables throughout the state without any need for the claimant to take any action to "perfect" the privilege. In other words, third parties are immediately and automatically affected by these general privileges on movables even though there may be no way for third parties to ascertain that they exist by examining the public records.

On the other hand, the general privileges on immovables fall into one of two categories: those that require recordation in the mortgage records to affect third parties and those that become effective as to third parties without recordation.

There are some general privileges on immovables, such as the funeral privilege, that require no recordation to affect third parties (see Section 29.2, below). Therefore, these general privileges are effective statewide on all immovable property owned by the debtor.

There are other general privileges on immovables, such as the clerks and secretaries privilege (see Section 29.7, below), that require recordation to affect third parties. For these, until the appropriate recordation occurs in a parish, the general privilege is not effective in that parish as to third parties. To create a state-wide effect of these general privileges, the holder of the privilege would have to record the necessary document in the mortgage records of each parish. Once the appropriate recordation occurs, however, the general privilege applies to all property the debtor then owns or may acquire in the future in the parish or parishes where the privilege is recorded.

29.2. The Funeral Privilege

The funeral privilege is a general privilege that extends to both movables and immovables (C.C. arts. 3191(1) and 3252(1)). The funeral privilege is effective on immovable property without any need to record any document in the public records (C.C. art. 3276). It is therefore a "secret lien"; it exists and affects all of the decedent's immovable property even though no one examining the public records can ascertain that it exists.

C.C. art. 3192 states that the funeral privilege secures the costs "*for the interment of the person deceased.*" Jurisprudence has extended this to those who dig the grave, furnish the coffin and drive the hearse, but not to those who furnish headstones.

Although courts typically hold that third parties who pay the claims of those who are entitled to a privilege cannot obtain legal or conventional subrogation to that privilege, the rule is different for funeral costs. Courts have held that third parties who pay the funeral bills can claim the funeral privilege.

As a practical matter, the funeral privilege is seldom asserted today, because by statute it can never exceed $500 (C.C. art. 3194). Most funerals today cost thousands of dollars.

In today's society, funeral benefits are paid from a variety of sources that do not require those who furnish funeral services to resort to the privilege. Policies of insurance covering funeral expenses are called "industrial life" policies and are regulated under R.S. 22:141 *et seq.* If you see an advertisement about a "life insurance policy" available to anyone, regardless of age and without having to answer any health questions, the advertisement is usually for what Louisiana terms an "industrial life" policy and is directed to those who want to acquire insurance to pay for funeral and burial expenses.

29.3. The Law Charge and Judicial Expense Privilege

The privilege for law charges and judicial expenses affects both movables and immovables (C.C. arts. 3191(2) and 3252(2)). Whether the law charge or judicial expense item qualifies as a privilege on immovables that can be obtained without recordation will depend upon the nature of the charge.

Only those items taxed as costs in a judicial proceeding are "law charges" that qualify for a privilege (C.C. arts. 3195, 3196, 3198). In addition, certain items are specifically included as part of law charges under C.C. art. 3197; these include the "*cost of affixing seals and making inventories for the better preservation of the debtor's property, those which occur in cases of failure or cession of property, for the general benefit of creditors, such as fees to lawyers appointed by the court to represent absent creditors, commissions to syndics; and finally, costs incurred for the administration of estates which are either vacant or belonging to absent heirs....*"

While law charges and judicial expenses always constitute a general privilege against movable and immovables, only certain of these charges affect immovables without the need to record the item. C.C. art. 3276 limits the general privilege on immovables, obtained without recordation, to the "*charges against a succession, such as ... law charges ... [and] lawyer fees for settling the succession.*" Therefore, if the law charge is not in connection with a succession, the privilege must be recorded in the mortgage records. As a practical matter, however, costs in a judicial proceeding are not taxed until the end of the proceeding when a judgment is rendered.

The recordation of the judgment operates as a judicial mortgage (see Chapter 17, above). Therefore, if a succession is not involved, all costs of proceedings that are included in a judgment end up being secured by the judicial mortgage.

29.4. The Last Sickness Privilege

The last sickness privilege is a general privilege that extends to movables and immovables (C.C. arts. 3191(3) and 3252(3)).

A last sickness is defined by C.C. art. 3199 as the sickness causing the debtor's death. The Civil Code privilege also covers the charges for "*chronic sickness*" (C.C. art. 3200). A chronic sickness is defined by C.C. art. 3200 as one "*which the deceased was attacked and of which he died, was a chronic disease, the progress of which was slow and which only occasioned death after a long while, then the privilege shall only commence from the time when the malady became so serious as to prevent the deceased from attending to his business and confined him to his bed or chamber.*" This description, which has remained unchanged since the year 1870, would cover cancer and AIDs.

The privilege covers more than doctor's bills and medicine; the jurisprudence has extended the privilege to include hospital bills and charges for medical equipment used in evaluating and diagnosing diseases.

While the last sickness privilege covers numerous items of medical care, the privilege is simultaneously expansive in one context (in that it covers the children) while being limited in both time and amount.

The last sickness privilege is expansive in that it covers the expenses of treating the last sickness of children under the "*authority*" of the debtor. Therefore, hospitals, pharmacies, and physicians treating a minor for a "last sickness" have a privilege on the property of the minor's parents.

The time limitation on the privilege is set forth in C.C. art. 3201, which provides that however long the sickness may have lasted "*after arriving at the point which prevented him from attending to his affairs, the privilege granted for the expense it has occasioned, can only extend to one year before the decease.*" In other words, the accessory privilege may not be as broad as the principal obligation—the medical bills it secures.

For example, many medical bills are essentially open accounts, and prescription on an open account is three years (C.C. art. 3494(4)). If someone's illness fit the definition of "*last sickness,*" and that person had been ill for two years, the physicians and hospital would have an open account claim for the entire two years' worth of bills; however, the privilege would only extend to cover those bills incurred within "*one year before decease*" (C.C. art. 3201). Even if there had been a contract with the hospital (so that prescription would be ten years, C.C. art. 3499), the privilege is still limited to bills incurred within one year before decease.

The limitation on the amount of the last illness privilege occurs because C.C. art. 3203 allows a court to reduce the claim to the *"true value"* of the services rendered or care afforded, unless there is a contract between the parties. If there is a contract, then the judge cannot separately rule on the *"true value."*

Whether a last sickness privilege can be asserted against immovables without recordation depends on whose last illness it was. If it is the debtor's last illness, no recordation is required, because C.C. art. 3276 exempts from recordation the *"charges against a succession."* On the other hand, if it is the children of the debtor who died from a last sickness, it appears that recordation may be required to affect the parents' immovable property. Of course, the general privilege always applies against movable property without recordation.

There are numerous other Louisiana statutes which give rise to privileges for doctors and hospitals and other medical service providers (such as R.S. 9:4751 *et seq.* and R.S. 23:1142).

Even though a last sickness privilege covers immovables, the holder of a last sickness privilege cannot seize the residence of the obligor. This is because R.S. 20.1, the homestead exemption statute (see Chapter 25, above), states that a person's homestead is exempt from seizure for any claim *"arising directly as a result of a catastrophic or terminal illness or injury."* Note that the exemption is broader than a last sickness; it applies to any *"catastrophic or terminal illness or injury."*

29.5. The Servants' Wage Privilege

C.C. arts. 3205–3207, which grants a privilege to certain "servants," was part of the amendments to the Civil Code when it was redrafted in 1870, during the Reconstruction era. It appears to have been designed to protect former slaves who continued to work in households.

For the time, this was progressive legislation, because it was written well before any federal wage and hour laws were enacted. It gave certain individuals who were not paid the right not only to sue for their wages, but also the right to seize and sell their employer's home and obtain a privilege on the sale's proceeds to satisfy the unpaid wages.

As a practical matter, however, this privilege is not utilized today, because C.C. art. 3205 limits it to *"servants or domestics"* who *"stay in the house of the person paying and employing them"* and because the post-Reconstruction society in the state made it dangerous for any person to claim such right. The

Reconstruction era ended in 1877 when federal troops were withdrawn from the South, and 1877 marks the beginning of the Jim Crow era.

Those *"servants"* included under C.C. art. 3205 are *"valets, footmen, cooks, butlers, and others who reside in the house."* In other words, if the person claiming the servant's wages privilege does not live in the house, there is no privilege.

Today, federal wage and hour laws, as well as state employment statutes, protect employees. For example, R.S. 23:631 provides a fifteen–day timeframe following an employee's termination in which an employer must pay all outstanding wages and certain other benefits. An employer who fails to timely act under R.S. 23:631 can be liable under R.S. 23:632 for an amount that may be equal to 90 days of the employee's wages as well as for the employee's reasonable attorney's fees.

29.6. The Suppliers of Provisions Privilege

The general privilege for suppliers of provisions extends only to movables (C.C. art. 3191(5)). There is no general privilege on immovables for this category of claimants.

The Civil Code includes retail dealers, innkeepers, and teachers in the category of *"suppliers of provisions"* (C.C. arts. 3208–3213).

The privilege is extended only to retailers, not wholesalers (C.C. arts. 3208, 3210). It applies only to store credit granted on an open account. No case has extended the privilege to include retailer-issued credit cards (like a Macy's charge card). There is no possibility under these Civil Code articles of the retailer claiming this privilege if the customer uses a non-retailer issued credit card (such as MasterCard, Visa, or American Express).

The retailer's privilege is limited to six months (C.C. art. 3209); debts older than that are unsecured.

The Civil Code privilege for innkeepers and masters of boarding houses is not used today, and under these articles there appears to be no reported case decided in the last sixty years. The Civil Code also contains provisions granting a special privilege to innkeepers (see C.C. arts. 3217(8) and 3232–3236). There are separate statutes governing the claims of those who provide temporary lodging (see R.S. 21:21 et seq.), and most hotels, motels, and bed-and-breakfasts require a credit or debit card and therefore obtain payment that way.

The Civil Code privilege for "teachers and preceptors" (C.C. art. 3212) is not used today as a practical matter because it applies only to those who *"receive in their house young persons to be brought up, fed and instructed."*

29.7. The Clerks and Secretaries Privilege

Clerks and secretaries are granted a general privilege on movables and immovables (C.C. arts. 3191(6) and 3252(5)). The privilege secures unpaid wages, but even if the clerk or secretary has an unsecured claim for wages that extends back over several years, the privilege is limited to the "*salaries for the last year elapsed and so much as has elapsed of the current year*" (C.C. art. 3214).

During the 1930s and 1940s, there were several cases brought by those asserting that they were entitled to this privilege even though the plaintiffs were not clerks or secretaries. Courts held that the privilege should be strictly construed (C.C. art. 3185) and that it does not extend to commission agents or others who do not strictly fit within societal notions of clerks and secretaries.

29.8. The Privilege of the Surviving Spouse

The surviving spouse and the minor children of the deceased have a general privilege only on immovables (C.C. art. 3252). The privilege does not extend to movables.

The privilege is narrow in scope; it is restricted to spouses and minor children who are left in "necessitous circumstances" and is limited to $1000 (C.C. art. 3252).

Chapter 30

An Overview of the Special Privileges in the Civil Code Pertaining to Movables

30.1. A Listing of the Special Privileges on Movables Covered by the Civil Code

There are more than a thousand special privileges on movables scattered throughout numerous Louisiana statutes (see Section 28.4, above).

Some of these privileges are possessory; they give the creditor or holder of the privilege the right to withhold the object from the owner until paid, and, failing that, a privilege on the proceeds of the object's sale.

Some of these privileges are non-possessory, meaning that the creditor or holder of the privilege does not physically possess the item but nonetheless may have it seized and sold and obtain a privilege on the proceeds of the sale.

The Civil Code deals with only a limited number of special privileges on movables. These include:

- Crop privileges (C.C. art. 3217(1), R.S. 3:207, R.S. 9:4521–4524, and R.S. 10:9-301 through 9-307).
- The privilege of worker's, artisans, and repairmen of movables (C.C. art. 3217(2) and R.S. 9:4501–4502; see Section 31.3, below).
- The lessor's privilege (C.C. art. 3217(3), 3219, and see Section 31.2, below).
- The pledgor's privilege (C.C. art. 3217(4); see Chapter 10, above).

- The depositor's privilege (C.C. art. 3217(5)).
- The privilege on those who preserve objects (C.C. art. 3217(6)).
- The privilege of vendor of movables (C.C. art. 3217(7), and see Section 31.1, below).
- The carrier's privilege (C.C. art. 3217(9)).

30.2. The Importance (or Unimportance) of the Civil Code's Special Privileges

Many of the special privileges dealt with in the Civil Code are not utilized today. The privilege may be obsolete (because of the changes in society that have arisen between the date the privileges were created in 1870 and today) or the privilege may have been superseded by more specific legislation contained in the Louisiana Revised Statutes.

The Civil Code's special privileges on movables that are used every day and which remain the subject of negotiation and litigation are primarily limited to the privileges of the vendor, the lessor, and the repairmen of movables.

Therefore, while a few of the privileges listed in Section 30.1 are discussed elsewhere in this Précis, although sometimes just in passing, the next sections will address in detail the special privileges on movables of the vendor, the lessor and the repairman.

Chapter 31

The Privilege on Movables of Vendors, Lessors, and Repairmen

31.1. The Vendor's Privilege on Movables

The vendor's privilege on movables is directly related to a Louisiana sale. If the sale occurs outside of Louisiana, no Louisiana vendor's privilege exists.

The Civil Code grants vendors a privilege on the movable item that has been sold; the privilege secures the obligation of the purchaser to pay the entirety of the purchase price.

If the item is not "*in the possession of the purchaser*" (C.C. art. 3227), the vendor's privilege is lost. One must be cautious, however, in reading too broadly the phrase "*the possession of the purchaser*." Both the Civil Code and jurisprudence allow the vendor's privilege to be enforced in certain circumstances where the purchaser does not have physical possession of the item. These instances appear to be limited to situations where a third party temporarily "possesses" the item and the original purchaser has the right to regain control and possession of the item. For example, if an item subject to a vendor's privilege is left in the possession of the repairmen, the vendor's privilege is not lost (R.S. 9:4501(B); see Section 32.2, below).

On the other hand, if the purchaser sells the item, the privilege of the vendor who originally sold the item to the purchaser is extinguished.

The vendor's privilege on movables is not dependent on the form of the document. Even if a sale of movables is styled a "cash sale," the vendor's privilege remains and can be exercised if the purchaser gave the seller a check that the bank rejected because of insufficient funds in the purchaser's account. A different result occurs, however, for a vendor's privilege on immovables because of the public records doctrine (see Chapter 33, below).

There are special statutes governing the seller of agricultural products and of perishable property. See, for example, R.S. 9:4541 *et seq.*

31.2. The Privilege the Lessor of Immovables Has on Movables

The Civil Code grants lessors of immovable property a privilege on the property of the lessor's tenants and subtenants (C.C. art. 3219).

The existence of the lessor's privilege is not dependent upon a written lease; an oral lease can give rise to a lessor's privilege, as can a written but unrecorded lease. Of course, an unrecorded or unwritten lease will not affect third parties concerning the immovable property (C.C. arts. 2712 and 3338(2)); however, the lessor's privilege on the movables will exist as long as the lease is in effect.

The lessor's privilege secures *"the payment of rent and other obligations arising from the lease of immovable property"* (C.C. art. 2707).

All the movable property of a tenant is subject to the lessor's privilege, subject only to the exceptions from seizure contained in R.S. 13:3881 (see Chapter 35, below).

The movable property of a subtenant is subject to the lessor's privilege, but *"only to the extent that the sublessee is indebted to his sublessor at the time the lessor exercise his right"* (C.C. art. 2708). In other words, if the tenant owes the landlord $1,000 in back rent, but the subtenant owes the tenant only $200 in back rent, the landlord's lessor's privilege on the property of the subtenant is limited to $200. For this reason, many leases expressly prohibit either an assignment of a lease or a sublease unless the landlord's consent is obtained, and that consent often requires the subtenant to become personally obligated on the lease. C.C. art. 2713 provides that a clause prohibiting assignment without the landlord's consent also suffices to prohibit subleasing, and vice-versa.

The property of third parties left with a tenant is subject to the lessor's privilege, but only if the landlord does not know that movable items belong to a third party (C.C. art. 2709). If movable items belonging to a third party are seized under the lessor's privilege by a lessor unaware of the ownership of the items, the third party may intervene under C.C.P. art. 1092 to regain possession.

If movable property is encumbered by a lessor's privilege, it may be seized by the landlord either on the leased premises or off of the premises, as long as the item has not been offsite for more than fifteen days (C.C. art. 2710). If the items are offsite for more than fifteen days and then are brought back onto the leased property, the lessor's privilege again encumbers those items.

There is no requirement that a landlord post a bond to sequester items subject to a lessor's privilege (C.C.P. art. 3575). A landlord may even sequester property before rent is due *"if the lessor has good reason to believe that the lessee will remove the property subject to the lessor's privilege"* (C.C.P. art. 3572).

The rights of a lessor of immovable property to receive a privilege on movables should not be confused with the rights of a lessor of movable property. A lessor of movable property owns the movables being leased. Louisiana has a distinct set of rules for this situation; see the Lease of Movables Act (R.S. 9:3301 *et seq.*).

31.3. The Repairmen's Privilege on Movables

The Civil Code grants a privilege on movables to a *"workman or artisan for the price of his labor, on the movable which he has repaired or made, if the thing continues still in his possession"* (C.C. art. 3217(2)). This codal privilege does not allow for recovery of the costs of parts installed in the movable as part of the repairs, and the privilege is lost if the item leaves the possession of the *"workman or artisan."*

Specialized statutes exist in the Revised Statutes governing the rights of repairmen. R.S. 9:4501 regulates the privilege granted to repairmen of *"automobiles and other machinery."* R.S. 9:4502 regulates the privilege accorded to repairmen who do not fit within the definitions of R.S. 9:4501 (see R.S. 94502(D)).

Both statutes (R.S. 9:4501 and R.S. 9:4502):

- Extend the privilege to materials furnished by the repairmen;
- Allow the repairmen to exercise the privilege for up to 120 days from the date the last parts were furnished or work was performed if the repaired item is removed from the repairmen's premises; however, note that the 120 day period runs not from the date the item is removed from the premises but rather from the date that the work was performed or parts furnished;
- Permit a writ of sequestration to be obtained without a bond; and
- Extinguish the right of an owner of the item subject to this privilege to claim exemptions from seizure and sale (R.S. 13:3881, see Chapter 35, below).

Both statutes have identical ranking provisions (R.S. 9:4501(B) and R.S. 9:4502(B)). A repairmen's privilege under either statute expressly is:

- Inferior to:
  - A vendor's privilege on the movable being repaired;
  - A "*previously perfected*" UCC9 security interest;
  - The rights of a "*bona fide*" purchaser who has both paid the purchase price without notice of the repairmen's privilege and received possession of the movable.

- Superior to:
  - A UCC9 security interest that was not perfected prior to the time the repairmen's privilege arose;
  - The rights of a purchaser: (a) who has not paid the purchase price; (b) who has paid the purchase price but with prior notice of the repairmen's privilege; or (c) who has not received possession of the movable.

Chapter 32

The Ranking of Privileges on Movables

32.1. Ranking Two Privileges under the Civil Code

The Civil Code contains four general rules concerning the ranking of any two privileges.

First, the ranking of privileges on movables must be done separately from the ranking of privileges on immovables. One cannot "rank" simultaneously privileges on immovables and movables.

Second, C.C. art. 3253 declares that when a privilege encompasses both movables and immovables (see Chapter 28, above), all rights in the movables must be dealt with first, and then only if there are insufficient funds to pay off the creditors may one turn to exercising rights on the immovable. C.C. art. 3270 notes, however, that when "*the debts privileged on the movables and immovables can not be paid entirely, either because the movable effects are of small value, or subject to special privileges which claim a preference, or because the movables and immovables together do not suffice, the deficiency must not be borne proportionally among the [debts] but the debts must be paid according to the order established above, and the loss must fall on those which are of inferior dignity.*" In other words, (a) in distributing the proceeds of the judicial sale of immovables, if there is a statutory priority order among the privileges affecting the immovables, that priority order must be followed, and (b) in distributing the proceeds of the judicial sale of movables, if there is a statutory priority order among the privileges affecting the movables, that priority order must be followed.

Third, as the title to C.C. art. 3254 states, "*special privileges prime general privileges on movables*." This is an example of a priority order for distribution of the proceeds of a judicial sale of movables to the holders of privileges on the property sold.

Finally, C.C. arts. 3255–3270 contain specific rules on ranking certain special privileges against one another as well as specific rules on ranking certain special privileges against certain general privileges. If there is a conflict between the general priority rules and of the specific rules of C.C. arts. 3255–3270, the latter control.

Thus, the Civil Code, the Revised Statutes, and UCC9 provide relatively easy solutions to ranking any two privileges against one another or against a UCC9 security interest.

For example:

- A vendor's privilege outranks a repairmen's privilege (R.S. 9:4501(B), 4502(B));
- A lessor's privilege outranks a vendor's privilege (C.C. art. 3263);
- A UCC9 security interest outranks the privilege of both the lessor and vendor (R.S. 9:4770); and
- A prior-perfected UCC9 security agreement outranks a repairmen's privilege (R.S. 9:4501(B) and 9:4502(B)).

Solving ranking problems on movables becomes far more complex, however, when three or more privileges are involved because, as the next Section demonstrates, there is the possibility of a "vicious circle." A "vicious circle" exists when Privilege A outranks Privilege B, when Privilege B outranks Privilege C, but when Privilege C outranks Privilege A. Vicious circles exist because there is no single, comprehensive statutory listing of all special privileges on movables ranking each one against all others.

32.2. An Example of a "Vicious" Circle Involving Ranking the Vendor's Privilege, the Lessor's Privilege, the Repairmen's Privilege, and a UCC9 Security Interest

Determining the rank of vendor's privilege, a lessor's privilege, a repairmen's privilege, and a UCC9 security interest on the same item requires considering the interrelationship among the Civil Code, the Revised Statutes, and UCC9.

On June 1, Seller sold a movable on credit to Buyer. On June 2, Buyer leased an apartment from Landlord and put the movable item on the premises; the item was not subject to an exemption under R.S. 13:1881 (see Chapter 35, below). On June 3, the movable broke and Buyer took it to Repair Shop, where the repairman promptly started to work on the repairs. On June 4, while the item was in the Repair Shop, Creditor of Buyer perfected a UCC9 security interest in the movable. On June 5, Buyer came to the repair shop to pick up the item but did not have funds to pay for the repairs. The Repair Shop seized the item in accordance with the applicable statute (R.S. 9:4501 or 4502) and the Seller, Landlord, and Creditor all intervened in the suit (under C.C.P. art. 1092) asserting their privileges. When the court is called upon to rank the privileges and determine which claimant is entitled to a preference on the proceeds of the sale, the following analysis is applicable:

- Seller's vendor's privilege outranks Repair Shop's repairman's privilege (R.S. 9:4501(B) and 4502(B)).
- While Landlord's lessor's privilege continues in effect (because the movable has been off the leased premises for less than 15 days, C.C. art. 2710), nonetheless, Repair Shop's repairman's privilege outranks the lessor's privilege (because the lessor's privilege is not listed in R.S. 9:4501(B) and 4502(B) as a privilege to which the repairman is inferior).
- The Repair Shop's repairman's privilege outranks Creditor's UCC9 security interest, because the UCC9 interest was not perfected prior to the time the repairmen's privilege arose (when work begun) (R.S. 9:4501(B) and 4502(B)).
- Creditor's UCC9 security interest outranks Landlord's lessor's privilege and Seller's vendor's privilege (R.S. 9:4770), although Creditor's UCC9 security interest is inferior to the repairman's privilege (R.S. 9:4501(B) and 4502(B)).
- Yet, Seller's vendor's privilege is superior to the Repair Shop repairmen's privilege (R.S. 9:4501(B) and 4502(B)).

There is no easy solution to vicious circle ranking issues, either in statutes or in the jurisprudence. The two main arguments utilized by those engaged in negotiating these issues revolve around claims that either one must look to the last amended statute or, because privileges are intended to serve an overall societal purpose, one must consider the ranking that best achieves an overall societal purpose.

The problem with looking at the last amended statute is that often this will not resolve the vicious circle, for almost never does the "last" amended statute expressly refer to the ranking of three or more privileges. The problem with looking at overall societal purpose is that there may be a multiplicity of competing purposes (when there are three or more privileges), there is a problem in ascertaining which purpose is most valuable to society, and there is the difficulty of arguing why the controlling "purpose" is not the one contained in the last amended statute. As can be seen, the analysis itself can lead to a vicious circle of reasoning.

Thus, there is no definitive answer to the "vicious circle" ranking problem. That is why lawyers are needed to help clients evaluate the risks and attempt to resolve these matters with the most persuasive arguments.

Chapter 33

The Vendor's Privilege on Immovables

33.1. Distinctions between the Vendor's Privilege on Movables and the Vendor's Privilege on Immovables

One must be careful to distinguish between a vendor's privilege on movables (see Section 31.1, above) and a vendor's privilege on immovables, because each operates differently and each has different effects on third parties.

A vendor's privilege on movables is not filed or recorded anywhere. It is not dependent upon the form of the contract; it matters not whether the contract states that the sales price has been paid in full. Rather, the critical elements are whether the seller actually has received payment in full for the item, whether the transaction is a Louisiana sale, and whether the property remains in the buyer's possession (see Section 31.1, above).

By contrast, a vendor's privilege on immovables requires consideration of the rules of registry (see Chapter 19, above). An unrecorded vendor's privilege on immovables has no effect on third parties. An act of sale that states the sales price was "paid in cash" will create no vendor's privilege, even if seller can prove that she did not receive cash but rather a check and that the check did not clear the bank. This is explored in further detail in the next section.

33.2. The Requirements for the Vendor's Privilege on Immovables to Affect Third Parties

A vendor's privilege on immovables must be filed for recordation in the mortgage records if it is to affect third parties (C.C. arts. 3271, 3273, 3338). The usual rules involving immovable property apply to the sale document; there must be a description of the property sufficient to identify it; usually a street address alone is not sufficient (see Chapter 19, above).

To affect third parties, no magic language is needed to create a vendor's privilege. The words "vendor's privilege" need not even be in the document, because a vendor's privilege arises by operation of law and not by consent of the parties. The only "form" requirement for a vendor's privilege on immovables is that the act of sale must reveal, on its face, that something remains to be paid. If so, then by operation of law a vendor's privilege exists.

If the act states, however, that the price was "paid in full" or "paid in cash," then a vendor's privilege cannot exist. Third parties may rely upon the absence from the public records of anything indicating the existence of a vendor's privilege (see Section 19.3(a), above).

Louisiana jurisprudence allows a seller to waive a vendor's privilege in the act of sale or in a later recorded document.

A vendor's privilege is different from a resolutory condition; every document creating a vendor's privilege gives rise to a resolutory condition, but not every resolutory condition is a vendor's privilege (see Sections 22.2(a) and 22.2(b), above).

33.3. Ranking the Vendor's Privilege on Immovables

C.C. art. 3274 sets forth the conditions under which a vendor's privilege on immovables may receive a unique retroactive rank.

Perhaps the rationale for the retroactive rank originated in the historic Louisiana differences between filing and recordation, and between recordation in the conveyance records and recordation in the mortgage records, a distinction that has now been abolished (see Section 19.7, above). Louisiana law formerly had indicated that conveyances could be valid against third parties if filed with the Clerk of Court, even though the documents were never recorded in the conveyance records, while mortgages were ineffective against third parties unless they were recorded in the mortgage records. This is no longer the law (see Chapter 19, above).

Under C.C. art. 3274, a vendor's privilege on immovables ranks retroactively to the date of execution of the act of sale under two conditions. There is a seven day retroactive rank and a fifteen day retroactive rank.

First, if the act of sale is passed in the parish where the immovable is located and the act of sale is "*recorded*" within seven days of the passage of the act of sale, the vendor's privilege affects third parties from the date the act of sale was signed, even though it was not recorded until later (within the seven day window). Second, if the act of sale is passed in a different parish from the one where the immovable is located and if the act of sale is "*recorded*" within fifteen days of the passage of the act of sale, the vendor's privilege takes effect from the date the act of sale was signed (see the example in Section 33.3(a), below).

Finally, there is the jurisprudentially-created rule that a timely recorded vendor's privilege (one filed within the seven-day or fifteen-day period, as appropriate), outranks a previously recorded judicial mortgage against the buyer (see the example in Section 33.3(b), below).

33.3(a). Example 1: Retroactive Rank of a Vendor's Privilege

On March 1 of this year, Seller and Buyer enter into an "act of credit sale" involving immovable property located in Tangipahoa Parish. The "act of credit sale," signed in Tangipahoa Parish, states that part of the purchase price was paid in cash and the remainder was represented by Buyer's note payable in monthly installments over a five-year period. Seller does not retain a mortgage to secure the unpaid portion of the purchase price.

The "act of credit sale" notes that it is "subject to" a 2015 mortgage granted by the Seller to Bank (see Section 21.5(b), above, on "subject to" sales).

On March 2, Buyer files the "act of credit sale" with the Tangipahoa Clerk of Court; however, the Clerk does not get around to recording it in the conveyance and mortgage records until March 5.

Meanwhile, on March 4, Buyer grants a mortgage to Creditor on this tract, and Creditor promptly files and records that mortgage in the Tangipahoa conveyance records and mortgage records on March 4.

Although Seller did not retain a mortgage to secure the unpaid portion of the purchase price, the fact that the "act of credit sale" reveals on its face that money remains to be paid to Seller, and the fact that this document was recorded in the parish mortgage records means that, by operation of law, Seller has retained a vendor's privilege on the property.

Although Creditor's mortgage was recorded on March 4 and the "act of credit sale" was not recorded until March 5, Seller's vendor's privilege will out-rank Creditor's mortgage under C.C. art. 3274, because the credit sale was recorded within the seven-day window. Under C.C. art. 3274, the vendor's privilege created by the credit sale affects third parties from its date (March 1), even though nothing was recorded until March 5.

Creditor's mortgage will affect third parties from March 5, not March 4, even though Creditor's mortgage was recorded on March 4. The reason Creditor's mortgage ranks only from March 5 is that this is the earliest concurrence of the recordation of the mortgage and the buyer's ownership. Under Louisiana Supreme Court jurisprudence (see Section 19.7, above), it appears that Buyer's ownership may not affect third parties until the credit sale is recorded in the conveyance records. Creditor's mortgage, recorded on March 4, was recorded at a time when nothing on the public records indicated that Buyer owned the property, so Creditor's mortgage cannot begin to affect third parties under the "after acquired title" doctrine until the property "*is acquired by the mortgagor*" (C.C. art. 3292).

On the other hand, the retroactive rank of Seller's vendor's privilege does not impact the preexisting mortgage that Bank holds against the property. The vendor's privilege may be retroactive to March 1, but the preexisting mortgage held by the Bank (recorded in 2015) affected third parties from the date of its recordation, which was years before the March 1 "act of credit sale."

Therefore these security interests will be ranked as: (a) Bank's 2015 mortgage; (b) Seller's Vendor's Privilege and Resolutory Condition (see Section 22.2, above); (c) Creditor's March 4, mortgage granted by Seller.

Note that this is a developing area of law (see Chapter 19, above).

33.3(b). Example 2: Retroactive Rank of a Vendor's Privilege versus a Preexisting Judicial Mortgage against the Buyer

The facts are the same as in Section 33.3(a), Example 1, above, except that the 2015 mortgage was not a consensual mortgage placed on the property by Seller in favor of Bank but rather was a judicial mortgage resulting from a judgment in favor of Judgment Creditor against Buyer.

The judicial mortgage, as a general mortgage, affected all of Buyer's immovable property, including property Buyer might acquire in the future (see Chapter 17, above).

Under the Louisiana jurisprudence, a timely filed vendor's privilege out-ranks a judicial mortgage against a purchaser. The underlying rationale is that Buyer's interest in the property attaches at the moment of sale; however, at that point Buyer's rights are already encumbered by the vendor's privilege in favor of Seller, and the judicial mortgage holder cannot expect to receive more rights than Buyer received in the sale.

Therefore, these security interests are ranked: (a) Seller's vendor's privilege and Resolutory Condition (see Section 22.2, above); (b) Judgment Creditor's 2015 judicial mortgage against Buyer; and (c) Creditor's March 4 mortgage.

Chapter 34

Extinction of Privileges

34.1. The Four Methods of Extinguishing a Privilege

C.C. art. 3277 describes the four ways that privileges "*become extinct.*" It provides: "*Privileges become extinct: (1) By the extinction of the thing subject to the privilege. (2) By the creditor acquiring the thing subject to it. (3) By the extinction of debt which gave birth to it. (4) By prescription.*"

The next four sections explore these concepts.

34.2. Extinction of a Privilege by Extinction of the Thing Subject to the Privilege

If the movable subject to the privilege is destroyed, then any special privilege and general privilege on it ceases to exist. The destruction of the movable, however, does not eliminate the debt that the privilege secures, because a privilege is merely an accessory obligation (see C.C. arts. 1891 and 3186 and Chapter 28, above). Therefore, if a creditor holds only a special privilege and the movable is destroyed, the creditor becomes an unsecured creditor.

On the other hand, because general privileges are "blanket" privileges affecting all movables of the debtor (see Section 28.3, above), the destruction of any one movable does not impact the general privilege on all other movables or immovables affected by the general privilege. The general privilege continues on all such items that the debtor owns now or more acquire in the future (see Chapter 29, above).

34.3. Extinction of a Privilege by the Creditor Acquiring the Thing Subject to the Privilege

If the creditor acquires ownership of the object that is subject to a special privilege, the privilege is extinguished. The extinguishment of the privilege, however, does not necessarily mean that the debt that the privilege secures is also extinguished.

There are mechanisms under the Louisiana Deficiency Judgment Act for a creditor to acquire the property for an amount agreed upon after default and still maintain the right to collect the balance owed (see the Louisiana Deficiency Judgment Act, R.S. 13:4106 and Chapter 40, below). A creditor must carefully comply with the requirements of the Deficiency Judgment Act, however, or the creditor may find that its ability to collect any remaining monies from the debtor has been eliminated.

34.4. Extinction of a Privilege by Extinction of the Debt Which Gave Rise to the Privilege

Because privileges are accessory obligations (see Chapter 28, above), the extinction of the debt that the privilege secures releases the accessory privilege (C.C. art. 1913).

The debt could be extinguished in several ways, including payment, prescription, or remission.

34.5. Extinction of a Privilege by Prescription

Prescription of a privilege (a real security) is distinct from prescription on the principal obligation (the obligation the privilege secures). If the principal obligation is prescribed, the accessory privilege is released (C.C. art. 3277(3) and Section 34.4, above).

But even if the principal obligation remains extant, the privilege can prescribe. For example, if a landlord does not sequester or judicially seize the tenant's movables within fifteen days after they are removed from the leased premises, the lessor's privilege is unenforceable (C.C. art. 2710 and Section 31.2, above). This is the type of "prescription" to which C.C. art. 3277(4) refers.

Chapter 35

Exemptions from Seizure: R.S. 13:3881

35.1. The Purpose of Exemptions from Seizure of Assets, Movable Property, and Immovable Property

The Civil Code states that every person who is bound for an obligation "*is obligated to fulfill it out of all of his property, movable and immovable, present and future*" (C.C. art. 3133). Even though this sets forth the general rule, the legislature has recognized that stripping a debtor of all assets does not permit the debtor to survive with dignity and makes that debtor a ward of the state. To allow debtors to maintain some semblance of autonomy and to retain the ability to earn a living, put food on the table, and protect certain personal possessions, the legislature created two sets of statutes, one protecting movable property and the other protecting the "homestead." The "homestead" exemption is discussed in Chapter 25, above. This Chapter 35 deals with exemptions from seizure and sale of certain movable items and non-immovable assets.

The general exemption statute is R.S. 13:3881, but it does not apply in all instances. For example, the exemptions from seizure under R.S. 13:3881 do not apply to a repairman's privilege under R.S. 9:4501 or 9:4502 (see Section 31.3, above). Likewise, if a debtor executes a UCC9 security interest in an asset otherwise protected under R.S. 13:3881, the exemption from seizure is waived (R.S. 13:3881(B)(2)).

35.2. The Exemptions from Seizure of Movables and Certain Other Assets: R.S. 13:3881

The exemptions from seizure under R.S. 13:3881 fall into six main categories:

- A portion of wages (R.S. 13:3881(A)(1));
- Items necessary to earn a living (R.S. 13:3881(A)(2));
- Certain personal effects (R.S. 13:3881(A) §§ (4), (5), and (8));
- The *"personal servitude of habitation"* and a C.C. art. 223 usufruct (R.S. 13:3881(A)(3));
- Motor vehicles, limited to $7,500 *"in equity value for one motor vehicle per household used by the debtor and his family household for any purpose,"* although there are special rules for a second motor vehicle that has been *"substantially modified, equipped, or fitted for the purposes of adapting its use to the physical disability of the debtor or his family and is used by the debtor or his family for the transporting of such disabled person for any use"* (R.S. 13:3881(A)(7) and (8)); and
- Certain insurance, annuity rights, pensions, and tax deferred retirement accounts (R.S. 13:3881(D)).

Note, however, that there are numerous items that do not fall within this exemption list. The following are examples of non-exempt items that remain subject to seizure by any creditor:

- Televisions;
- Computers (other than those used in the *"exercise of a trade, calling or profession,"* R.S. 13:3881(A)(2));
- Artwork (other than family portraits, R.S. 13:3881(A)(4)(b)); and
- Electronic gear (other than musical instruments played by a member of the family, R.S. 13:3881(A)(4)(d)).

35.2(a). The "Tools of the Trade" Exemption: R.S. 13:3881(A)(2)

R.S. 13:3881(A)(2) exempts from seizure and sale *"property necessary to the exercise of a trade, calling or profession by which he earns a livelihood."* The exemption is a narrow category of items and is limited to *"(a) Tools; (b) Instruments; (c) Books; (d) One utility trailer."*

Each of these listed items, to be exempt, must be "*necessary*" to the debtor's "*trade, calling, or profession.*" Thus, not all tools, instruments, and books owned by a debtor are exempt from seizure and sale.

35.2(a)(1). Example #1: "Tools of the Trade" Exemption

Debtor is a carpenter by trade whose hobby is astronomy. Debtor owns hammers, electric nail guns, drills, and saws that she uses in her work. Debtor has a fancy telescope she uses to observe the stars. Debtor owns books on carpentry and astronomy.

If Debtor had borrowed money from Creditor on an unsecured basis, did not repay the loan, and Creditor obtained a judgment and attempted to seize Debtor's assets to pay the judgment, Creditor could seize the telescope and books on astronomy, because these items are not necessary to the debtor's trade, calling, or profession. Debtor, however, could claim an exemption from seizure under the R.S. 13:3881(A)(2) on the hammers, electric nail guns, drills, saws, and books on carpentry.

35.2(a)(2). Example #2: "Tools of the Trade" Exemption and a UCC9 Security Interest

The facts are the same as in Section 35.2(a)(1), Example #1, above, except that, to purchase the fancy telescope, Debtor took out a loan from Lender and gave Lender a perfected UCC9 security interest in the telescope.

In this situation, while Creditor may not seize the telescope to satisfy the judgment (see Example #1, above), Lender may seize the telescope if Debtor does not pay. Debtor may not claim an exemption from seizure under R.S. 13:3881 against Lender, because these exemptions do not apply if a debtor has given a lender a UCC9 security interest in an item that otherwise would be exempt under R.S. 13:3881. This is because R.S. 13:3881(B)(2) states: "*No property upon which a debtor has voluntarily granted a lien shall, to the extent of the balance due on the debt secured thereby, be subject to the provisions of this Chapter or be exempt from forced sale under process of law.*"

35.2(a)(3). Example #3: The "Family Portraits," "Military Accoutrements," "Firearms," and "Musical Instruments" Exemptions under R.S. 13:3881

R.S. 13:3881(A)(4) exempts from seizure and sale "*(b) The family portraits; (c) His military accoutrements; (d) The musical instruments played or practiced on by him or a member of his family*" and "*(g) All firearms, arms and ammuni-*

tion, and accessories thereto, not exceeding a total maximum value of two thousand five hundred dollars, which may be used for any purpose."

Debtor #2 comes from a family of art collectors. Debtor #2 has inherited from her mother a portrait of her grandmother painted by a famous artist as well as works of art from Degas, Monet, and Picasso. Debtor #2 also inherited from her mother a baby grand piano. Debtor #2 owns a Glock pistol worth $5,000, which she had used while she served in the Army. She also owns two shotguns, each worth $3,000; she bought these shotguns to use for duck hunting.

If Debtor #2 had borrowed money from Creditor on an unsecured basis, did not repay the loan, and Creditor obtained a judgment and attempted to seize Debtor #2's assets to pay the judgment, Creditor could seize the paintings by Degas, Monet, and Picasso, because these are not "family portraits." Debtor #2 may claim, however, that her grandmother's portrait is exempt from seizure.

Debtor #2's ability to claim an exemption from seizure on the piano would depend on whether Debtor #2 or a member of her family "played or practiced" on it. It should be noted that there is a potential conflict between R.S. 13:3881(A)(4)(d) concerning musical instruments and R.S. 9:4561, which states that *"pianos may be seized to enforce a vendor's privilege thereon."* There is no jurisprudence on this potential conflict, but it would appear that R.S. 13:3881, as the later-amended statute, should control. Further, the piano seller could not use R.S. 13:3881(B)(2), because a vendor's privilege on movables arises by operation of law and thus is not property *"upon which a debtor has voluntarily granted a lien."*

Debtor #2's Glock pistol, even though it is worth more than $5,000, would be exempt from seizure, because the term "military accoutrements" has been judicially interpreted to mean weapons used in the context of military duty. On the other hand, Debtor #2's shotguns would not be exempt and are subject to seizure by Creditor, because they are not related to Debtor #2's military service and because they exceed "a total maximum value" of $2,500.

Chapter 36

Materialmen's Liens and Privileges Affecting Immovables

36.1. An Overview of Materialmen's Liens and Privileges

Louisiana law gives a privilege to workers, contractors, architects, engineers, and others who help improve immovable property. The privilege allows them to seize and sell the property and get a privilege on the proceeds of the sale. In some instances, this privilege can outrank preexisting mortgages on the property (see C.C. art. 3186 and R.S. 9:4821). This privilege is generically known among lawyers as the "materialmen's lien," although the term "lien" stems from common law, not civil law.

This privilege is an accessory obligation that, depending on the party claiming the privilege, secures the payment of wages and benefits of workers, the costs of materials and supplies, and the contract price for the work performed. The privilege is not necessarily dependent on privity of contract between the property owner and the one asserting the privilege. The specifics of the statute under which the privilege is claimed will determine whether the privilege extends to supplies and provisions as well as whether the privilege extends beyond those who work for a "contractor" (as defined in the statute under which the privilege is claimed).

There are four main statutes systems dealing with the materialmen's liens:

- The Louisiana Private Works Act (R.S. 9:4801 *et seq.*, see Chapter 37, below);

- The Louisiana Oil, Gas and Water Well Lien Act (R.S. 9:4861 *et seq.*), which some lawyers refer to as the "Oil Well Lien Act."
- The Louisiana Public Works Act, detailing the rights of those who work on immovable property owned by the state or political entities (R.S. 38:2241 *et seq.*); and
- The Miller Act, concerning the rights of those who work on federal projects (40 U.S.C. §3131 *et seq.*). This statute applies not only to federal projects in Louisiana, but also to federal projects nationwide.

The Louisiana Public Works Act and the federal Miller Act prevent the lien claimant from having a right against the immovable property, but under these acts the lien claimant does have a right to pursue not only a claim against the governmental owner of the property but also a claim against the bonding company on the job. The problem for lien claimants under these two acts, however, is that a judgment against a governmental entity does not result in a judicial mortgage (see Section 17.6, above); the lien claimant must seek satisfaction from the bonding company or wait until the governmental entity approves payment of the judgment.

The Louisiana Private Works Act and the Oil Well Lien Act permit the lien claimant to seize and sell the immovable property in addition to having claims against the owner and bonding company.

The four listed lien laws are not the only Louisiana materialmen's lien statutes. There are specialized statutes for certain industries. Each statutory regime has its own unique scope on who is entitled to the lien, rules on how to obtain and preserve the lien, lists of items to which the lien applies, and rules on the rank of lien claimants against each other and against third parties.

36.2. The Historical Background on Materialmen's Lien Privileges

Since its enactment in the nineteenth century, the Louisiana Civil Code has protected workers and contractors who assist an owner in improving or repairing immovable property. The Civil Code provided this protection by granting workers and contractors a privilege on the immovable. The property could be seized and sold to satisfy the unpaid wages and monies owed to those who performed the improvements.

Historically, at the time of the enactment of the Code Napoleon in France in 1804, privileges were granted to architects, contractors, masons, and those who built houses. No privilege, however, was granted to suppliers of materials. The Louisiana legislature added suppliers of materials to those entitled to the privilege when it revised the Civil Code in 1825.

When the Civil Code was revised again in 1870, C.C. arts. 3249 and 3274 were enacted and they have remain unchanged since that date. The privileges created by these articles are not dependent on whether those claiming the privilege had privity of contract with the owner of the property.

The area dealt with in these provisions in terms of materialmen's liens is now covered in much greater depth and detail in the Louisiana Private Works Act (R.S. 9:4801 *et seq.* and Chapter 37, below) and the Oil Well Lien Act (R.S. 9:4861 *et seq.*). The jurisprudence today relies on these latter two acts rather than on the terms of the Civil Code articles.

Chapter 37

The Louisiana Private Works Act

37.1. Scope and Structure of the Louisiana Private Works Act

The Louisiana Private Works Act ("PWA," R.S. 9:4801 *et seq.*) grants a privilege on immovable property to a broad scope of workers, contractors, vendors, and others who improve or repair the property. Those who are entitled to claim the privilege (the "lien claimants") may seize and sell the property. Once the property has been sold, the lien claimants are entitled to a privilege on the sale's proceeds; the rank of these claims is controlled by R.S. 9:4821 (see Section 37.11, below).

The privilege secures two types of lien claimants: (a) those who have privity of contract with the owner (R.S. 9:4801); and (b) those who do not have privity of contract with the owner (R.S. 9:4802).

The scope of lien claimants include:

- Laborers, whether they work for the owner of the property (R.S. 9:4801(2)) or are employed by a general contractor, contractor, or subcontractor (R.S. 9:4802(A)(2));
- General contractors as well as all contractors who have privity of contract with the owner (R.S. 9:4801(1));
- Sellers of movables that become component parts or are consumed at the site or in machinery at the site, as long as the seller has sold to the owner of the immovable (R.S. 9:4801(3)) or to a contractor or subcontractor (R.S. 9:4802(A)(3));

- Lessors of movables used at the job site, as long as the lessor has a written contract with the owner of the immovable (R.S. 9:4801(4)) or with a contractor or subcontractor (R.S. 9:4802(A)(4)); and
- A defined group of architects, engineers, and land surveyors, as long as they have a contract with the owner of the immovable (R.S. 9:4801(5)) or with a contractor or subcontractor (R.S. 9:4802(A)(5)).

Louisiana jurisprudence has declared that the rights of lien claimants are personal to them and that lien claims are strictly construed against the lien claimants. Louisiana courts generally have held (and Louisiana privilege concepts appear to mandate) that an inferior lien claimant may not pay off a lien claimant with superior rank and claim that superior rank; the key cases held that subrogation to the rank of liens under the Private Works Act does not apply to lien claimants, although there have been some intermediate Louisiana appellate decisions to the contrary.

The scope of lien claimants does not include any of the following individuals or entities listed below. These individuals and businesses are not entitled to a PWA privilege, although they may pursue whatever rights they have under contract:

- Sellers or suppliers who do not have a contract with the owner, contractor, or subcontractor but who nonetheless supply other sellers or suppliers. For example, no PWA privilege can be claimed by seller of lumber who delivers the lumber to a cabinet maker, who then creates a cabinet and then delivers it to the job site. The reason is that the cabinet maker, by merely delivering the cabinets to the job site, will be treated as a "vendor" under the PWA, and vendors of vendors are not entitled to a PWA lien under either R.S. 9:4801 or 9:4802.
- Laborers who work for vendors, suppliers, or lessees of movable property used in the improvement of the immovable property. For example, the laborer who worked for the seller of lumber (described above) would not be entitled to a PWA privilege.

If an owner fails to follow the PWA rules concerning notice of contract and bond (see Sections 37.3, below), the owner may be exposed to personal liability. That personal liability is not limited to those with whom the owner has privity of contract, but it also extends to all lien claimants even though the owner has no privity of contract with them (see Section 37.2, below).

The PWA is very broad. It covers more than commercial construction. It covers more than major residential renovations. All those who make a repair or "physical change of an immovable or its component parts" (R.S. 9:4808(A)) may be entitled to a PWA privilege if they fit within one of the categories listed in R.S. 9:4801 and 9:4802. Thus, the PWA privilege extends to the roofing company that repairs a homeowner's roof, to the plumber who installs a new sink in a house, and even to the repairman who fixes a home's central air conditioning unit (for this unit would be considered a component part under C.C. art. 466).

A word of caution to those reading this Chapter. At the time of the writing of this edition of the Précis, the Louisiana State Law Institute is in the process of reworking and redrafting the PWA; at some point that draft will be submitted to the legislature for consideration. Therefore, readers should check to see whether any legislative changes have been enacted after the publication date of this edition of the Précis.

37.1(a). Critical Definitions and Concepts in the Louisiana Private Works Act

The PWA contains definitions of "owner," "work," "general contractor," "contractor," and "subcontractor." A detailed understanding of these terms is necessary to understand the scope and implications of the PWA.

37.1(b). PWA Definition of "Owner"

"Owner" is defined in R.S. 9:4806(A) as including not only the owner of the immovable but also the "*naked owner, owner of a predial or personal servitude, possessor, lessee, or other person owning or having the right to the use or enjoyment of an immovable or having an interest therein shall be deemed to be an owner.*"

The definition is not as broad as it appears. It is limited in two respects. First, it is limited to only those "owners" who are personally impacted by privilege. Second, the definition limits the scope of the privilege that impacts each owner's rights in the property.

When there is more than one owner of the property, the non-privity personal claims against an owner under R.S. 9:4802 (see Section 37.2, below) do not apply to those owners who have not contracted with the contractor or who have not "*agreed in writing to the price and work of the contract of a lessee*" (R.S. 9:4806(B)).

Even if a PWA claim exists against an owner, the privilege is limited to that owner's interest in the immovable (R.S. 9:4806(C)). Both landlords and tenants can be "owners" under the PWA. For example, if a tenant makes physical improvements to leased immovable property, the lien claimants will have a privilege on the tenant's rights in the lease, but the privilege is inferior to the claims of the landlord (R.S. 9:4806(D)). If a tenant makes improvements, lien claimants do not have either a personal claim against the landlord or a privilege on the immovable property itself unless the landlord has "*specifically agreed to be liable for any claims*" in writing (R.S. 9:4806(B)).

37.1(c). PWA Definition of "Work"

"*Work*" is used in different contexts in two provisions of the PWA—R.S. 9:4808 and R.S. 9:4820.

R.S. 9:4808 "*work*" defines the kinds of activities entitling a lien clamant to a PWA privilege. Every lien claimant who does R.S. 9:4808 "*work*" may assert a PWA privilege. This "*work*" is the "*single continuous project for the improvement, construction, erection, reconstruction, modification, repair, demolition, or other physical change of an immovable or its component parts*" (R.S. 9:4808(A)).

R.S. 9:4820 "*work*," by contrast, is a narrower scope of activities than that encompassed in R.S. 9:4808. Once any lien claimant performs R.S. 9:4820 "*work*," then not only is that lien claimant entitled to a PWA lien, but also all lien claimants who work on the property at any point in time thereafter as part of this project are entitled to a PWA lien.

For example, the worker on the bulldozer who clears and levels vacant property is entitled to a PWA lien for this kind of "*work*" (that is, R.S. 9:4808 work), but these activities do not operate to entitle any other lien claimant to assert a PWA lien (see R.S. 9:4808(C)). By contrast, a carpenter who helps put up a wall in a new building in February is doing the kind of R.S. 9:4820 work that will entitle the painting contractor, who does not come on to the job until August, not only to have a lien but also to assert that the lien began either (i) back in February when the carpenter came onto the job, or (ii) to such earlier time as the notice of contract was filed, if the notice of contract was filed prior to the time that "work" under R.S. 9:4820 began (see R.S. 9:4820(A)).

37.1(d). PWA Definitions of "General Contractor" and "Contractor"

The definitions of "general contractor," "contractor," and "subcontractor" are contained in R.S. 9:4807. General contractors and contractors are those who have privity of contract with the owner; subcontractors do not.

There can be more than one general contractor on a job, because R.S. 9:4807 defines a general contractor as one who either performs "*all or substantially all of a work*" or one who is deemed to be a general contractor under R.S. 9:4808(B).

R.S. 9:4808(B) is in the same part of the PWA that defines "work." It appears to permit separate lien periods to run on different portions of the same immovable tract if there are separate, timely filed notices of contract with appropriate bonds.

37.1(e). Examples of How the Definitions of "Work" and "Contract" Can Interact

The statutory definitions of "work" and "contract" appear to allow an owner to have separate lien periods running on the same tract of land by using different "contracts" (even if there is only one general contractor) or by having different general contractors. There is no case, however, that either validates or invalidates this reading of the statute. The following examples give illustrations of potential situations.

37.1(e)(1). Example #1

Owner is building two separate apartment structures on the same tract, with apartment building #1 started on March 1 and completed on October 1, and apartment building #2 started on April 1 and completed on December 1. No notice of contract was filed.

If this is all part of a "*continuous project*" (R.S. 9:4808(A)), those who worked on building #1 on March 2 would not have to file their liens until after December 1, the completion of work on building #2. This is because the R.S. 9:4820 "work" on building #1 started the date that PWA liens became effective against third persons (see R.S. 9:4820(A)).

37.1(e)(2). Example #2

The facts are the same as in Section 37.1(e)(2), Example #1, above, but here Owner had entered into separate contracts with the general contractor for each building and had timely filed a notice of contract with a proper bond on each building (R.S. 9:4808(B)).

In this instance, it can be argued that the owner may file a separate notice of termination for each building (R.S. 9:4822(F)). When this occurs, those who worked on building #1 would have to timely file their liens when building #1 was completed and could not wait to file until building #2 was finished (see Section 37.4, below).

37.1(f). PWA Definition of "Subcontractor"

R.S. 9:4807(C) defines a subcontractor as *"one who, by contract made directly with a contractor, or by a contract that is one of a series of contracts emanating from a contractor, is bound to perform all or part of a work contracted for by the contractor."* In other words, a subcontractor is one who has a contract with a general contractor, a contractor, or another subcontractor.

There is no limit to the number of levels of subcontracts that can qualify for a PWA lien. Once someone is classified as a contractor or subcontractor, then all those who subcontract through them entitled to PWA lien. One must be careful, however, to distinguish this situation from other contractual relationships that may not qualify for PWA lien status.

The critical inquiry is distinguishing among a contractor, subcontractor, and supplier. The jurisprudence has held that if a company installs a product on the site or works on the site, that entity can be classified as a contractor or subcontractor (depending on whether the entity has privity of contract with the owner of the immovable). By contrast, an entity that merely delivers movables or product to the job site is a vendor or supplier.

Subcontractors can be individuals as well as business entities; however, one must be careful to distinguish between laborers (who are employees of the owner, contractor or subcontractor) and individuals who operate as a contractor or subcontractor. If the person claiming the privilege is an employee of someone, that employee is classified as a laborer and must claim his or her lien under R.S. 9:4801(2) or 9:4802(A)(2).

37.1(f)(1). Example #1

The subcontractor of a subcontractor of a subcontractor is entitled to file a PWA lien (R.S. 9:4802(A)(1)). If the subcontractor is entitled to a PWA lien, the subcontractor's laborers are entitled to a lien (R.S. 9:4802(A)(2)). Likewise, the laborers of a subcontractor of a subcontractor of a subcontractor are entitled to a PWA lien.

37.1(f)(2). Example #2

One who sells movable property to a contractor or subcontractor (or even to a subcontractor of a subcontractor of a subcontractor) is entitled to a PWA lien if the movable becomes a component part or is used or consumed in the construction process (R.S. 9:4801(3) and R.S. 9:4802(A)(3)).

On the other hand, laborers of the seller and subcontractors of the seller are not entitled to a PWA lien. Likewise, those who sell movables or product to the seller (such as a wood mill that sells lumber to a cabinet maker who uses the lumber to make cabinets and then sells the cabinets to a subcontractor) are not entitled to a PWA lien.

37.2. An Owner's Liability under the Louisiana Private Works Act

An owner always has contractual liability to those with whom the owner has privity of contract. The terms of the contract set forth the limits of the owner's liability to those with whom the owner contracts.

Under the PWA, however, all of the lien claimants without privity who are entitled to a lien under R.S. 9:4802 have a personal claim against the owner for the work performed (R.S. 9:4802(A)). The owner's personal liability is secured by the PWA lien against the owner's property. In other words, the PWA lien is an accessory obligation to the owner's personal liability to the lien claimant, and this personal liability arises by statute, not contract.

The owner's non-privity liability is not limited by the amount of any contract that the owner may have with the contractor or general contractor; the only limit is the total amount of all claims of those who properly and timely assert and preserve their PWA liens.

37.2(a). Example #1

Owner enters into a $1 million construction contract with General Contractor; no notice of contract is recorded and no bond is provided. Owner has paid General Contractor $600,000. It turns out that General Contractor has bid too little for the job; the costs are far more than the General Contractor had anticipated. It will cost an additional $700,000 to complete the job (a total cost of $1.3 million, which is $300,000 more than the original contract).

Owner can enforce its contract rights. Owner can insist General Contractor complete the job, and Owner is liable only for an additional $400,000 (the difference between the $1 million contract amount and the $600,000 the Owner had already paid General Contractor).

37.2(b). Example #2

The facts are the same as in Section 37.2(a), Example #1, above; however, in addition, General Contractor has not paid any of its subcontractors or suppliers. The subcontractors and suppliers are owed $1.5 million. The subcontractors and suppliers timely file and preserve their PWA liens.

In this situation, Owner personally owes the subcontractors and suppliers the entire $1.5 million. The $1.5 million is secured by a PWA lien on Owner's property where the work is being performed. Owner cannot limit its liability to the $1 million contract with General Contractor. Owner cannot claim a set-off or take a deduction for the $600,000 already paid to the General Contractor.

37.2(c). The General Contractor's Liability under the Private Works Act

Just as an owner can have unlimited personal liability to those lien claimants with whom the owner has no privity of contract (see Section 37.2, above), a contractor can have identical unlimited personal liability to lien claimants with whom the contractor has no privity of contract (R.S. 9:4802(A)).

The claim against the contractor in such instances, however, is an unsecured claim, unlike the claim against the owner, which is secured under the PWA by a privilege on the owner's property where the work is being performed.

37.3. How an Owner May Avoid Personal Liability to Those without Privity of Contract with the Owner

Owners have an incentive to try to limit their liability under the PWA because, under the Act, an owner may have unlimited personal liability to lien claimants even if the owner did not know the identity of these parties while they were working on the property and even though the owner has no privity of contract with them (see Section 37.2, above). General contractors likewise have an incentive to limit personal liability because contractors can have unlimited non-privity liability to lien claimants (see Section 37.2(c), above).

The way that both an owner and general contractor can limit personal liability to those without privity of contract is by timely filing a notice of contract with a proper bond.

The form for a notice of contract is controlled by R.S. 9:4811. The requirements of a proper bond are contained in R.S. 9:4812. A PWA bond is a legal suretyship (see Section 2.2(b), above).

A notice of contract is timely filed only if it is filed prior to R.S. 9:4820 "work" beginning. Note that the time frame is hinged to R.S. 9:4820 "work," not R.S.

9:4808 "work." See Section 37.1(c), above, about the distinctions between "work" under R.S. 9:4808 and R.S. 9:4820. For example, if the only thing that has occurred on a tract of land is that a tractor operator clears an owner's property of trees and underbrush, the tractor operator has done R.S. 9:4808 "work" and can obtain a PWA privilege, but the tractor operator has not performed R.S. 9:4820 "work." Thus, a notice of contract filed after the tractor operator has completed the clearing operations can still be timely as long as no R.S. 9:4820 "*work*" has begun. If, on the other hand, while the tractor operator was engaged in the land-clearing operations, a lumber supplier delivered $500 worth of lumber to the property to be used to construct forms for concrete pouring, the delivery of the lumber in that amount would constitute R.S. 9:4820 "*work*" and thus a notice of contract filed after the delivery of lumber would be untimely.

If a timely notice of contract with a proper bond is filed, the owner escapes all personal liability to those lien claimants with whom the owner has no privity of contract (R.S. 9:4802(C)). In this instance, these lien claimants may (a) sue only those with whom they have privity, and (b) pursue the surety under the bond (R.S. 9:4813).

37.3(a). Where Are PWA Filings Made?

All filings under the PWA must be made in the mortgage records of the parish where the immovable property is located (R.S. 9:4831). This applies to notices of contract, notices of termination or default, and notices of liens.

All filings under the PWA must contain a legal property description; using only the street name or mailing address is insufficient to preserve any rights or claims (R.S. 9:4831(C)).

37.3(b). How All Lien Claimants, Other Than the General Contractor, Assert and Preserve Their Privileges

Those lien claimants who have privity of contract with the owner may always elect to sue the owner directly on the contract, regardless of whether they have timely preserved their PWA privilege. On the other hand, those lien claimants who do not have privity of contract with the owner must timely preserve their PWA claim in order to pursue both the owner and the contractor personally (R.S. 9:4823(A)).

There are two main time periods to preserve liens under the PWA—30 days and 60 days (see Sections 37.5 and 37.6, above). Which period is applicable depends upon whether the lien claimant has privity of contract with the owner and, if not, whether a timely notice of contract has been filed.

Each lien claimant must file, within the proper time period, a "*statement of claim or privilege*." The requirements for this statement are contained in R.S. 9:4822(G).

The 30-day lien period is triggered by a notice of substantial completion or of termination (see Section 37.4, below). The 60-day lien period is triggered by either notice of substantial completion or abandonment of the work (see Section 37.4, below).

37.4. Notice of Substantial Completion and Notice of Termination

"Substantial completion" is defined in R.S. 9:4822(H). If the work has been substantially completed, the owner may file a notice of termination in the mortgage records (R.S. 9:4831). The notice of termination starts the time from which the lien claimants must file their statement of claim (R.S. 9:4822(G)) in order to timely claim the PWA lien.

If the work is not substantially completed but work on the job has terminated (for instance, because the contractor is in default and has left the job or has been kicked off the job by the owner), the owner may file a notice of termination in the mortgage records. A notice of termination may be filed in relation to a specified portion of the work (R.S. 9:4822(F)).

37.5. The 30-Day Lien Period

All claimants have 30 days to file their statement of claim if the notice of contract is timely filed (R.S. 9:4822(A)). A timely filed notice of contract is one that is filed before "*work*" under R.S. 9:4820 begins. The fact that a bond was not attached to the notice of contract does not make the notice invalid or change the 30-day lien period (R.S. 9:4811(C)); however, if a proper bond is not attached, the owner has unlimited personal liability to the lien claimants.

The thirty-day period begins when the notice of termination is filed for recordation in the mortgage records (R.S. 9:4822(A)).

In addition, a copy of the statement of claim must be delivered to the owner, unless the owner's address is not contained in the notice of contract (R.S. 9:4822(A)(2)).

37.6. The 60-Day Lien Period

The sixty-day lien period applies to all those lien claimants if a notice of contract was not timely filed (R.S. 9:4822(C)).

Note that the sixty-day period is triggered by the failure to timely file the notice of contract.

The statement of claim (R.S. 9:4822(G)) must be filed within sixty days of the owner's filing a notice of termination or within sixty days of substantial completion or abandonment (R.S. 9:4822(C)).

37.7. The 70-Day Lien Period

There is a special seventy-day time frame to file a statement of claim. It applies, however, only when a notice of contract is not filed and is applicable only to *"the seller of movables sold for use or consumption in work on an immovable for residential purposes"* (R.S. 9:4822(D)(2)).

37.8. Special Rules for Those Who Sell or Lease Movables to a Contractor or Subcontractor

Those who lease or sell movables to contractors or subcontractors must give timely notice of their contracts to the owner and others (R.S. 9:4802(G)). A failure to give a timely notice at the start of the contract will prevent these lessees and sellers from filing any lien claim; without that timely notice at the start of the project, any subsequent statement of claim that they file will be invalid.

37.8(a). How a General Contractor Preserves Its Privilege

A general contractor whose contract is under $25,000 is entitled to file a PWA lien (R.S. 9:4811(D)).

A general contractor whose contract is greater than $25,000 is entitled to a PWA lien only if a notice of contract is timely filed (R.S. 9:4811(D)).

If a notice of contract is timely filed (which must before R.S. 9:4820 *"work"* begins), the general contractor has sixty days from the *"notice of ter-*

mination or substantial completion" to file its statement of claim (R.S. 9:4822). Note, however, that at least one intermediate Louisiana appellate court has held that the General Contractor's notice of lien must be filed within sixty days of actual substantial completion, not within sixty days of the owner's filing of a notice of substantial completion. This is a developing area of the law.

Once the general contractor has timely filed its statement of claim, it must then timely file a lawsuit to enforce the PWA lien. A failure to timely file the suit will result in the lien being extinguished (R.S. 9:4823; see Section 37.8(c), below).

37.8(b). How Lien Claimants without Privity of Contract Preserve Their Claims against the General Contractor

The PWA creates the possibility that the general contractor and other contractors (but not subcontractors) can have unlimited personal liability to those lien claimants with whom the contractor does not have privity of contract (R.S. 9:4802(A)).

The special rules on how these lien claimants can preserve and assert their claim against the contractor are in R.S. 9:4823(B). In essence, delivering certain timely statutory notification to the contractor may be sufficient, but only if a suit is later timely filed.

37.8(c). How All Lien Claimants Enforce Their PWA Liens and Prevent Their Liens from Being Extinguished

Merely filing a timely statement of claim is not enough to preserve a lien claimant's rights. The only thing a timely filing of a statement of claim accomplishes is to preserve the lien against the owner's property (R.S. 9:4822). The lien claimant, however, cannot assert the lien against the owner without doing more.

Once a timely statement of claim has been filed, each lien claimant must take the additional step of timely filing a lawsuit. The lawsuit must be filed *"within one year after filing the statement of claim or privilege"* (R.S. 9:4823(A)(2)).

37.8(d). The Amount of the PWA Bond and the Liability of a PWA Surety

One who supplies a bond under the PWA is a legal surety (see Section 2.2(b), above).

The amount of the PWA bond varies depending upon the amount of the contract. R.S. 9:4812 contains the requirements for calculating the proper amounts of the PWA bond.

37.9. The Liability of the PWA Surety: Payment and Performance Bonds

Every PWA bond is always a "payment bond." The phrase "payment bond" is not one contained in the PWA but rather is an informal way to describe this legal suretyship. It secures the general contractor's obligation to timely pay those lien claimants with whom the general contractor has privity of contract and to make sure that lien claimants who do not have such privity of contract with the general contractor are timely paid by subcontractors. It also secures the general contractor's obligation to the owner (a) to make payments to lien claimants to prevent them from filing personal claims against the owner and (b) to remove any liens that may arise from such claim.

In this legal suretyship, the debtor is the general contractor. The lien claimants and the owner are the creditors (R.S. 9:4812(C)(1); also see the next diagram). No matter what kind of terminology the surety uses in drafting the bond, it will be deemed a payment bond (R.S. 9:4812(D)).

Diagram 37.9

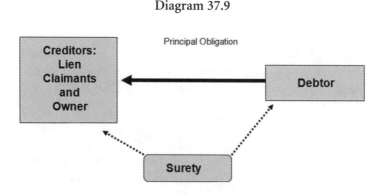

A PWA bond may also include what is sometimes called a "performance bond." This is a suretyship contract by which the surety agrees to pay the owner a set amount if the general contractor does not build the work as called for in the agreement with the owner. Under a performance bond, the debtor is the general contractor and the only creditor is the owner.

The PWA surety, by express language in the bond, may exclude the "performance bond" obligations (R.S. 9:4812(C)(2)); however, the PWA surety may not use language to eliminate its obligations under the payment bond, and any such attempt to do so will be invalid (R.S. 9:4812(D)).

37.10. The Liability of a PWA Surety to 60-Day Lien Period Claimants under the Payment Bond

The liability of the PWA surety under the payment bond (R.S. 9:4812(C)(1) and Section 37.9 above) is set forth in two separate statutes—R.S. 9:4813 and R.S. 9:4822(J).

The latter statute was added in 2001. In essence, R.S. 9:4822(J) supersedes some of the provisions of R.S. 9:4813 and indicates that the surety may have no liability to those who have contracted through a subcontractor unless certain notices are given to the surety. Therefore, while it is possible that lien claimants who do not timely file their statement of claim may still have a right against the surety (R.S. 9:4813(B)(2)), if these lien claimants' contracts are with a subcontractor (rather than a contractor), they must also give timely notice under R.S. 9:4822(J) to preserve their claim against the surety.

R.S. 9:4822(J) requires that the written notice be given "*to the contractor within thirty days from the recordation of notice of termination of the work, stating with substantial accuracy the amount claimed and the name of the party to whom the material was furnished or supplied or for whom the labor or service was done or performed. Such notice shall be served by mailing the same by registered or certified mail, postage prepaid, in an envelope addressed to the contractor at any place he maintains an office in the state of Louisiana.*"

37.10(a). The Concursus Proceeding

A concursus proceeding (C.C.P. art. 4651) may be brought by an owner "or any interested party" (R.S. 9:4841). The purpose of the concursus proceeding is to remove the statements of claims from the public records and to compel the lien claimants to be satisfied from the surety's bond rather than from the seizure and sale of the owner's property.

If a notice of contract was timely filed with a proper bond, the concursus proceeding has two important benefits for the owner of the property: removal of privileges and termination of the owner's R.S. 9:4802 personal liability.

First, the concursus proceeding allows the owner to get a court order erasing the PWA liens from the public records, thereby freeing the owner's property of any PWA privileges. This is especially important if there is a mortgage on the owner's property. This is because most mortgages contain clauses allowing the lender to declare a default in the loan and foreclose on the property if there are liens or privileges filed against the land, even if those liens and privileges are inferior to the mortgage (see Chapter 27, above).

Second, the owner will be able to obtain a court order barring any lien claimant (other than those who have privity of contract with the owner) from asserting any claim against the owner personally under R.S. 9:4802.

37.10(b). The "After-the-Fact" 125% Bond

An owner who has failed to timely file a notice of contract and with the proper bond cannot escape personal liability to those with whom the owner has no privity of contract (see Section 37.2, above). Moreover, the PWA privileges remain on the property; the mere existence of these privileges not only impacts an owner's ability to sell or finance the property in the future but may also trigger a default under existing mortgages on the property (see Chapter 27, above).

R.S. 9:4835 provides the owner in such instances with the ability to remove the privileges from the property. It permits an owner to remove the PWA liens by filing a bond in the amount of 125% of all the liens that have been filed. With this bond in place, the owner may invoke a concursus and have the liens erased from the public records affecting the immovable. The claimants may now seek recovery of the amounts owed to them under the 125% bond (R.S. 9:4823(D) and (E), and R.S. 9:4841(E)(2)).

Note that this 125% bond is provided after liens are filed; this is in contrast to the bond that should have been attached to the notice of contract before "work" began. Also note that this 125% bond apparently relieves the owner of all personal liability the owner may have to lien claimants with whom the owner has contractual privity under R.S. 9:4801, because R.S. 9:4823(E) states that the filing of the 125% bond extinguishes the "*claim against the owner and the privilege securing it.*"

37.10(c). Example #1

Owner enters into a $300,000 construction contract with General Contractor. A notice of contract is timely recorded along with a proper bond in the amount of $100,000 (R.S. 9:4812(B)(3)). Owner has paid General Contractor $75,000 and General Contractor defaults. Lien Claimants who have no privity of contract timely file statements of claim totaling, in the aggregate, $500,000 (because the General Contractor has paid nothing to Lien Claimants and because General Contractor underestimated the cost of the job).

In these circumstances, Lien Claimants will assert that Owner is personally liable to them for the entire $500,000, that Owner cannot limit its liability by pointing to the $300,000 figure in the General Contractor's contract, and that Owner cannot argue that the $75,000 already paid to General Contractor should be considered.

In this situation, because there was a timely notice of contract and proper bond, Owner has the ability to remove R.S. 9:4802 (non-privity) claims of personal liability and the ability to erase the PWA liens.

Owner files a concursus and joins Lien Claimants, Surety, and General Contractor (R.S. 9:4841(A)). Surety can be required to place the amount of its bond—$100,000—into the registry of court (*cf.* R.S. 9:4841(E)). Owner, upon proving that the notice of contract was timely filed with a proper bond, is entitled to obtain a judgment removing the lien filings from the public record and relieving Owner of all liability (R.S. 9:4841(D)) to all R.S. 9:4802 (non-privity) Lien Claimants. Of course, Owner always has liability under any contract it may have (see R.S. 9:4801).

Although Owner escapes both personal liability to non-privity Lien Claimants and all PWA liens against the Owner's property in this instance, Lien Claimants who have $500,000 in claims are relegated to fighting over the $100,000 bond. The amount of the bond is insufficient to pay all lien claims in full. Thus, liens will be paid according to their rank (see R.S. 9:4821 and Section 37.12, below).

37.10(d). Example #2

The facts are the same as in Section 37.10(c), Example 1, above, but in this case the notice of contract was not timely filed and no bond was provided by the General Contractor at the inception of the contract.

In this instance, (a) Owner has personal liability for the entire $500,000 in claims; (b) Owner's immovable property is encumbered by $500,000 in PWA liens; and (c) the existence of the PWA liens may cause a default under provisions of Owner's mortgage (see Chapter 27, above).

Nonetheless, under R.S. 9:4823(E), R.S. 9:4835, and R.S. 9:4841(E)(2), Owner or "any interested party" may remove the PWA liens by putting up a bond equal to 125% of the liens, which is $625,000 ($500,000 x 1.25%). The liens can now be erased.

Note that the amount of this bond, which is given after the liens are filed, is measured by the face amount of the timely-filed liens. The amount of the bond is not determined by whether timely filed liens are valid or are in the proper amount. Only by putting up the 125% bond in the amount of $625,000 can the liens be erased. It will take litigation, after the 125% bond is filed, to determine the actual validity and amount of those liens.

Also note that if Owner had made General Contractor put up an appropriate bond at the start of the transaction, the amount of the bond would have been only $100,000; however, because a bond was not properly given along with a timely notice of contract, the after-the-fact bond now must be in the amount of $625,000.

37.10(e). Bonded Jobs Cost More Than Jobs That Are Not Bonded

A PWA bond is supplied by a legal surety in exchange for payment of a premium. The general contractor, who is supplying the bond, pays the premium and builds the cost of the premium into the price that the general contractor charges the owner for the job.

Bonded jobs, therefore, are more expensive for the owner initially than unbonded jobs. A bonded job, however, may be far cheaper for the owner in the long run because it assists the owner in avoiding unlimited personal liability (see Section 37.2, above) and allows liens to be removed from the property even if all lien claimants are not paid in full (see Section 37.10(d), Example 2, above).

Before the start of every job that may trigger a PWA lien, an owner must make a business decision whether to require the general contractor to furnish a PWA bond. Certain disclosures are required to residential homeowners in this regard concerning home improvements (R.S. 9:4851 *et seq.*), but the failure of the general contractor to make these disclosures does not affect the rights of the lien claimants.

37.11. The PWA Can Transform the Rights of Creditors

The PWA can transform an unsecured creditor into a secured creditor of an immovable. This is because the PWA allows workers, vendors, and others who (without the PWA) would have only a personal claim against the owner for work performed or materials sold to claim a privilege on the owner's property to secure the payment owed to them by the owner.

The PWA also can transform a creditor who has a privilege on a movable into a creditor who has a right to seize and sell an immovable. This is because the PWA permits those with privileges on movables, such as vendors (see Section 31.1, above) and repairmen (see Section 31.3, above), to claim a PWA lien when the movable on which they have a privilege is transformed into an immovable or a component part of an immovable.

The following examples help illustrate these concepts.

37.11(a). Example #1

Gasoline Seller A sells 50 gallons of gasoline on credit to Owner so that Owner can operate her car. Gasoline Seller A delivers the gasoline to Owner's house in a 50-gallon drum.

Gasoline Seller B sells 50 gallons of gasoline on credit to General Contractor so that General Contractor can operate a generator used for power tools in making repairs to Owner's roof. Gasoline Seller B delivers the gasoline to General Contractor, at Owner's house, in a 50-gallon drum and gives written notice of this fact to Owner.

In this situation, Gasoline Seller A may have a vendor's privilege on the gasoline (see Section 31.1, above), but that privilege is lost when the gasoline is used in operating the car. Gasoline Seller A does not get a PWA privilege because the gasoline is not used in the erection, construction, repair or improvement of an immovable.

Gasoline Seller B also loses its vendor's privilege when General Contractor uses the gasoline to power the generator. Yet, Gasoline Seller B can claim a PWA lien under R.S. 9:4802(A)(3) (also see R.S. 9:4802(G)(2)). If Gasoline Seller B properly preserves the PWA lien, Gasoline Seller B not only can sue both General Contractor and Owner for the price of the gasoline (R.S. 9:4802(A)) but also can seize and sell Owner's house pursuant to the PWA lien (R.S. 9:4802(B)).

37.11(b). Example #2

Owner buys an HDTV on credit from Store #1. The HDTV breaks. Repairman #1 comes to Owner's house to repair the HDTV but cannot complete the repairs there. Repairman #1 takes the HDTV to its shop, fixes the HDTV, and returns it to Owner's house.

Owner also buys a central air conditioning unit on credit from Store #2, which installs the unit at the house. The unit breaks. Repairman #2 comes to Owner's house to repair the unit but cannot complete the repairs there. Repairman #2 takes the unit apart, takes it to her shop, fixes the unit, and returns it to Owner's house and reinstalls it.

In this situation, Store #1 has a vendor's privilege on the HDTV, a movable (see Section 31.1, above), and Repairman #1 has a repairman's privilege on the HDTV as long as the repairmen takes appropriate legal action within 120 days of the repairs being made (see Section 31.3, above). Store #1's vendor's privilege outranks Repairman #1's privilege (see Section 31.3, above, R.S. 9:4501(B), and R.S. 9:4502(B)). If the judicial sale of the HDTV brings sufficient funds to pay off only Store #1, Repairman #1 will have an unsecured claim against Owner.

By contrast, because the central air conditioning unit is a component part of an immovable (C.C. art. 466), Store #2's vendor's privilege on the unit (which was movable when it was at Store #2) was lost the minute the unit was installed and became a component part of an immovable. Yet, because Store #2 installed the unit and did work on the premises, Store #2 is a "contractor" (R.S. 9:4807 and Section 37.1(d), above) that improved an immovable (the house) and is entitled not only to sue Owner personally but also to obtain a PWA lien against Owner's house and seize and sell the house to obtain a privilege on the proceeds of the sale.

Likewise, while the unit may have been a movable while at Repairman #2's shop (and thus subject to a repairman's privilege while in the shop), the minute the unit was reinstalled, it became a component part, and the repairman's privilege was lost (because this privilege applies only to movables, and only to those seized within 120 days of the repair if the movable is no longer on the repairman's premises). Yet, because Repairman #2 worked on a component part of an immovable, Repairman #2 is entitled to either a contractor's privilege or laborer's privilege under the PWA (depending on whether Repairman #2 is operating as an individual or as a business entity) because Repairman #2 has privity of contract with Owner and is improving immovable property.

37.12. The Ranking of Private Works Act Privileges

The PWA contains a statutory rule on ranking PWA privileges against each other and against other privileges and mortgages affecting the immovable property. Determining rank involves a consideration of: (a) when PWA liens start to affect third parties (see Section 37.12(a), below) and (b) the ranking rules contained in R.S. 9:4821 (see Sections 37.12(b) and 37.12(c), below).

37.12(a). PWA Privileges Affect Third Parties from the Earlier of Notice of Contract or R.S. 9:4820 "Work"

R.S. 9:4820(A) sets forth the rule that third parties are affected by PWA privileges from the earlier of (i) a proper and timely notice of contract, or (ii) R.S. 9:4820 "work" being performed on the property.

PWA privileges can be "secret," in the sense that one cannot know by looking at the public records whether a PWA lien exists or when the lien begins to affect third parties. If no notice of contract has been filed, third parties cannot ascertain by looking at the public records whether R.S. 9:4820 "work" has begun. Even if a notice of contract has been filed and recorded in the mortgage records (R.S. 9:4811 and 9:4831), PWA liens could have previously attached to the property because "work" began before the notice was recorded. There is no way for third persons checking the public records to ascertain whether the notice of contract was filed prior to the start of R.S. 9:4820 "work" (see Section 37.1(c), above), because "work" under R.S. 9:4820 refers to physical actions affecting the property.

If no notice of contract has been filed, third parties may only discover the existence of PWA liens when a lien claimant files a notice of claim in the mortgage records (see Section 37.3(b), above). The lien notice need not be filed until after the job is completed or terminated, which may be months (or, in some cases, years) after the R.S. 9:4820 "work" began. The timely filing of a notice of claim makes the lien effective against third parties retroactive to the earlier of (i) R.S. 9:4820 "work" beginning or (ii) the recordation of the notice of contract.

Creditors who wish to take a mortgage on property where "work" may be ongoing often obtain what is called a "no-work" affidavit (R.S. 9:4820(C) and Section 37.12(d), below). The "no work" affidavit can protect the rank of a creditor taking a mortgage.

37.12(b). The Six "Classes" of Ranking under the Private Works Act

Once PWA liens have been properly preserved (see Sections 37.3(b), 37.8(a), and 37.8(b), above) and lawsuits have been brought to enforce them (see Section 37.8(c), above), a court will determine in what order the PWA liens are to be paid from the proceeds of the judicial sale. This priority order of distribution is called "ranking."

R.S. 9:4821 controls the ranking of PWA privileges, both as against each other and as against mortgages and other privileges affecting immovable property. Thus, if there are mortgages and PWA privileges affecting immovable property, the only way to properly ascertain how they rank against one another is to use R.S. 9:4821.

In general terms, proceeds are distributed in the following order:

- First, for *ad valorem* taxes and certain other specified governmental assessments.
- Second, to laborers, whether they have privity of contract with an owner or whether they work for a general contractor, contractor, or subcontractor.
- Third, to mortgages and immovable property privileges that became effective before the earlier of (a) filing of a notice of contract, or (b) the commencement of R.S. 9:4820 "work" (see Section 37.1(c), above).
- Fourth, to all other lien claimants (except those in Class 2, above, and those in Class 5, below).
- Fifth, to the following persons and entities that have privity of contract with the owner: contractors, architects, engineers, and surveyors.
- Sixth, to all other mortgages and privileges.

These six groupings are sometimes called "classes" of claims. For example, *ad valorem* taxes are sometimes said to be in the "first class" or "first rank." This Précis will use the term "class" in referring to the ranking of claims under the PWA.

37.12(c). The Ranking of PWA Privileges by Nature and by Date

Under R.S. 9:4821, the rank of PWA privileges depends upon which class (first through sixth, see Section 37.12(b), above) they are and the types of claims in that class. In some of the classes, the claims rank against other classes by nature. This is the case for the first, second, fourth, and fifth classes. The remaining classes rank against the others depending upon the time of perfection of the security interest. In addition, one must consider how the claims in each class rank against one another within the same class.

A rank by nature is one that depends on the type of obligation in each class, not upon the time the privilege was perfected. Thus, *ad valorem* taxes are the first ranked (and first paid) under the PWA, regardless of when the taxes were assessed. It is possible that the PWA privilege arose in March and the taxes were not assessed until December; nevertheless, under R.S. 9:4821, the *ad valorem* taxes rank first and must be paid first from the sales' proceeds.

Similarly, laborer's privileges rank second. It matters not when the laborer performed the work or filed a statement of claim. As long as the laborer properly and timely preserved the privilege, the laborer outranks a mortgage recorded twenty years earlier. If there is more than one laborer in this Class 2, it does not matter when each filed a statement of claim or when each filed suit to assert the lien; if all acted timely, they all share equally with others in Class 2.

Some of the ranking under R.S. 9:4821 occurs by date. For example, determining which mortgages fall into Class 3 (R.S. 9:4821(3)) requires ascertaining (a) the date when the mortgage began to affect third parties; (b) the date when the PWA privileges began to affect third parties (the earlier of a timely notice of contract or the start of R.S. 9:4820 "*work*," see Section 37.1(c), above), and (c) that the mortgage remains effective as to third parties. Once all the mortgages that fall into Class 3 are ascertained, they rank against each other within that grouping by date as well.

37.12(d). A "No-Work" Affidavit Can Alter the Class a Mortgage Holder Would Otherwise Receive under R.S. 9:4821 of the Private Works Act

Because PWA privileges start to affect third parties from the earlier of notice of contract or R.S. 9:4820 "*work*" (see Sections 37.1(c) and 37.12(a), above), third parties cannot ascertain whether PWA liens affect the property solely by examining the public records.

R.S. 9:4820(C) provides protection for third parties who wish to obtain a "*mortgage privilege or other right*" in or on immovable property by obtaining and filing what is sometimes called a "no-work affidavit." If timely and properly obtained, a no-work affidavit results in the creditor being in Class 3 rather than in Class 6 (see Section 37.12(b), above).

R.S. 9:4820(C) requires that the no-work affidavit must be obtained from *"a registered or certified engineer or surveyor, licensed architect, or building inspector employed by the city or parish or by a lending institution chartered under federal or state law."* The person executing the affidavit inspects the property and must state in the affidavit the time of the inspection and that, as of that moment, *"work had not then been commenced nor materials placed at its site...."*

The affidavit provides protection to the person relying on it only if *"the affidavit is filed within four business days after the execution of the affidavit, and the mortgage, privilege, or other document creating the right is filed before or within four business days of the filing of the affidavit."* The time frames given in this provision are critical. If the affidavit is filed outside of this timeframe, or if the mortgage is not timely filed in relation to the timely-filed affidavit, then the holder of the mortgage may not "rely" on the no-work affidavit, and the no-work affidavit does not protect the mortgage holder. As a practical matter, lawyers involved in a mortgage closing try to have the no-work affidavit filed and recorded within two days of its execution and the mortgage filed immediately after the filing of the affidavit.

The person executing the affidavit is personally liable for any damages caused if the affidavit is incorrect; however, the person relying on the affidavit is fully protected *"unless actual fraud by such person is proven."*

37.12(e). Examples of Ranking Under the PWA

The following examples are illustrations of ranking issues under the PWA.

37.12(e)(1). Example #1

On February 1, Creditor was granted a mortgage on Property by Owner; the mortgage secured a note payable in monthly installments over 30 years. The mortgage was filed and recorded that day in the parish mortgage records.

On July 1, Owner of Property entered into a $20,000 construction contract with General Contractor and recorded it that day in the parish mortgage records. The next day, on July 2, R.S. 9:4820 work began on the Property.

On August 1, Owner of Property granted a mortgage on the property to Finance Company. The mortgage was filed and recorded that day in the parish mortgage records.

On September 1, Owner filed a notice of termination of General Contractor's contract in the parish mortgage records.

Between September 1 and September 30, statements of claim were filed by lien claimants in the mortgage records concerning work on Property:

September 2: Statement filing by Subcontractor X

September 3: Statement filing by Subcontractor Y

September 4: Statement filing by General Contractor

September 10: Statement filing by Lumber Supplier who delivered to the job site lumber used in the construction work on the Property

September 20: Statement filing by Larry Laborer, who was employed by Subcontractor Y and who worked on the property.

If a timely suit had been filed to preserve the PWA liens (R.S. 9:4823) and to rank them and all other security interests, and if all parties entitled to a privilege or mortgage met their burden of proof, the result of that ranking analysis would be:

- First, for *ad valorem* taxes and certain other specified governmental assessments. There are none here.
- Second, to laborers. Larry Laborer ranks second, even though he was last to file a statement of claim.
- Third, to mortgages and immovable property privileges that became effective before the earlier of (a) filing of a notice of contract, or (b) the commencement of R.S. 9:4820 "work" (see Section 37.1(c), above). The February 1 mortgage held by Creditor ranks here.
- Fourth, to all other lien claimants (except those in Class 2, above, and those in Class 5, below). Subcontractors X and Y rank here as well as Lumber Supplier. Note that all are in Class 4, even though Lumber Supplier filed its statement of claim after Subcontractors X and Y. The reason all are in Class 4 is that each fits within the category described in R.S. 9:4821(A)(4) and each acted timely to file its statement and to file suit to prevent its lien from being extinguished.
- Fifth, to the following persons and entities that have privity of contract with the owner: contractors, architects, engineers, and surveyors. General Contractor ranks here because (a) its contract is less than $25,000 (R.S. 9:4811(D) and section 37.8(a), above), and (b) in any event, the notice of contract was timely.
- Sixth, to all other mortgages and privileges. Finance Company's August mortgage ranks here.

37.12(e)(2). Example #2

The facts here are similar to those in Section 37.12(e)(1), Example #1, but instead of the first event being the February mortgage to Creditor, there is activity in January.

On January 15, Owner and General Contractor entered into a handshake deal to add an addition to Owner's home. General Contractor started work that day by bringing a load of $200 worth of lumber to the site. General Contractor also had his workers start that day by tearing down a wall that separated the kitchen from the den in Owner's home.

On February 1, Creditor was granted a mortgage on Property by Owner; the mortgage secured a note payable in monthly installments over 30 years. The mortgage was filed and recorded that day in the parish mortgage records.

On July 1, Owner and General Contractor formalized their handshake deal and entered into a written construction contract totaling $50,000. On that same day, General Contractor filed and recorded a proper notice of contract in the parish mortgage records.

On August 1, Owner granted a mortgage on the property to Finance Company. The mortgage was filed and recorded that day in the parish mortgage records.

On September 1, Owner filed a notice of termination of General Contractor's contract in the parish mortgage records.

Between September 1 and October 15, statements of claim are filed by lien claimants in the mortgage record concerning their work on Property:

September 2: Statement filing by Subcontractor X

September 3: Statement filing by Subcontractor Y

September 4: Statement filing by General Contractor

September 10: Statement filing by Lumber Supplier, who supplied the lumber used in the construction work on Property

October 15: Statement filing by Larry Laborer

If a timely suit had been filed to preserve the PWA liens (R.S. 9:4823) and to rank them and all other security interests, and if all parties entitled to a privilege or mortgage met their burden of proof, the result of that ranking analysis would be:

- First, for *ad valorem* taxes and certain other specified governmental assessments. There are none here.

- Second, to laborers. Larry Laborer ranks second, even though he was last to file a statement of claim. Larry's claim is timely even though made more than 30 days from the notice of termination. The 60-day rule applies (see Section 37.6, above) because the notice of contract was filed untimely. It was untimely because it was filed after R.S. 9:4820 "work" began.
- Third, to mortgages and immovable property privileges that became effective before the earlier of (a) filing of a notice of contract, or (b) the commencement of R.S. 9:4820 "work" (see Section 37.1(c), above). There are no mortgages that fit this criteria in this situation.
- Fourth, to all other lien claimants (except those in Class 2, above, and those in Class 5, below). Subcontractors X and Y rank here as well as Lumber Supplier. Note that all are in Class 4, even though Lumber Supplier provided the lumber on January 15, before any other lien claimant, and even though Lumber Supplier filed its statement of claim after Subcontractors X and Y. The reason all are in Class 4 is that each fits within the category described in R.S. 9:4821(A)(4) and each acted timely to file its statement and to file suit to prevent its lien from being extinguished. As among X, Y, and Supplier, all rank equally within this group.
- Fifth, to the following persons and entities that have privity of contract with the owner: contractors, architects, engineers, and surveyors. The General Contractor does not have a claim in this instance because its contract was more than $25,000 (R.S. 9:4811(D) and section 37.8(a)) and because the notice of contract was not filed before R.S. 9:4820 "work" began.
- Sixth, to all other mortgages and privileges. Both Creditor's January mortgage and Finance Company's August mortgage rank here. As between Creditor and Finance Company, Creditor outranks Finance Company because Creditor's mortgage was recorded first.

Chapter 38

Foreclosures in Louisiana

38.1. The Interrelationship between Foreclosure Rules and Mortgages

Those who draft or analyze Louisiana mortgages must be aware of the Louisiana procedural requirements for foreclosures. If a mortgage does not contain the necessary terminology and if it is not in the required form, then executory process will not be available (see Section 38.1(c), below).

Louisiana foreclosure procedures involving immovable property must be by judicial procedure. There is no non-judicial foreclosure in Louisiana on immovable property (see Section 39.1(a), below).

A proper successful foreclosure action and sale will extinguish inferior mortgages, liens and encumbrances, as well as extinguishing the owner's rights in the property. Because judicial process is used, federal due process rules apply.

Any creditor whose claim is not paid in full through the foreclosure sale may wish to pursue the debtor (and any sureties) for the balance. In Louisiana, the process of collecting this remaining balance is called an action for a "deficiency judgment." Those who foreclose on mortgages and immovable property rights must be aware of the deficiency judgment rules applicable in Louisiana (see Chapter 40, below).

The comments in this Chapter also apply to any privilege on immovables that is created by a written document that must be filed in the mortgage records to affect third parties, such as a vendor's privilege on immovables (see Section 33.2, above).

38.2. The Differences between Ordinary Process Foreclosure and Executory Process Foreclosure

There are two different procedures available to creditors who wish to foreclose on a mortgage—ordinary process and executory process.

Ordinary process is a regular lawsuit in which a creditor seeks a personal judgment against the debtor and judicial recognition of the mortgage. Once a judgment has been rendered, the creditor may obtain a writ allowing seizure and sale of the property (C.C.P. arts 2291–2343, and 2721–2725).

Ordinary process requires the issuance of a citation and service of process on the debtor (C.C.P. arts. 1201–1267). Typically, the sheriff serves these papers on the debtor. Once the debtor is served with the proper paperwork, the debtor is afforded a time to file exceptions, to answer the suit, and to seek discovery.

Executory process is Louisiana's "quick-taking" mechanism. There is no citation and no service of process (C.C.P. arts. 2631, 2640). With the proper documentation and a properly verified petition, a creditor may obtain, on the day the suit is filed, a judgment ordering the seizure and sale of the mortgaged property (C.C.P. art. 2638). The first time the debtor learns of the lawsuit is the day the sheriff serves the notice of seizure; however, at that point, the judgment already has been rendered.

An executory proceeding does not result in a personal judgment against the debtor; it merely orders the seizure and sale of the property. To obtain a personal judgment against a debtor after a judicial sale held pursuant to an executory proceeding, the creditor must either convert the executory proceeding into an ordinary proceeding (C.C.P. art. 2644) or file a separate suit for a deficiency judgment (see Chapter 40, below).

38.3. Requirements for Use of Executory Proceedings

Louisiana statutes formerly required that almost every document forming the basis of an executory proceeding be in authentic form. A document in authentic form, under Louisiana law, is one executed in the presence of a notary public and two witnesses (C.C. art. 1833).

C.C.P. art. 2635 was amended in the 1980s to eliminate the requirement that almost everything be in authentic form. The current version of C.C.P. art. 2635 requires that only the following documents be in authentic form:

- "*The note, bond, or other instrument evidencing the obligation secured by the mortgage, security agreement, or privilege*";
- "*The authentic act of mortgage or privilege on immovable property importing a confession of judgment*"; and
- "*The act of mortgage or privilege on movable property importing a confession of judgment whether by authentic act or by private signature duly acknowledged.*"

As can be seen, the two critical elements are an authentic act of mortgage containing a confession of judgment and an authentic "*note, bond, or other instrument evidencing the obligation secured by the mortgage, security agreement, or privilege.*"

If executory process is to be utilized, the mortgage must be in authentic form and must contain a confession of judgment. The note that the mortgage secures, however, need not be in authentic form if the requirements of C.C.P. art. 2636 or R.S. 9:5555 are met (see Section 38.5, below).

38.4. The Confession of Judgment

A "confession of judgment clause" is a statement in the mortgage that the borrower "confesses judgment" in favor of the creditor.

This clause is "magical" in the sense that a creditor cannot properly obtain a valid executory judgment unless a "confession of judgment" clause is contained in the document creating the real security (C.C.P. art. 2635).

This language is merely procedural; it does not create any presumption that the debt is valid, that the debt is due and owing, or that the debtor has waived any defenses. The presence of the language simply permits the use of executory process.

38.5. Things That Are in Authentic Form, Things That Are Deemed to Be in Authentic Form, and Things That Need Not Be in Authentic Form

While C.C.P. art. 2635 requires that some documents be in authentic form (see Section 38.3, above), Louisiana statutes permit some of these same documents to be treated as if they were in authentic form even though the form requirements have not actually been met.

For example, a note paraphed for identification with an act of mortgage (see Section 12.4(c), above) is "deemed" to be in authentic form, even though it is not executed before two witnesses and a notary public (C.C.P. art. 2636(1)). If a mortgage secures a principal obligation relating to one or more notes that have not been paraphed for identification with an act of mortgage, executory process can be utilized if the executory suit contains an affidavit or verified petition conforming to the requirements of R.S. 9:5555.

C.C.P. art. 2637 sets forth a non-exclusive list of items that need not be in authentic form for executory process. This statute was significant prior to the 1980s when, under the former provisions of C.C.P. art. 2635, everything had to be in authentic form unless there was a specific exception. Now, however, there is no need for anything to be in authentic form unless a statute expressly requires authentic evidence.

It should be emphasized that a mortgage is valid and affects third parties, even if it is not in authentic form, as long as it is in writing, signed by the debtor, and contains a description of both the property and the debt being secured (C.C. art. 3288 and Sections 12.1, 12.2, 12.3, and 12.4, above). If such a mortgage is not in authentic form, the creditor will have to prove the validity of the signatures on the mortgage in order foreclose by ordinary process. The lack of authentic form will make executory process unavailable as a remedy.

Chapter 39

The Relationship of Federal Due Process and Certain Other Federal Laws to Louisiana Foreclosures

39.1. Louisiana Foreclosures and Due Process Issues

Property owners, tenants, servitude holders, usufructuaries, naked owners, and the holders of mortgages and privileges possess property rights protected by the Fifth Amendment to the U.S. Constitution. The Fifth Amendment prohibits deprivation of property rights without due process of law. Because Louisiana foreclosures on immovable property must take place through judicial proceedings (see Chapter 38, above), the foreclosure process involves state action under color of state law. Due process requirements must be met, because a foreclosure extinguishes the rights of the holders of mortgages and privileges as well as the rights of owners, tenants, servitude holders, usufructuaries, and naked owners (C.C.P. art. 2376).

The due process jurisprudence requires that the sheriff or foreclosing creditor must attempt to notify, at least by mail, all those whose property rights will be affected or extinguished by the foreclosure process, if they can be reasonably identified. The identity of the holders of these inferior property rights usually can be ascertained from the conveyance and mortgage records (see

Chapter 19.3, above). Therefore, as part of the foreclosure process, a foreclosing creditor should examine the conveyance and mortgage records to identify all holders of inferior property interests to ensure that notice is sent to those entitled to due process notice.

The jurisprudence hinges the requirement of giving notice to those inferior property interest holders whose identity can be ascertained from the public records. The due process jurisprudence emphasizes that if a creditor makes reasonable attempts to give this notice, the fact that the notice was not received does not invalidate the sale. On the other hand, the jurisprudence also holds that if a creditor is aware that notice was not received—such as sending a notice letter by certified mail and finding that the letter is returned unclaimed— the creditor must make further attempts at notification. The jurisprudence is emphatic that notice by publication in a newspaper is never sufficient for purposes of due process.

The failure to give due process notice can invalidate the judicial sale. R.S. 13:3886.1 provides a mechanism for those property interest holders who were not notified to contest the sale. This statute sets forth the burden of proof that must be met and the time frame for bringing a suit attacking the sale. While the Louisiana Supreme Court has not yet addressed R.S. 13:3886.1, intermediate appellate courts in the state have utilized the statute in evaluating claims of those alleging that a judicial sale was invalid because of due process concerns.

In addition to constitutional due process notice, there are Louisiana statutes that require notice in foreclosure proceedings. These include but are not limited to R.S. 9:3260.1, mandating that a lessor *"disclose in writing to the lessee and any prospective lessee any pending foreclosure action to which the residential dwelling is subject and the right of the lessee to receive a notification of a foreclosure action pursuant to this Section."*

39.2. Other Federal Laws That Impact Louisiana Foreclosures

There are numerous federal laws that must be considered by any creditor who seeks to bring a Louisiana foreclosure action. These include but are not limited to:

- The Bankruptcy Code (11 U.S.C. § 101 *et seq.*), particularly the sections dealing with the automatic stay (11 U.S.C. § 362) and preferential and fraudulent transfers (11 U.S.C. §§ 547–548);

- The Fair Debt Collection Act (15 U.S.C. § 1601 and § 1692 *et seq.*), dealing with collection practices and lawsuits involving consumers;
- The Servicemember's Civil Relief Act (50 U.S.C. Appx. § 501 *et seq.*), dealing with protections afforded to borrowers and others who are in active military service; it covers matters such as mortgages, credit card debt, and lease terminations;
- Federal tax lien statutes (see 26 U.S.C. §§ 6321–6322) and other federal laws protecting certain federal lenders. These statutes create special rules under which federal mortgages may last longer than the rules for non-federal mortgages (see Section 20.6, above);
- The Protecting Tenants at Foreclosure Act, (12 U.S.C. § 5220).

Chapter 40

The Louisiana Deficiency Judgment Act and Deficiency Judgments under UCC9

40.1. Deficiency Judgments — An Overview

A creditor is entitled to seize and sell collateral on which it has a security interest and to obtain a privilege on the proceeds of the sale. If the proceeds of the sale are insufficient to satisfy the entire debt, the creditor may want to collect the balance personally from the debtor. This balance owing after the sale is called the "deficiency," and a creditor would like to have the right to obtain a judgment allowing collection of the deficiency from the debtor's other assets.

Deficiency judgments are regulated by two separate regimes, depending on the type of collateral involved. If the collateral is immovable property or any asset not secured by a UCC9 security interest, the rules are contained in the Louisiana Deficiency Judgment Act (R.S. 13:4106 and C.C.P. art. 2771). If the collateral consists of an asset subject to a UCC9 security interest, the rules are contained in the UCC (R.S. 10:9-615, 9-616, 9-620, and 9-625).

40.2. Preserving a Deficiency Judgment after a Judicial Foreclosure on Immovable Property and Non-UCC9 Assets

Louisiana's Deficiency Judgment Act (R.S. 13:4106) prohibits a creditor from obtaining a deficiency judgment if the property has not been foreclosed on through a judicial process with appraisal. The Louisiana Deficiency Judgment Act is an express declaration of public policy; the debtor cannot waive its application (R.S. 13:4107).

Although a creditor may elect to proceed to a judicial sale without an appraisal if the debtor has waived the appraisal requirements in the loan or mortgage documents (C.C.P. art. 2332), a judicial sale without an appraisal bars a deficiency judgment (C.C.P. art. 2771 and R.S. 13:4106).

The property must be appraised prior to the judicial sale; the appraisal must be of the value of the property at the time of the foreclosure. The appraisal procedures are set forth in R.S. 13:4363.

The minimum bid at the judicial sale is the greater of two-thirds the appraised value or the amount of liens, mortgages, and encumbrances that are superior to that of the seizing creditor (C.C.P. arts. 2336, 2337). If no one bids the minimum at the first sale, a second sale can be scheduled, with appropriate notice and advertising. At that second sale, the minimum bid is the greater of outstanding court costs in the suit or the amount of liens, mortgages, and encumbrances that are superior to that of the seizing creditor (C.C.P. arts. 2336, 2337).

At the second sale, even if there are no superior liens and encumbrances (meaning that the minimum bid is for court costs only), the debt for which the deficiency is sought must be reduced "*by the greater of either one-half of the appraised value, less superior security interests, mortgages, liens, and privileges, or the amount by which the price bid exceeds superior security interests, mortgages, liens, and privileges*" (C.C.P. art. 2336).

Violating the Deficiency Judgment Act does not extinguish the obligation the debtor owes the creditor; it merely removes the creditor's right to pursue the debtor personally for the balance due. This fact is demonstrated by R.S. 13:4106(B). Under this provision, a creditor who forecloses without appraisal on one piece of property encumbered by a mortgage may later foreclose on other tracts encumbered by that same mortgage even though a deficiency judgment is no longer available against the debtor. If the Deficiency Judgment Act had extinguished the entire debt, the accessory obligation of mortgage (see Section 11.1, above) would have been rendered unenforceable. Thus, the Deficiency Judgment Act, by its own terms, does not extinguish any obligations;

rather it bars claims that constitute a "personal obligation of the debtor" (R.S. 13:4106(A)). The mortgage continues "*in rem*" on the remaining tracts (see Section 12.11, above, concerning *in rem* mortgages).

40.3. Exceptions to the Deficiency Judgment Act

The legislature has crafted two types of exceptions to the Deficiency Judgment Act: (a) those relating to certain types of assets or certain types of dispositions of assets; and (b) those relating to voluntary agreements between debtor and creditor.

Under R.S. 13:4108, certain transactions and actions are listed as exceptions to the Deficiency Judgment Act; therefore, a creditor is not prohibited from obtaining a deficiency judgment in these situations. These include:

- Sales of stocks and commodities through national exchanges (R.S. 13:4108(1) and (2));
- Disposition of property through bankruptcy courts (R.S. 13:4108(3)) or, when the property is outside of Louisiana, pursuant to the laws of the state where the property is located (R.S. 13:4108(4)); and
- Disposition of cash and cash equivalents, such as cash deposits and insurance refunds (R.S. 13:4108(5)–(7)).

The other exception to the Deficiency Judgment Act concerns voluntary agreements between debtors and creditors, but the ability to come within the parameters of these exceptions requires careful drafting of such agreements.

R.S. 13:4108.1 is an exception that applies when the agreement concerns commercial transactions. R.S. 13:4108.2 applies when the agreement concerns a consumer transaction. Both of these statutes mandate that, prior to the disposition of the collateral, the debtor and creditor reach an agreement on the value of the collateral and consent that this value shall be attributed to the outstanding debt. As a result, the debtor will remain liable after the disposition of the collateral for no more than the difference between the outstanding amount of the debt and the agreed-upon value of the collateral. Further, if the disposition does not involve a transfer of the collateral to the creditor but rather a sale to a third party, and if the sales price is greater than the previously agreed-upon value of the collateral, then the debtor is liable only for the balance of the debt minus the disposition price.

If the debt arises from a consumer transaction, R.S. 13:4108.2 requires the consumer be informed of the right to an appraisal and that the consumer be given certain notices.

40.4. Preserving a Deficiency Judgment under UCC9

Unlike R.S. 13:4106, UCC9's deficiency judgment rules are not concerned with the procedural niceties of a foreclosure sale but rather look to whether the disposition of collateral was "commercially reasonable" (R.S. 10:9-610(b)).

UCC9 allows a disposition of collateral by public or private sale. The presumption is that every sale of secured collateral results in the satisfaction of the debt and that, therefore, the creditor may not obtain a deficiency judgment unless the creditor proves that the sale was conducted in a commercially reasonable manner (R.S. 10:9-626(a)(2)).

A judicial sale is always considered to be commercially reasonable, but UCC9 does not contain a definition of what constitutes a commercially reasonable sale. The jurisprudence around the country has created two broad categories of non-judicial sales that are deemed commercially reasonable.

One category of commercially reasonable sales involves a creditor who gives the property to a seller of such goods, and the seller disposes of the collateral in the ordinary course of the seller's business. For example, assume a creditor had a UCC9 security interest in jewelry and, after default, has a jewelry store sell that jewelry in the ordinary course of its business. This type of sale could be deemed commercially reasonable.

Another category of commercially reasonable sales occurs when the price of the property sold is the same as could be obtained by a seller in the ordinary course of business. To take the jewelry example, for instance, if the creditor did not give the jewelry to a jewelry store to sell but rather sold it through Craig's List or E-Bay, and the price obtained was the same or higher than would have been received had the jewelry store sold it, that sale could be deemed commercially reasonable.

This is a developing area of the law, and courts are increasingly being asked to rule whether online private sales are commercially reasonable. As of the date of the publication of this edition of the Précis, no Louisiana case has addressed this issue.

Chapter 41

The Louisiana Version of UCC9

41.1. A Limited Discussion of the Louisiana Version of UCC9

Louisiana's version of the Uniform Commercial Code tracks the numbering system of the model version approved by the Uniform Law Commission. By and large, Louisiana's UCC is very similar to the model version, but changes have been made to conform to Louisiana's civil law system. For example, Louisiana did not adopt UCC art. 2 dealing with sales, because the Louisiana State Law Institute (which proposes changes to Louisiana's UCC) believed that UCC art. 2 incorporated a number of common law precepts that were inapplicable in Louisiana or which were unenforceable under civil law principles.

This Chapter is not intended to be a comprehensive look at Louisiana's UCC9 or even to constitute an overview of its provisions. Rather, this Chapter will point out some major differences between Louisiana's version and the model version, will discuss certain aspects of Louisiana's UCC9 that are necessary to understand collateral mortgages and the impact of fixture filings, and to point out some traps for the unwary in dealing with UCC9 issues.

41.2. Items and Collateral That Are Outside the Scope of Louisiana's UCC9

Louisiana's UCC9 covers the perfection of consensual security interests only in assets and rights explicitly brought within the scope of UCC9 by specific statutory provisions (see R.S. 10:9-109). Assets on which a UCC9 security interest cannot be perfected include:

- An immovable. Creditors may obtain consensual real security through a mortgage (see Chapter 12, above).
- A tenant's rights in a lease of an immovable. Creditors may obtain consensual real security of a tenant's rights in a lease through a mortgage (see Chapter 12, above).
- A landlord's rights in the rental income stream derived from the lease of an immovable. Creditors may obtain consensual real security through a pledge (see Chapter 10, above).
- "Assignments" of interests in property and casualty policies. Creditors may obtain consensual real security through a pledge (see Section 15.2, above).
- Fixtures that constitute "consumer goods." Creditors may not obtain any type of consensual security interest in these items. R.S. 10:9-102(40) expressly prevents fixture filings from affecting residential property when the fixture is bought by a consumer. This is because fixture filings by definition do not attach to "consumer goods." R.S. 9:102(23) defines "consumer goods" as "goods that are used or bought for use primarily for personal, family or household purposes."

41.3. The Security Agreement and the Separate Financing Statement, Which Is Sometimes Called the "UCC 1" Form

The "security agreement" is the document setting forth the "deal" between the creditor and debtor stating that the debtor grants a security interest in collateral to secure a debt (R.S. 10:9-102(73)). A security agreement must be "authenticated" (R.S. 10:9-203(a)), but "authenticated" is a term that is not restricted to a written instrument and does not refer to what Louisiana law terms an "authentic act." R.S. 10:9-102(a)(7) states that authenticate means "to sign" or "to execute or otherwise adopt a symbol, or encrypt or similarly process a record in whole or in part, with the present intent of the authenticating person to identify the person and adopt or accept a record."

The security agreement is a private document retained by the creditor. It is not filed or recorded in any public record.

To perfect the security agreement against third parties, for most collateral, the creditor files a "financing statement" (R.S. 10:9-502) in the UCC9 records. The "financing statement" is a short-form, one page document that states the name of the debtor, gives other required information, provides the name of the secured party, and "*indicates the collateral covered by the financing statement*" (R.S. 10:9-502(a)(3)). A "financing statement" is sometimes called a "UCC-1" form because the number of the form used for this document is number 1 in all states.

R.S. 10:9-503 contains detailed rules on how to properly set forth the name of the debtor and secured party; trade names are not sufficient.

R.S. 10:9-504 contains detailed rules on how one must describe the collateral. In general, one may use generic descriptions of collateral. Unlike a mortgage on immovable property, which must describe with particularity the encumbered property (C.C. art. 3288, see Section 12.3, above), a proper UCC-1 "financing statement" may be able to contain a description of some types of collateral by generic type, such as "equipment" (R.S. 10:9-102(a)(33)), "inventory" (R.S. 10:9-102(a)(48)), or "accounts" (R.S. 10:9-102(a)(2)), although often a UCC-1 gives more information. A third party looking at the UCC records cannot ascertain precisely what property is being encumbered. A third party may ascertain, however, the identity of the debtor and creditor and the general type of property that is encumbered by the security interest.

On the other hand, "*supergeneric descriptions*," such as "*all of the debtor's assets*," will never suffice to create a valid security interest (R.S. 10:9-108(c)).

There are certain types of collateral for which a generic description will not suffice. Specific descriptions are needed to obtain a security interest in items such as:

- Consumer goods (R.S. 9:102(a)(23) and R.S. 10:9-108(e));
- Life insurance policies (R.S. 10:9-108(e));
- A collateral mortgage note (R.S. 10:9-108(e) and Section 13.4, above); and
- A security interest in "fixtures" (R.S. 10:9-102(a)(41)); a fixture filing must include a "*description of the real property to which the collateral is related sufficient to cause the mortgage to be effective against third persons if the description were contained in a mortgage of real property filed for registry*" (R.S. 10:9-502(b)(3)).

41.4. Where to File a Financing Statement in Louisiana and Where to Check the UCC9 Indices

When Louisiana was working on the adoption of UCC9 in the 1980s, the Clerks of Court were opposed to having Louisiana enact a law like that of most states, where the UCC-1 "financing statement" would be recorded with the Secretary of State. They were concerned about the loss of income that might ensue, for prior to the advent of UCC9 in Louisiana, filings affecting movable property had been done at the parish level.

A compromise was reached. If the UCC9 filing must be made in the state of Louisiana, the UCC9 "financing statement," the UCC-1 form, may be filed with any clerk of court in the state (R.S. 10:9-501(a)(2)), except for motor vehicles and certain other titled vehicles, which must be filed with the Louisiana Department of Public Safety and Corrections (R.S. 10:9-501(a)(1)), and certain other items, such as titled watercraft, which must be filed with the Department of Wildlife and Fisheries (R.S. 10:9-502(a)(3)).

The indices for all filings are kept by the Secretary of State (R.S. 10:9-519), but the physical location where the UCC-1 is filed (except as noted above) is any clerk of court's office.

For example, if a debtor in East Baton Rouge Parish grants a security interest in "equipment" to a lender located in West Baton Rouge Parish, the lender may file the UCC-1 filing statement in any parish of the state. The lender is not required to file in any particular parish as long as the filing is accomplished somewhere in the state.

41.5. UCC9 Security Interests and Collateral Mortgages

The only way to perfect a security interest in a collateral mortgage note is by delivery of the collateral mortgage note to the creditor (R.S. 10:9-312(b)(4) and R.S. 10:9-313(a)). One can never perfect a security interest in a collateral mortgage note by filing a UCC-1 in the UCC records (R.S. 10:9-313).

One must not confuse a perfection of a security interest in the collateral mortgage note with a perfection of real security in the collateral mortgage itself. The collateral mortgage must be filed for registry in the parish mortgage records. Any attempt to file something in the UCC9 records concerning the collateral mortgage or collateral mortgage note will not affect third parties (see Section 13.5, above).

There is some question whether, in addition to possession of the collateral mortgage note, a security agreement is required for perfection of a security interest in a collateral mortgage note. This is because a collateral mortgage note is possessory collateral (see R.S. 10:9-313(a), requiring perfection by "*taking possession*"). Nonetheless, cautious creditors prefer to have debtors enter into security agreements to avoid any later disagreements over the scope of the principal obligations secured by the "pledge" of the collateral mortgage note (see Section 13.5, above).

41.6. Traps for the Unwary in Louisiana's Version of UCC9

UCC9 is a highly technical statute with its own choice-of-law rules (R.S. 10:9-301 *et seq.*), its own priority provisions (R.S. 10:9-317 *et seq.*), its own filing and duration of inscription provisions (R.S. 10:9-501 *et seq.*), its own private, non-judicial collection proceedings and deficiency judgment rules (R.S. 10:9-601 *et seq.*), and even its own rules for judicial foreclosure and executory proceedings if a creditor desires to execute on collateral through litigation (R.S. 10:9-629).

There are a few areas, however, that seem to create traps for the unwary in Louisiana. The most commonly reoccurring of these are described below.

41.6(a). Fixture Filing Issues

In general, an item that would qualify for a UCC9 fixture filing is a movable that becomes a component part of a building or other construction under C.C. art. 466.

To be effective against third parties, Louisiana UCC-1 fixture filings: (a) must contain a description of the real property where the fixture is to be located, and (b) must be filed prior to the item becoming a component part of an immovable (see R.S. 10:9-102(a)(41) and R.S. 10:9-502(b)(3)).

In Louisiana, UCC-1 fixture filings can never be made on residential property when the item was a consumer good (see Section 41.1(b), above) prior to becoming a component part (and therefore a "fixture").

UCC-1 fixture filings on items that become fixtures under Louisiana law can be made only in Louisiana (R.S. 10:9-301(3)(A)).

41.6(b). Security Interests in Accounts Receivable

A security interest in accounts can be perfected only by filing a UCC-1 financing statement in the debtor's "*place of business*" (R.S. 10:9-307).

"Accounts" is a defined term under UCC9 (R.S. 10:9-102(a)(2)). The definition is long and complex and includes accounts receivable as well as items such as a "*right to payment of a monetary obligation, whether or not earned by performance, (i) for property that has been or is to be sold, leased, licensed, as-*

signed, or otherwise disposed of, (ii) for services rendered or to be rendered, (iii)
for a policy of insurance issued or to be issued, (iv) for a secondary obligation in-
curred or to be incurred, (v) for energy provided or to be provided...."

The same statute states that the term "accounts" does not encompass a number of items, such as "*... (ii) tort claims, (iii) deposit accounts, (iv) investment*
property, (v) letter-of-credit rights or letters of credit...."

An exploration of the intricacies of the what is and is not an "account" under
UCC9 is beyond the scope of this Précis.

The following are general rules to perfecting a security interest in accounts:

If the debtor is an individual, the "*place of business*" is the state of the debtor's
"principal residence" (R.S. 10:9-307(b)(1)).

If the debtor is a "*registered organization*" (R.S. 10:9-102(a)(70)), such as a
corporation, limited partnership, or limited liability company, the "*place of*
business" is the state under whose law the debtor was organized (R.S. 10:9-
307(e)). Thus, if a creditor wants to take a security interest in the accounts receivable of a store operating in New Orleans, it would not be sufficient to file
a UCC-1 in Louisiana if the store was owned and operated by a Delaware corporation. Under the UCC, Delaware would be the only proper location to file
the UCC-1 financing statement affecting the accounts receivable, even if the
receivables were being generated in the New Orleans location.

Finally, if the debtor is neither an individual nor a "*registered organization,*"
then the proper filing location is (a) if the organization has only one place of
business, the state where the business is located, or (b) if the organization "*has*
more than one place of business is located" then filing must occur in the state
where "*its chief executive office*" is located (R.S. 10:9-307(b)).

41.6(c). Security Interests in Equipment

As in the case of the accounts, a security interest in equipment located in
Louisiana may be perfected only by recordation of the UCC1 in the state of
the debtor's "place of business" (see Section 41.6(b), above).

41.6(d). Security Interests in Life Insurance Policies

A security interest in a life insurance policy may be obtained only by taking possession of the policy, notifying the insurer, and obtaining consent of
any permanent beneficiary; however, no consent is needed if the owner of the
policy can change the beneficiary designation (see R.S. 10:9-107.1, 9-108(e)(3),
9-312(b)(5), and 9-314(a)).

Appendix

Key Cases and Other Resources

The following is a selective listing of key cases and other
resources that relate to discussions in this Précis.

<u>Section 1.1</u>: See the Official Louisiana Law Institute Comments to C.C. art.
476 for a discussion of real rights.

<u>Section 1.2</u>: *Shell Offshore, Inc. v. M. H. Marr*, 916 F.2d 1040 (5th Cir. 1990)
holds that Louisiana all contracts create, by default, personal rights and
not real rights.

<u>Chapter 2</u>: For a more detailed discussion of the suretyship jurisprudence, see
Rubin, "Ruminations on Suretyship," 57 Louisiana Law Review (1997).

<u>Section 2.1(b)</u>: For a definition of suretyship under French law, see Planiol,
"TRAITE ELEMENTAIRE DE DROIT CIVIL," (La. State Law Institute
translation), Vol. 2, Nos. 2323–2326.

<u>Section 2.1(h)</u>: Cases on whether the language of a contract is sufficient to cre-
ate a contract of suretyship:
- *Amory v. Boyd*, 5 Mart. (O.S.) 414 (La. 1818) please assist [X,] a bill (sent
  to me) for funds he may need ... will be honored (by me)—suretyship;
- *Lobre v. Pointz*, 5 Mart. (N.S.) 443: "[X] is honest. If I had the money I'd
  lend it to him"—no suretyship;
- *Herries v. Canfield*, 9 Mart. (N.S.) 385 (La. 1821), "[X] is honest and will
  pay his debts.... if he should not, we will be responsible"—suretyship;
- *Hickey v. Dudley*, 9 Rob. 502 (La. 1845), where the surety agrees to either bring back the sugar or the money—suretyship;
- *Trefethen v. Locke*, 16 La. Ann. 19 (La. 1861), "This letter will be your
  guarantee"—suretyship;

- *Ball Marketing Enterprise v. Rainbow Tomato Co.*, 340 So.2d 700 (La. App. 3d Cir. 1976), "This will confirm our understanding with you that [we] will take such steps as are necessary to assure payment to you by [the debtor] of amounts due …"—no suretyship.

Section 2.4: *Texas Company v. Couvillion*, 148 So. 295 (La. App. Orl. Cir. 1933), holds that suretyship may be limited in both time and amount.

Section 3.5(a): Two key pre-1988 suretyship cases are: *Louisiana Bank Trust Company, Crowley v. Boutte*, 309 So.2d 274 (La. 1975), and *Aiavolasiti v. Versailles Gardens Land Development Co., et al.*, 371 So.2d 755 (La. 1979).

Section 8.4(a): *Felix Bonura v. Christiana Brothers Poultry Co. of Gretna, Inc.*, 336 So.2d 881 (La. App. 4th Cir. 1976) holds that a creditor's knowledge that a surety is no longer a shareholder of the corporation which guaranteed the debt is not sufficient "notice" to terminate a contract of suretyship.

Section 9.3: Compare: *Fidelity National Bank of Baton Rouge v. Calhoun*, 2008-1685 (La.App. 1 Cir. 3/27/09), 11 So.3d 1119, holding that suspensive appeal bond in the wrong form is not a bond at all and therefore the suspensive appeal is converted into a devolutive appeal; with *Brumley v. Akzona, Inc.*, 2009-0021 (La.App. 4 Cir. 2/18/09), 7 So.3d 1223, holding that a bond in the incorrect amount still suffices to support a suspensive appeal under the judgment creditor affirmatively attacks the bond.

Section 10.1: See Rubin, "Ruminations on the Louisiana Law of Pledge," 75 Louisiana Law Review 698 (2015).

Section 10.6: The "constant acknowledgment" rule was first recognized in *Scott v. Corkern*, 231 La. 368, 91 So.2d 569 (1956) (pledge of a life insurance policy) and reiterated in *Succession of Picard*, 238 La. 455, 115 So.2d 817 (1959) (pledge of negotiable notes; the pledged notes may prescribe but prescription remains interrupted on the principal obligation) and *Kaplan v. University Lake Corporation*, 381 So.2d 385 (La. 1979) (pledge of collateral mortgage note).

Section 11.1: *Randolph v. Starke*, 51 La. Ann. 1121, 26 So. 59, 62 (La. 1899) holds that an indivisible mortgage may secure divisible debts; *Federal Land Bank v. Rester*, 164 La. 926, 114 So. 839 (1927) holds that there is no marshalling of assets in Louisiana.

Section 12.3: The following language has been deemed an acceptable property description, but it is at the remote edge of permissible descriptions: "All property I own in Ascension Parish, bounded by the Mississippi River, and acquired from John Doe." See: *City National Bank v. Barrow*, 13 La. App. 229, 21 La. Ann. 396 (1869).

The following language has been deemed not an acceptable description: "All property I own in Ascension Parish," *State ex rel Brisbois v. Recorder* 13 Teiss 229 (La. App. Orl. Cir. 1915) (invalid even between the parties); "All property belonging to the succession of Joseph Schalatre." *Edwards v. Caulk*, 15 La. Ann. 123 (1850); and "The home I own." *Kieffer v. Starn*, 27 La. Ann 282 (1875).

Section 12.4(d): *Linton v. Purdon*, 9 Rob. 482 (La. 1845) holds that a mortgage must specifically describe past advances if it is to secure past advances; *Pickersgill & Co. v. Brown*, 7 La.Ann. 297 (1852) holds that a mortgage which appears to secure contemporaneous advances may secure future advances if that was the intent of the parties at the time of the creation of the mortgage.

Section 12.8: *Chevron U.S.A., Inc. v. State*, 2007-2469 (La. 9/8/08) 993 So.2d 187 describes the after-acquired title doctrine.

Section 13.4: Law review articles on collateral mortgages include: Rubin and Grodner, "Recent Developments, Security Devices," 53 La. L. Rev. 969 (1993); Willenzik, "Future Advance Priority Rights of Louisiana Collateral Mortgages: Legislative Revisions, New Rules, and a Modern Alternative," 55 La. L. Rev. 1 (1994); Rubin, Willenzik, and Moore, "Is the Collateral Mortgage Obsolete?" 41 La. Bar Journal 529 (1994); Willenzik, "Louisiana Future Advance Mortgages: A 20-Year Retrospective," 75 La. L. Rev. 613 (2015).

Section 13.5(d): *First Guaranty Bank v. Alford*, 366 So.2d 1299 (La. Dec 15, 1978), held that a collateral mortgage package does not automatically secure all future obligations, despite language to that effect in the collateral mortgage. The court held that a collateral mortgage secures only the debts the mortgagor intended to secure, and that can be determined only by looking at the intent of the mortgagor at the time of the pledge of the collateral mortgage note.

Section 13.12: *Diamond Services Corp. v. Benoit*, 2000-0469 (La. 2/21/01), 780 So.2d 367, held that a collateral mortgage package given by a third party to secure the debt of another is an *in rem* obligation; the maker of the collateral mortgage note cannot be sued for a deficiency judgment on the collateral mortgage note.

Section 13.13: *Texas Bank of Beaumont v. Bozorg*, 457 So.2d 667 (La. 1984) discusses how a creditor's rank on loans secured by a collateral mortgage package can be properly (or improperly) transferred from one creditor to another.

Section 14.3: *Carriere v. Bank of Louisiana*, 95-3058 (La. 12/13/96) 702 So.2d 648 (a tenant may mortgage its right of possession and use without mortgaging and imposing on the mortgage creditor the obligation to pay rent).

Section 17.3: *Baker & McKenzie Advokatbyra v. Thinkstream Inc.*, 2008-2535 (La.App. 1 Cir. 6/19/09), 20 So.3d 1109, held that the Louisiana Enforcement of Foreign Judgments Act (R.S. 13:4241) and the Full Faith and Credit Clause applies to judgments of federal courts and to other states, not to foreign jurisdictions outside of the United States.

Section 18.1: *Miller v. Shotwell*, 38 La.Ann. 890 (1886) (a mortgage "disguised" as a sale does not transfer title if it is apparent on the face of the public records that the purpose of the sale was to secure a debt that the seller owes to the buyer).

Section 18.2(d): *Levine v. First National Bank of Commerce*, 2006 0394 (La. 12/15/06), 948 So.2d 1051, holds that, under federal law, mortgages held by national banks are deemed to contain due-on-sale clauses triggered by bond-for-deed contracts.

Chapter 19: *Hans Wede v. Niche Marketing USA, LLC*, No. 2010-0243 (La. 11/30/10), 52 So.3d 60, held that a judgment filed with the clerk of court's office and recorded in the conveyance but not recorded in the mortgage records does not create a judicial mortgage affecting third parties.

Section 20.6: The federal cases holding that certain mortgages to federal agencies are essentially imprescriptible are *Farmers Home Administration v. Muirhead*, 42 F.3d 964 (5th Cir. 1/24/95), and *United States v. Oliver*, 2008 WL 215398 (W.D. La. 1/24/08). The Louisiana case rejecting that view is *L.L.P. Mortgage, Ltd. v. Food Innovisions, Inc.*, 08-422 (La.App. 5 Cir. 10/28/08), 997 So.2d 628.

Section 21.11: *Glass v. Ives*, 169 La. 809, 126 So. 69 (La. 1929), is the key decision on how the proceeds of a judicial sale are to be distributed when a third party possessor is involved; those principles are now incorporated into C.C. art. 3318.

Section 22.2: *Louis Werner Saw Mill Co. v. White*, 205 La. 242, 17 So.2d 264 (1944) holds that a resolutory condition ceases to affect third parties ten years from the date the lending obligation comes due. The case was legislatively overruled when C.C. art. 2561 was amended; however, the changes in C.C. art. 2561 affect only transactions arising after January 1, 1995.

Section 22.3(c): *Travis v. Felker*, 482 So.2d 5 (La.App. 1st Cir. 1985) held that a first right of refusal is imprescriptible. The case has been legislatively overruled when C.C. art. 2628 was amended; however, the changes in C.C. art. 2728 affect only transactions arising after January 1, 1995.

Section 22.4: *Latiolais v. Breaux*, 154 La. 1006, 98 So. 620 (1924), holds that a sale with a right of redemption may constitute a mortgage as between the parties.

Section 26.2: *May v. Market Ins. Co.*, 387 So.2d 1081, 1083 (La.1980), discusses the difference between "simple" and "standard" loss payee clauses.

Chapter 28: For a historical overview of privileges, see Dainow, "Ranking Problems of Chattel Mortgages and Civil Code Privileges in Louisiana Law," 13 Louisiana Law Review 537 (1953), and Dainow, "Vicious Circles in the Louisiana Law of Privileges," 25 La. L. Rev. 1 (1964).

Section 29.2: *Alter v. O'Brien*, 31 La.Ann. 452 (1879), stated: "Were it not for the privilege which the law allows to those who dig the grave, furnish the coffin and drive the hearse, many a lifeless frame, deprived of sepulture, would rot in unnoted or forsaken homes. Were it not for that privilege, when Death enters a city and knocks at every door—watchful and indefatigable as it is, Charity would inevitably be unequal to the increased task which—otherwise—would be imposed upon it."

Suc. of Holston, 141 So. 793 (La. App. 2d Cir. 1932), held that those who pay the funeral and last illness expenses are subrogated to those rights and can claim the privilege; however, Holston also held that the funeral privilege did not cover monuments and tombstones.

Section 29.4: *Pelican State Associates, Inc. v. Winder*, 253 La. 697; 219 So. 2d 500 (1969), held that the last sickness privilege includes "whatever charges may come about in this vast and complex cycle of our modern civilization and all its progressive ramparts in treating of the sick...."

<u>Section 32.1:</u> One of the premiere law review articles on ranking privileges is Dainow, "Vicious Circles in the Louisiana Law of Privileges," 25 La. L. Rev. 1 (1964).

<u>Section 33.3(b):</u> *Lawyers Title Ins. Corp. v. Valteau*, 563 So.2d 260 (La. 1990), holds that a preexisting judicial mortgage against the buyer is outranked by the seller's vendor's privilege on immovables.

<u>Chapter 37:</u> on the Private Works Act, see Rubin, "Ruminations on the Louisiana Private Works Act," 58 Louisiana Law Review 570 (1998).

<u>Chapter 39:</u> The key federal due process cases impacting foreclosures include:
- *Mullane v. Central Hanover Bank & Trust Company*, 339 U.S. 306, 70 S.Ct. 652, 94 L.Ed. 865 (1950);
- *Sniadach v. Family Finance Corp.* 395 U.S. 337, 89 S.Ct. 1820, 23 L.Ed.2d 349 (1969);
- *Fuentes v. Shevin*, 407 U.S. 67, 92 S.Ct. 1983, 32 L.Ed.2d 556 (1972); *reh. denied* 409 U.S. 902, 34 L.Ed.2d 165, 93 S.Ct. 177, 180;
- *Buckner v. Carmack*, 263 La. 627, 272 So.2d 326 (La. 1972), *writ refused* 417 U.S. 901 (1974);
- *Mitchell v. W.T. Grant & Co.*, 416 U.S. 600, 94 S.Ct. 1895, 40 L.Ed.2d 406 (1974);
- *Flagg v. Brooks*, 436 U.S. 149, 98 S.Ct. 1729, 56 L.Ed.2d 185 (1978);
- *Lugar v. Edmondston Oil Co., Inc.*, 457 U.S. 922, 102 S.Ct. 2744, 73 L.Ed.2d 482 (1982);
- *Mennonite Board of Missions v. Adams*, 462 U.S. 791, 103 S.Ct. 2706, 77 L.Ed.2d 180 (1983);
- *Magee v. Amiss*, 502 So.2d 568 (La. 1987);
- *Allain v. Martco Partnership*, 851 So.2d 974 (La. 5/23/03); and
- *Jones v. Flowers*, 547 U.S. 220, 126 S.Ct. 1708, 164 L.Ed.2d 415 (2006)

<u>Chapter 40:</u> on deficiency judgments, see Rubin and Seymour, "Deficiency Judgments: A Louisiana Overview," 69 La.L.Rev. 785 (2009).

Index

deceased persons, judgment
against (C.C. art. 3306), 17.5
definition (C.C. art. 3284), 17.1
discussion applies to (C.C.P. art.
5151), 17.4
as general mortgages, 17.2
registry rules of, 17.3(a), 19.7(c)
reinscription of, 20.8(c)
state/governmental entity, effect
of judgment against, 17.6
vendor's privilege rank *vs.*,
33.3(b)
judicial proceedings (C.C. art.
3319), 20.9(d), 29.3

L

last sickness privilege, 29.4
leases, mortgages on, 14.3
legal mortgages (C.C. art. 3299),
16.1–16.4. *See also* conventional
mortgages; judicial mortgages
in Civil Code, 11.3
creation of (C.C. art. 3283),
16.3
definition, 16.1
discussion applies to (C.C.P. art.
5154), 16.4
as general mortgages, 16.2
reinscription of, 20.8(d)
legal suretyship (C.C. art. 3063),
9.1–9.8
agreement, parameters of (C.C.
art. 3067), 9.2(b)
cash *vs.* (C.C. art. 3068), 9.6,
9.6(1) *illus.*
definitions (C.C. art. 3043), 9.1
judgment, necessity of (C.C.
art. 3069), 9.7

qualifications of (C.C. art.
3065), 9.2(a)
release, from security bond
(R.S. 9:3911, 3912), 9.8
requirements, generally (C.C.
art. 3064), 9.2
testing, effect on (C.C.P. art.
5123.), 9.5
testing, for meeting legal requirements, 9.3(a)–(c)
"three strikes and you're out"
rule (C.C.P. art. 5123), 9.4
lessors of immovables, privilege on
movables by, 31.2
life insurance. *See* insurance
*Louisiana Bank Trust Company,
Crowley v. Boutte* (La. 1975),
3.5(a)
Louisiana Deficiency Judgment Act
(R.S. 13:4106), 40.1–40.4
Louisiana Oil, Gas and Water Well
Lien Act, 36.1
Louisiana Private Works Act (R.S.
9:4801), 36.1, 37.1–37.12
"contractor," definition, 37.1(d)
contractors, selling/leasing movables to, 37.8
creditors' rights, transformation
of, 37.11, 37.11(a)–(b)
filings, location for, 37.3(a)
"general contractor," definition,
37.1(d)
liability, of general contractors,
37.2(c)
liability, of owners, 37.2,
37.2(a)–(b)
liability, of PWA surety, 37.8(d),
37.9 *illus.*

liability, of PWA surety under payment bonds, 37.10(a)–(e)

liability avoidance, by owners, 37.3

lien periods, 37.5–37.7

liens, enforcement and extinguishment prevention of, 37.8(b)

"owner," definition, 37.1(b)

preserving privileges, by general contractors, 37.8(a)

preserving privileges, by lien claimants, 37.3(b), 37.8(c)

ranking, of privileges under, 37.12(a)–(e)

scope, structure and, 37.1

"subcontractor," definition, 37.1(f), 37.1(f)(1)–(2)

subcontractors, selling/leasing movables to, 37.8

substantial completion notice, 37.4

termination notice, 37.4

"work," definition, 37.1(c)

"work" vs. "contract," examples, 37.1(e)

Louisiana privileges (R.S. 9), 28.4

Louisiana Public Works Act, 36.1

Louisiana Title Insurance Act (R.S. 22:511), 23.1(b)

Louisiana Uniform Commercial Code (UCC9), 41.1–41.6

accounts receivable, security interests in, 41.6(b)

collateral outside scope of, 41.2

equipment, security interests in, 41.6(c)

filing/indices location, 41.4

fixture filing issues, 41.6(a)

life insurance policies, security interests in, 41.6(d)

security agreement, financing form and, 41.3

UCC9 security interests, collateral mortgages and, 41.4

M

materialmen's liens and privileges, 36.1–36.2

Miller Act, 36.1

mortgages (C.C. art. 3278), 11.1–11.4, 18.1–18.2. See also conventional mortgages

bond-for-deed contracts (R.S. 9:2941), 18.2(a)–(d)

creditor-drafted insurance documents, 26.1–26.4

creditor's burden of proof, 24.3

creditor's rights (C.C. art. 3280), 11.1(a), 11.1(a)(1) illus.

debtor's rights (C.C.P. Art 2295), 11.1(b)

definition, 11.1

"disguised" as sales, 18.1

extinction of (C.C. art. 3319), 20.9(a)–(f)

filing, recordation and (C.C. 3338), 11.4

limits (C.C. art. 3286), 11.2

recordation, cancellation and, 20.3

types (C.C. art. 3283-3284, 3299), 11.3

"multiple-indebtedness mortgages." See "future advance mortgages"

"multiple-obligation mortgages." See "future advance mortgages"

scope of, "continuing guarantees," 3.4

solidary sureties (C.C. art.
3037), 3.5, 3.5(a)(1) *illus.*,
3.5(a)(2) *illus.*, 3.5(a)(3)
illus.

surety's rights (C.C. arts. 1829,
3048-3051), 3.3

suretyships, debtor-surety relationships in, 4.1–4.5(b)

formation, of relationship,
2.1(c)(1) *illus.*, 4.1

reimbursement right (C.C. arts.
3049-3050), 4.4, 4.4(a)(1)
illus., 4.4(b)

right of security, forms of,
4.5(a)

right of security, from debtor,
4.5, 4.5(a)(1) *illus.*

right of security, when security
unavailable, 4.5(b)

rights, overview (C.C. art.
3047), 4.2

subrogation rights, 4.3,
4.3(a)(1) *illus.*

subrogation rights, attorney's
fees, 4.3(c)

subrogation rights, limits on,
4.3(b)

surety's rights, if no security,
4.5(b)

surviving spouse privilege, 29.8

T

10-year-rule, on recorded conventional mortgages, 20.2,
20.2(a)(2), 20.2(a)T

termination
of "future advance mortgages,"
13.3(b)(4)

of mortgages, by extinction,
20.9(a)–(f)

of suretyship contracts,
8.1–8.4(c)

third parties (C.C. art. 3343)

conventional mortgages
(recorded), time affecting,
20.2, 20.2(a)(1)–(2)

examination of "future advance
mortgages" by, 13.3(c)

judicial mortgages, (recorded),
time affecting, 20.4, 20.5

legal mortgages, (recorded),
time affecting, 20.5

mortgage-secured federal obligations, time affecting, 20.6

mortgage-secured principal obligations, amending, 20.7,
20.7(a)–(b)

registry rules of, 19.3, 19.4, 19.7

reinscription, 20.8

resolutory condition, effect on,
22.2(b)

vendor's privilege on immovables, 33.2

third party possessors, rights of
(C.C. art. 3315), 21.1–21.22(e)

definitions, acts giving status of,
21.2

generally, 21.2

liability of, 21.3

right of payment, 21.6

right to arrest the seizure/sale,
21.7

right to claim enhanced value,
21.8

right to claim enhanced value,
limits on, 21.9

right to claim enhanced value,
procedure, 21.10

right to claim enhanced value,
  sheriff's sale and,
  21.11(a)–(e)
seller's warranty, against eviction, 21.5(a)
seller's warranty, cash sales and,
  21.5(c)
seller's warranty, quit-claim
  deeds and, 21.5(e)
seller's warranty, sales "subject
  to a mortgage" and, 21.5(b)
seller's warranty, sales with assumption and, 21.5(d)
seller's warranty of title, 21.5(a)
title examinations
  abstracts of title, 23.2,
  23.3(a)–(h)
  litigation issues concerning,
  24.1–24.2
  overview, definitions, 23.1

process, 23.4
title insurance. *See also* title examinations
  Louisiana Title Insurance Act
  (R.S. 22:511), 23.1(b)
  overview, definitions, 23.1
title opinions, 23.1(a)

U
usufructs, mortgages on, 14.2

V
vendor's privilege
  on immovables, ranking, 33.3,
  33.3(a)–(b)
  on movables, 31.1
  on movables *vs.* immovables,
  33.1
virile share of surety, 5.2